THE WES ANDERSON COLLECTION
THE GRAND BUDAPEST HOTEL

THE WES ANDERSON COLLECTION
THE GRAND BUDAPEST HOTEL

by
MATT ZOLLER SEITZ
with an introduction by
ANNE WASHBURN

featuring interviews with
Writer and director **WES ANDERSON**
Actor **RALPH FIENNES**
Costume designer **MILENA CANONERO**
Score composer **ALEXANDRE DESPLAT**
Production designer **ADAM STOCKHAUSEN**
and
Cinematographer **ROBERT YEOMAN**

Critical essays by members of the
Society of the Crossed Pens
ALI ARIKAN
STEVEN BOONE
DAVID BORDWELL
OLIVIA COLLETTE
and
CHRISTOPHER LAVERTY

ABRAMS, NEW YORK

To **DAVID PIERCE ZOLLER**,
the author's father, friend, and
inspiration.

The
CONTENTS

A

1,418–Word

INTRODUCTION

WE LIKE TO THINK THAT CIVILIZATIONS are solid, foundational creations, but they are generally confections: concocted as much from color and air and spun sugar as they are from butter, cream, flour. Half vital force, half uninterrogated tradition, they become more glorious, as they grow in confidence, and more unstable—not so very unlike the Courtesan au Chocolat offered by Mendl's, the revered bakery in Wes Anderson's fictional Mitteleuropean town of Nebelsbad, Zubrowka.

Mendl's pastel, cream-puff tower, tottering and a little slapdash, is less culinary masterpiece than an institution; those pink boxes passports more reliable than any set of travel documents.

With *The Grand Budapest Hotel*, Wes Anderson has created a confection of curious depth and substance—the lightest, airiest movie about cataclysm, and one of the more moving.

Anderson's movies deliberately recall the childhood pleasures of world-making, and a childlike sense of conviction and focus. You won't see hands reaching into the frame, shifting the characters, and you can't hear the muttering of dialogue and the special-effect plosives, but you can feel the traces of those hands, those lips, in the devoted way in which every frame is handled, in the performance idiom he has created, and in the physical and emotional worlds that are particularly his own.

His movies are not only about the love of the tale, but always, also, about the love of telling it. His characters are often engaged in the act of making stories; if they aren't actual artists, they are deeply and consciously involved in crafting the stories of their own lives through adventures, escapes, and escapades. The physical life of Anderson's films—the miniatures, painted backdrops, annotations, and stop-motion animation—is as much a part of the tale as the telling of it, the detail and precision and visual conviction an important offset to the carefully offhand tone he employs.

by Anne Washburn

Uncharacteristically, Anderson doesn't attempt to seduce us with the big pink pastry box that is the Grand Budapest Hotel in its heyday. It is persuasive and impressive, and nicely ridiculous, but it isn't the fully articulated playscape in which so many of his movies are set. The Grand Budapest Hotel is, as Zero the lobby boy notes reverently, an "institution" tirelessly upheld by M. Gustave, himself either sharp tool or cream filling, nestled in the center of the confection.

Most of Anderson's dreamers are created—and shown actively *creating*—in contradiction to an established order they both crave and fiercely despise. His characters are rascals, pitting themselves against a status quo they wish they could respect enough to obey. M. Gustave's passion for the hotel, however, is reciprocated—he doesn't merely serve the institution; he defines it. Zero's fierce dedication to M. Gustave, to his own role as lobby boy, to the Grand Budapest itself, is clearly comic; is not fealty to a commercial establishment, traditionally, the sign of an immature protagonist, or one with a lack of scope, whom we are free to mock? Over the course of the movie, we learn what Zero has lost; what an institution can mean.

In *The Grand Budapest Hotel*, a fictional hotel is represented by a miniature against a painted backdrop in an imaginary nation populated with a delightful but improbable secret society of concierges, the made-up masterpiece *Boy with Apple*, an alternate version of European history, an absurd cologne. It is a movie that continually signals it's a comedy, until it confounds us, and it isn't. The horrible is delightfully cartoonish (Willem Dafoe in black leather and sharpened teeth—perfect; may he never appear to us in any other guise), until it is not. Anderson's films are always shades darker and grimmer than they seem to be, but in no other movie of his is the gulf between the tone and weight so large. Made-up worlds, in the current aesthetic fashion, are for comedies, or fantasies, seldom a place to explore the consequential.

M. Gustave is the possessor of a more contradictory set of characteristics than are generally felt to be plausible in art (and really only allowed in comedy), perhaps an example of the dictum that the best art is made by disobeying its principles. In a movie full of capers and menace and plot gimcracks, the largest point of suspense—and one not resolved until toward the very end—is the question of M. Gustave's integrity, its capacities and limits. His last act, the one that decides him for us, is a brave miscalculation in which he stakes everything on the existence of a set of assumptions that have evaporated; a culture has ended. A completely different way of life has begun.

The dilapidation of the Grand Budapest in its 1968 incarnation, a shabby resort in a Soviet satellite state, is rendered with disconcerting beauty and clarity, its ugliness described with a loving exactitude. History here is a twilight world where old gossip slowly becomes legend.

In drawing inspiration for the movie from the luminous, essential work of Stefan Zweig, the renowned, forgotten, now-revived Austrian memoirist and fiction writer, Anderson utilizes more than a milieu and a series of fun, nested storytelling devices; he inherits the loss of a world. Anderson's movies are always about the loss of a world, often childhood, sometimes family, sometimes the world we've created out of our own self-identity. But this is the first time he has concerned himself with the destruction of a civilization, the end of an era, and the terrible ways in which our lives—our own personal and super-absorbing dramas—are deformed by the larger histories we are embedded within.

Reality, in a Wes Anderson film, is a vulgarity, a cruelty, and a necessity—for although his films are populated with people trying as best they can to create a superior cubbyhole of an illusion to live in, and for all that he adores and glorifies this effort, stubbornly, still, he always allows his beautiful worlds to be shattered. Like kids on the beach after a wave has sluiced through their sandcastles, Anderson's protagonists are left working up the will to rebuild again. We have faith that they will rebuild, perhaps less ambitiously but with more success. In *The Grand Budapest Hotel*, however, after the loss of illusion, only death remains. In the character of Zero Moustafa, we see a man who has adapted to his losses but has never rebuilt his life, choosing instead to enshrine his past; he is a testament, rather than a true survivor.

Moustafa's one real legacy is his story, and in the first and final framing device—that of a young girl offering homage to the Author who made Moustafa's life a revered fiction—it is suggested that although some stories are too terrible for an individual to move through and past, perhaps these are the stories that have the most meaning for the rest of us.

There's a wonderful quote from *The World of Yesterday*, Zweig's memoir, which he completed and mailed to his editor in 1942, two days before he and his wife took their own lives in Brazil:

"The generation of my parents and grandparents was better off, they lived their lives from one end to the other quietly in a straight, clear line. All the same, I do not know whether I envy them. For they drowsed their lives away remote from all true bitterness, from the malice and force of destiny. . . . We . . . for whom comfort has become an old legend and security, a childish dream, have felt tension from pole to pole of our being, the terror of something always new in every fiber. Every hour of our years was linked to the fate of the world. In sorrow and in joy we have lived through time and history far beyond our own small lives, while they knew nothing beyond themselves. . . . Every one of us, therefore, even the least of the human race, knows a thousand times more about reality today than the wisest of our forebears. But nothing was given to us freely; we paid the price in full."

Anderson has taken the dark sorrow of Stefan Zweig and joined it to his own sly melancholies to make a film that moves us because it is infinitely capable of disarming before it wounds us. In creating an imaginary world to speak about the end of illusion, Anderson courts a kind of literary double jeopardy. As with the best fables, however, his unreality is more emotionally vibrant than the truth.

A
384–Word
PREFACE

THE GRAND BUDAPEST HOTEL IS THE CULMINATION of Wes Anderson's career to date, gathering together everything he's learned and applying it to a tale that contains literary and visual echoes of every other thing he's done. It's a twelve-layer wedding cake of a film, yet, as you're devouring it, you don't necessarily think about all the work that went into it—only that it's delicious.

The film's sheer complexity and scope seemed to argue for something more, so although we've approached this book with a mind-set similar to that of *The Wes Anderson Collection*, trying to create a portrait of a director's aesthetic—a volume that looks and feels somehow "like" a Wes Anderson movie without being too imitative of his style—this time, we've tried to go a bit deeper.

The "portrait of an artist's style" conceit is reflected in the three-part interview with Anderson. Interspersed among these three "Acts" are self-contained sections covering different aspects of the production. There's an interview with Ralph Fiennes on acting, followed by a costume analysis by Christopher Laverty, and an interview with costume designer Milena Canonero. The section on production design features an essay by film critic Steven Boone and a long interview with production designer Adam Stockhausen; the section on music pairs an essay by critic Olivia Collette and an interview with composer Alexandre Desplat. Film critic Ali Arikan contributes an appreciation of the works of Stefan Zweig, whom Anderson has acknowledged as a primary inspiration for his screenplay; selected excerpts from Zweig's fiction and memoirs follow. The cinematography section closes the book and pairs an interview with Anderson's regular director of photography, Robert Yeoman, with an essay by the great film theorist and historian David Bordwell, whose books on the evolution of film storytelling (written solo or with Kristin Thompson, his partner in both writing and life) have served as touchstones for generations of movie buffs and filmmakers. I like to think of all these remarkable writers as members of their own intrepid organization: The Society of the Crossed Pens.

The end goal was to make a book that has a sense of architecture—of floors and rooms—not unlike that of the remarkable movie that inspired it. Here you are in the Grand Budapest Hotel, the book: I hope you enjoy your stay.

by Matt Zoller Seitz

A
1,751-Word
CRITICAL ESSAY

ALL OF WES ANDERSON'S FILMS ARE COMEDIES, AND none are. There is always a melancholic undertone, buried just deep enough beneath artifice and artistry that you don't sense it right away.

Such is the case with *The Grand Budapest Hotel*, Anderson's eighth and most structurally ambitious film. After one viewing, you come away recalling the wit and motion, and wit in motion, of this tale within a tale within a tale within a tale. A dowager countess is murdered, a foppish concierge named Gustave is framed for the crime and robbed of his inheritance, and a nation is plunged into war as fascism's specter looms—but these dire events are cushioned by vibrant colors, lush textures, and madcap chases. When you recall the film, you quote the quotable lines: "She was dynamite in the sack, by the way." "I apologize on behalf of the hotel." "May I offer any of you inmates a plate of mush?" You remember brazenly farcical set pieces: the normally unflappable Gustave trying to escape the cops sent to arrest him by turning tail and sprinting; the Rube Goldberg–esque prison break, complete with tools hidden in pastries, a seemingly endless rope ladder, and the rhythmic tapping of hammers on bars; Gustave and his lobby boy Zero on a bobsled, chasing the assassin Jopling down a tree-lined slalom. And you savor the details of costuming, special effects, set design, and cinematography: the pink hotel; the funicular; Madame D.'s Marie-Antoinette-by-way-of-Elsa-Lanchester hairdo; a dresser-top packed with Gustave's signature scent, L'Air de Panache; Jopling's skull-shaped knuckle-dusters; those exquisite pastries in those exquisite boxes; the way the frame changes shape, depending on where you are in the story. The film's second half has the pace and bright energy of an early Coen brothers picture (the middle section, especially, has the comic velocity of the prologue to *Raising Arizona*).

by Matt Zoller Seitz

The whole picture is buoyed not just by a sense of invention, but reinvention. The heroes are people who have re-created themselves, or tried to. Madame D., weighed down by propriety, matriarchal responsibility, and memories of youthful vigor, escapes into fantasy with Gustave, the only person who treated her tenderly in her dotage, and wills him *Boy with Apple*, the painting that will change his life, then Zero's. Three inmates escape prison along-side Gustave, pile into a bus, and disappear into the wider world. Agatha, an apprentice baker, becomes an action heroine, helping her love retrieve *Boy with Apple* at great risk to herself.

We never find out the details of Gus-tave's history, but we don't need to. We see through his cultivated facade each time he intersperses his coy "darling"s with exple-tives or momentarily (sometimes tactically) forgets to be a gentleman. The L'Air de Panache stands in for his handmade per-sona. The man has perfumed his life.

But with each successive viewing of *The Grand Budapest Hotel*, a funny, really *not*-so-funny thing happens: We realize that all these acts of self-reinvention and self-determination will nonetheless be trampled by the greedy and powerful, then ground up in the tank treads of history. The film's veil of lightness lifts to reveal a reality that's inconsolably sad. You find yourself dread-ing dark moments more acutely: Jopling hacking off Deputy Kovacs's fingers with a sliding metal door; Gustave getting dragged off by police while a train whistle shrieks; Agatha marrying Zero on a mountaintop as old Zero informs us that she, and their infant son, died just two years later of the Prussian *grippe*. Speak the film's title again,

after a second or third viewing, and the emblematic image becomes the face of old Zero, who's so shattered by the deaths of his best friend and his great love that he can't bear to describe their demises in detail.

Like so many Wes Anderson movies, this one is about loss, and how we come to terms with loss, or never do. The most important parts of any story are the parts people omit: the abysses they sidestep. Zero keeps the hotel because it reminds him of Agatha. *Boy with Apple*—a cheeky vision of innocence that he encouraged Gustave to steal, setting the film's main plot in motion—now hangs behind the concierge desk and is featured on the backs of the hotel's menus, where every guest's dining companion must at least briefly regard it. In some sense, Zero lives in the past. He invites the Author into that past, but not too deeply. Whenever he prepares to revisit his personal history, the lighting in the room changes, and theat-rical shadows darken his face. He gifts the Author with details about Gustave, Agatha, assorted colorful supporting characters, the hotel, the country, the war, and the art of being a lobby boy and a concierge; in so doing, he hands his young dining compan-ion a legacy that transforms him into a rare author so beloved that his country claims him as a favorite son.

Zero remains a guarded soul, how-ever. His need to share his story is keen (he approaches the Author, not the other way around), but his cup never runs over. He allocates just six words to Gustave's execu-tion by "pock-marked, fascist assholes," a moment presented in plain-facts black-and-white: "In the end, they shot him." Agatha's death gets three sentences, one of which describes the illness that killed her as "An absurd little disease." *De nada, it's nothing; and now we move on.* Whenever he's about to get lost in reverie for Agatha, he catches himself and changes the subject. We often see her from a distance: riding her bike as the soundtrack swells; gazing adoringly at Zero, carousel lights haloing her face. She is a nearly absent presence, by Zero's choice: a door marked "Do Not Enter." The buoyant tone of his narration eventually comes to seem like a cushioning device—a means of distracting the Author, and us, from the tale's grimmer aspects.

The Grand Budapest Hotel is inspired, as a closing title card informs us, by the works of Stefan Zweig. The Austrian author fled his beloved Vienna (his personal Grand Budapest Hotel, perhaps) as World War I ramped up and the Continent burned. He watched it spiral further into madness during the Second World War, then eventually settled in Petropolis, Brazil, where he and his second wife, Lotte Altmann, committed suicide together. His memoir, *The World of Yesterday*, is a Proustian love letter to Vienna, the city he adored then left because he couldn't bear to see it soiled by anti-intellectualism and thuggish tribalism. We see bits of Zweig represented in the film's story, setting, and images (including the young Author, the old Author, and Gustave, all of whom physically resemble Zweig in various ways), but as is so often the case in Wes Anderson's films, *The Grand Budapest Hotel* comes at reality, historical and personal, in an oblique and fanciful way. This Europe is no more "real," in the Encyclopedia Britannica sense, than the Rushmore Academy, the 375th Street Y, or Pescespada Island. And yet the characters' emotions are real. Their deaths feel as real as the blood that spills from Richie Tenenbaum's slashed wrists and that clouds the water near Zissou's wrecked helicopter. Anderson's movies are filled with personal abysses; if the scripts tread lightly around them, it's only because the characters are living in the abyss already and have been there for years, or for their whole lives. On some level, we know this, and we can feel it.

In this way—glancingly, discreetly—the movie honors Zweig's losses: of national identity, of youthful idealism, of life itself. Fear of loss, and agonizing knowledge of loss, fuels the film's characters, as surely as it fuels motherless Max Fischer's restless productivity, Mr. Fox's reckless adventurism, and the Whitman brothers' journey across India. Loss fuels Zero, a man described by the Author as the only person in the hotel who struck him as "deeply and truly" lonely, and who confirms that impression tenfold.

Why does Zero speak to a young writer he meets in the baths? Perhaps it's for the same reason that Steve Zissou makes films; that Max Fischer writes and directs plays; and that Dignan chronicles a "seventy-five-year plan" in his spiral notebook: to channel those unexpressed anxieties, give them shape, and, ideally, master them, rather than be mastered by them. To ensure that some part of themselves lives on. The decay of the body is irreversible. Death is nonnegotiable. After that, what's left? Stories. But not just the stories as the storytellers remembered them, and then recounted them to others: the stories that people adapt from *other people's* stories, which then are retold, remade, and handed down, until only their essence remains. *The Grand Budapest Hotel* treats storytelling itself as an inheritance bequeathed to anyone who's willing to listen, feel, and remember, then repeat the story, with whatever embellishments are necessary to personalize it and make it mean something to the teller.

And so the film begins with a young woman visiting a statue of the Author and glancing down at the (nonexistent) novel that supplied the story we're about to see: a story set in a (nonexistent) country that's been remade by war; a story told in a (nonexistent) hotel that's been remade first by brute force and then by brutish ideology; a story recounted by a writer who first heard it from a lonely old man who ended it with what sounds like a benediction: "I think *his* world had vanished long before he ever entered it," he says of Gustave, his mentor, his father figure, his brother, speaking also of himself, and the Author who'll spin his yarn into literary gold. "But, I will say:

he certainly sustained the illusion with a marvelous grace!" Shortly thereafter, the elevator doors slide shut like a book's covers closing.

The final shots drive home the notion of stories as inheritances. We see the old Author sitting quietly on a couch beside his grandson; he's wearing a version of the Norfolk suit he wore the night that he spoke to Zero—a night that we now sense was the most important of his life—and he's in a study (uncompleted, judging from the half-painted walls in the room beyond) whose décor echoes that of the hotel in 1968. The old Author's voice supplants the younger's: "It was an enchanting, old ruin—but I never managed to see it again." Then we return to the young woman in the cemetery as she closes the book.

Life destroys. Art preserves.

· UNICUS · FILIUS
DUCATI · UNDECIMI ·

ANNO · D ·
MDCXXVII

The Idea of Europe

A 188-Word Note

MY FIRST CONVERSATION WITH WES ANDERSON about *The Grand Budapest Hotel* happened in early November 2013, just a few days after I'd seen a nearly finished cut of the film at the Fox screening room in Midtown Manhattan.

He'd warned me beforehand that the sound mix and music weren't set, that the timing of some scenes would change, and that certain visual-effects shots might seem distractingly unfinished. "It's a little rough," he said.

Of course, Wes Anderson's "a little rough" is another filmmaker's pristine. What I saw that afternoon did not differ in any significant way from the final theatrical release. It felt like a complete statement. From the intricate layering of storytelling devices to the clockwork interplay of character and incident, the film also seemed a leap forward in degree of complexity, so much so that I was daunted by the prospect of interviewing Wes about it after only one viewing.

Our conversation took place via telephone. I was in my editor's office at Abrams Books in Lower Manhattan on a chilly Friday morning. The director was in London, embroiled in post-production. He spoke from his hotel.

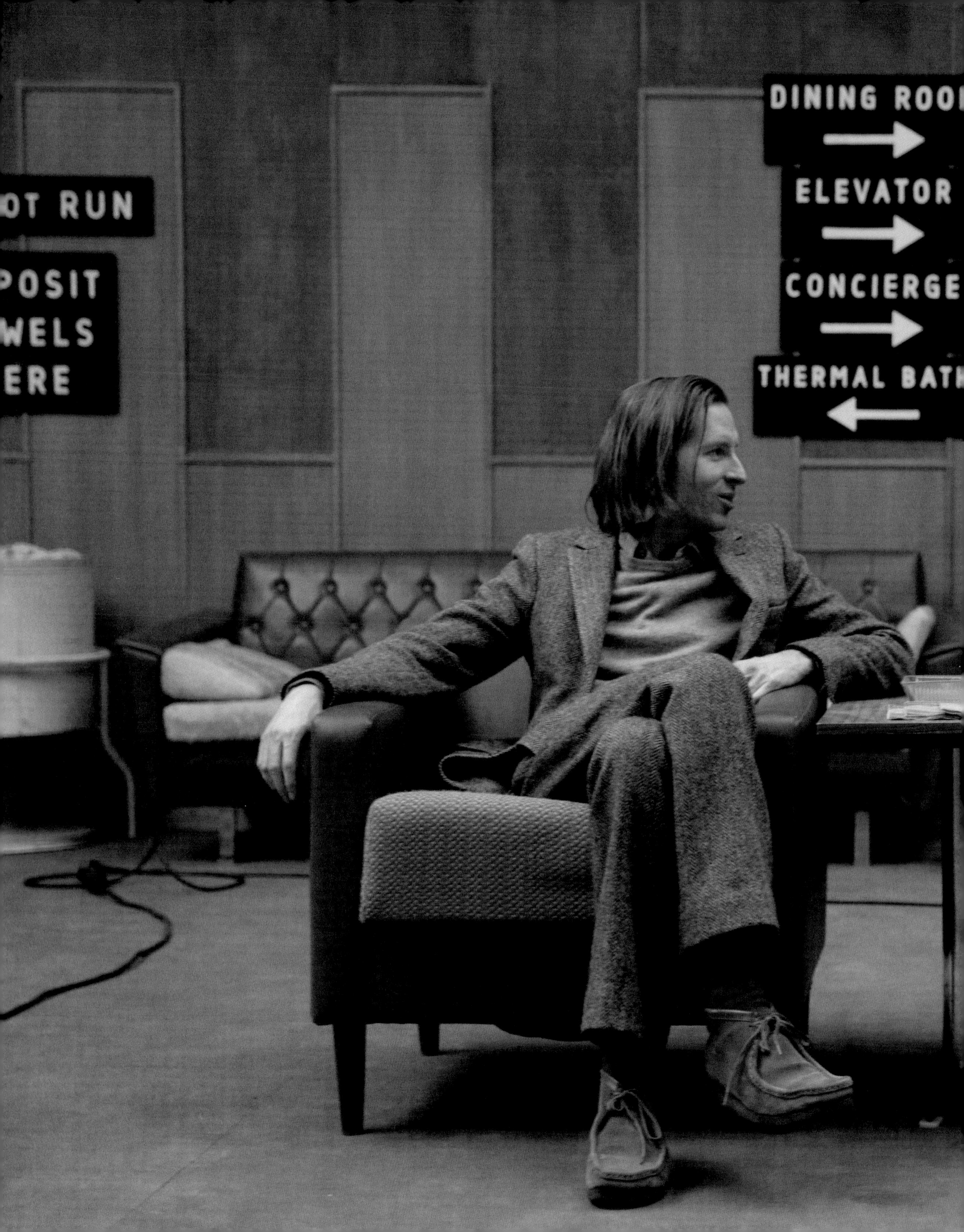
RUN
DINING
ELEVATOR
CONCIERGE
THERMAL

The

7,269-Word

FIRST

Interview

OPPOSITE: Wes Anderson and Tom Wilkinson in the Author's study during the shooting of the film's 1985 scenes. The patterns on the wallpaper and curtains faintly evoke the paintings of Gustav Klimt, as well as the carpets in the hallways of the Overlook Hotel in Stanley Kubrick's *The Shining* (1980). The painting of woolly mammoths suffering through the Ice Age connects with the film's themes of eras passing and ways of life becoming extinct.

BELOW: Stefan Zweig, the Austrian author whose work inspired Wes Anderson's screenplay. Note the physical resemblance to both Gustave (Ralph Fiennes) and the young Author (Jude Law); the latter is shown here in a film still-frame.

---

*   Joseph Conrad's *Heart of Darkness* is one of the best-known novels to use the literary conceit of a frame narrative.

MATT ZOLLER SEITZ: Let me start with a quote from your screenplay: "It is an extremely common mistake: people think the writer's imagination is always at work, that he is constantly inventing an endless supply of incidents and episodes, that he simply dreams up his stories out of thin air. In point of fact, the opposite is true. Once the public knows you are a writer, they bring the characters and events to *you*—and as long as you maintain your ability to look and carefully listen, these stories will continue to seek you out."

So: did this story seek you out?

WES ANDERSON: Well, in fact, that's all from Zweig! That's not my thought; that's his.

Stefan Zweig, the fiction writer and essayist whose work you acknowledge in the film's dedication as an inspiration for *The Grand Budapest Hotel*.

Yes. What Zweig describes is a person coming to him and telling him their story. That didn't happen to me. What *did* happen is, my friend who made up the story with me, Hugo Guinness—he and I based the character on our other mutual friend. We had this fragment of a story that was about a character based on our friend, who maybe I'll tell you about in more detail in a little bit. We had this idea for a few

years. It took us a long time to decide what would happen to him.

At the same time, I had been thinking of doing something related to Zweig, whose work I had gotten to know a little bit well over the past few years. He's a writer I'd never heard of until six or eight years ago, and I had become very interested in his work. I really love his stories, and also his memoir, *The World of Yesterday*.

I remember you had mentioned Zweig during the interview that later became the *Moonrise Kingdom* chapter of *The Wes Anderson Collection*. We were talking about stories that are to some extent *about* storytelling—or stories that are presented to the reader or viewer as having been told *to* someone.

Exactly. It's sort of like what we see in Conrad.* I mean, this is obviously not something that's Zweig's exclusive territory, but almost everything he's written, other than the biographies and the memoir, takes that form. And that's why we did it. The character in the movie who's sort of supposed to be the author, and then the character who's sort of supposed to be like the author as a younger person in his story? They're both, theoretically, Zweig himself, more or less.

You have stories within stories in this movie. Perhaps more so than any other film of yours, this one is about stories and storytelling, and our relationship to stories, and why we *need* stories. And yet, at the same time, there's a cushioning effect, a sense of distance.

Well, we do take about three or four steps to get to the main event. I mean, we do take a pretty long time before you get to meet Ralph Fiennes's character. But hopefully, the other parts that lead up to it are setting the mood, and with any luck, the characters you meet along the way are kind of entertaining by themselves.

Yes, I like the narrator—or I guess I should say the *first* narrator, the author of the book.
     I also like that, right off the bat, you're puncturing the pomposity of this narrator by having his—I guess that's his son coming in and shooting a pellet gun at him?

Or maybe his grandson.

Is the story in any part inspired by your fascination with travel, which seems to have become more important to you as you've gotten deeper into your career?

I think it probably does relate to the fact that I've spent a lot of time in Europe over the past ten or twenty years. It's interesting to be able to go out and see the world.
     But it also relates, as much as anything in my own life, to what I've been reading. The movie is personal in that it's telling a story that lets me move around in a world I've been very interested in for a long time, that I've wanted to learn more about, and that will let me use all the stuff I've gathered and picked up along the way—stuff that comes as much from reading as from traveling.
     And then there's another thing, which is that there's sort of an American, or you could say *Hollywood*, interpretation of Central Europe that's made mostly by Europeans, specifically by Europeans working in Hollywood. This film is partly informed by that type of film, too. I feel like we were taking it more from movies made in the 1930s.

Ernst Lubitsch. *The Shop Around the Corner*.

Lubitsch, and that whole 1930s Hollywood version of Europe.

Michael Powell and Emeric Pressburger: Were they in your mind?

I'm sure they were. I feel like they *always* are. I can give you one example right now: You remember Adrien Brody in the scene where he notices that the painting has been stolen? He's dressed as Lermontov, you know. Anton Walbrook in *The Red Shoes*. I mean, he's wearing his dressing gown, and he's actually wearing red shoes! In fact, now that I think of it, part of our structure comes from *The Life and Death of Colonel Blimp*. In that movie, they even go into a thermal baths, and then the story goes back into the past from the thermal baths, which is something we sort of do, too, in our own way.

You've definitely created a dream space. But at the same time, if I were to describe the tone of this film, I would say it has a light tone, but it's only light if you are comfortable with, shall we say, a less American and perhaps more European way of seeing the world.
     By that I mean: In this movie, there's violence, there's war, but there is no sense of innocence, at least not in the way that Americans use the word "innocence," as in "that thing that we're constantly losing every decade throughout our history." There is no innocence in this movie. There's sweetness and kindness, but that's not the same thing as innocence. These are tough people. When we hear that war is imminent, your characters don't seem terribly shocked. It's like, "Oh, OK—well, I guess we'll have to get ready for that." There is a sense that this is not the first time something like this has happened. War is something these people recognize as a part of life. The movie is a comedy, and yet there's a sense of history and suffering.

Maybe you're right. But in that scene you're talking about, you know, it's also partly a gag. Zero brings M. Gustave the paper, and it says a war is coming, and maybe the world's about to end, but the big news is: The rich old woman dropped dead.

LEFT: Still-frame from Ernst Lubitsch's *The Shop Around the Corner* (1940), a lighthearted, fast-paced comedy about two store clerks (Margaret Sullavan and James Stewart, pictured) who at first despise each other, but ultimately fall in love. The German-born Lubitsch was one of many European directors who relocated to Hollywood in the 1920s. His buoyant sensibility was meticulous yet somehow never overbearing; studio executives and critics called it "the Lubitsch touch."

RIGHT: Still-frame of Tony Revolori as young Zero in *The Grand Budapest Hotel*.

OPPOSITE: Still-frames from one of Tom Wilkinson's two scenes in the film as the old Author; he's interrupted by his grandson (Marcel Mazur) shooting a toy gun at him. This unbroken take encapsulates Wes Anderson's aesthetic: precise décor, costuming, and lighting, plus intricately choreographed camerawork, capturing a moment that's serious but not self-serious, and interrupted by a burst of cheerful, childlike anarchy.

True! But you see what I'm driving at: There's a sense of physical reality to this movie. The physicality is rooted in history, and in an understanding of history. And yet, at the same time, the movie is almost whimsically fantastic—particularly the exteriors. The hotel itself is like a spread from a pop-up book; same thing with the mountains around it. And then you have that elevator, the funicular that takes you up the side of the mountain: It's based on something real, but like the rest of that panorama, it's stylized.

Touches like those gave me the sense that what we're seeing here is a well-traveled and well-read and curious American trying to imagine his way into this past.

Well, remember, also, in a case like this, we aren't even in a real country. The part of the story with young Zero and Gustave, that's 1932, but it isn't a real 1932. I mean, Mussolini was in power in the real 1932, but Hitler wasn't appointed until a year later. We're not on that timeline. Nothing can be fully historically accurate if the place never actually existed. I guess that goes without saying.

We're kind of combining the First World War with the Second World War, and making it all into three periods. One period is what Zweig called the "world of yesterday," which is before World War I. The second period is this period of war and fascism. And then, finally, there's the period of Communism in Central or Eastern Europe, which comes after that but that was already beginning, anyway. It's sort of a riff on something, I guess. I don't know what you call it!

Well, it is consistent with the strategy of your other films. You often have stories that occur in unspecified locales, or in made-up places, and sometimes you add made-up creatures. In this one, you've added history to the list of things that you're messing around with.

We made up our own money for this one. The Klubeck. The countries are all fictional in the movie—except there does seem to be a Maltese Riviera, for some reason. And a few French people. I wouldn't want to break it all down too carefully. It might start to come unglued.

This is not Europe. This is the *idea* of Europe.

Well, either way, most of what is in the movie I can't claim we *invented*. So much of our own little version of this region just comes from us traveling around and seeing things. You might find yourself a view next to a railroad track or, you know, a bakery, or whatever it is—all the landscapes and cityscapes—and for the film, you transform them a bit.

On top of that, the movie is about seeing things from another time, and then gathering it all up and making it into a kind of *Reader's Digest* version of Central Europe. You know, its Greatest Hits. It's kind of a concoction.

VISITORS
ARE REQUESTED
TO REFRAIN
FROM CIGAR SMOKING
IN THE LOBBY

ABOVE LEFT: Still-frame from *The Red Shoes* (1948), a film by Michael Powell and Emeric Pressburger. Actor Anton Walbrook wears an outfit whose patterns are echoed in *The Grand Budapest Hotel*, in the dressing gown and red shoes that Adrien Brody's Dmitri wears in the scene where his character realizes that *Boy with Apple* has been stolen (ABOVE RIGHT).

BELOW LEFT: More Powell and Pressburger references: in the duo's epic *The Life and Death of Colonel Blimp* (1943), which spans World Wars I and II, the "present day" sequences in a bath trigger flashbacks that take us into the title character's youthful adventures.

BELOW RIGHT: F. Murray Abraham as Mr. Moustafa in the 1968 sequences of *The Grand Budapest Hotel*.

ABOVE: Abraham napping on the set.

The Grand Budapest Hotel is also what I like to call a "Contraptionist" movie. A big narrative machine with all these interlocking parts, organized around a complicated plot—like you'd find in a farce or a mystery, two modes that this movie sort of borrows from. This movie is constantly moving the audience forward, toward the goal of getting the painting back. To do that, the characters have to accomplish all these related tasks, like busting Gustave out of prison.

But, in another sense, the particulars of the plot are not as important as how people are feeling when things are happening to them.

We were lucky to have a good gang of actors to help us out with that part of it. We got very lucky. Ralph and Tony Revolori, plus Saoirse Ronan. Those three— and especially the relationship between Gustave and Zero—that's really the center of the movie. I feel like that's what the thing is ultimately about: the friendship between the two of them.

It's a master-and-apprentice movie, too.

Yes, right.

There's a constant sense that it's important that things be done in a certain way, in a certain manner, at a certain time, for a certain reason—you know, using certain materials, and so forth. Rituals are important, and it is these rituals that are passed down from the master to the apprentice in your movie.

And then you have this framing device within the framing device within the framing device—the F. Murray Abraham version of Zero, who is very wise, telling his story to the young Author, who in the flashbacks seems almost as naive as the young Zero in the 1932 scenes.

Old Zero is a figure of mystery and power. Although we don't yet know his story when we meet him as an older man, it's clear that he has, in some sense, over time, become a master.

Kind of a sadder one, I guess. You know, Murray Abraham—he's really something. That's a guy who knows how to give a line reading.

Yes—as the record-label owner in *Inside Llewyn Davis* who tells the hero, "I don't see a lot of money here."

He's been in a couple or three of the plays Ethan Coen has written.

He has an extraordinary voice.

He sure does.

And, of course, that's how most people got to know him thirty years ago, as the narrator of *Amadeus*, playing Salieri opposite Mozart. *Amadeus* is also, it occurs to me, a film in which an older narrator recalls his life when he was young. It's F. Murray Abraham's voice that we recall when we recall *Amadeus*.

I think he's probably nearly as old in real life as he was for the old-man part of *Amadeus*. But he looks about twenty years younger than that character. And he's at least as great as he ever was.

Tell me about Tony Revolori, who plays the young Zero.

His father, Mario, directed some shorts. His older brother—also Mario—has been in a film or two. Mario and his brother both came in to read for the part in Los Angeles. We were mainly looking more in the Middle East.

The character is kind of half-Arab, half-Jew, maybe? He's from another made-up country. The history and the ethnicity of this character are also

AUTHOR
Don't do it. Don't!

The boy hesitates, then fires. A yellow, plastic pellet ricochets off the author's chest and rings against a whiskey glass as the author makes a violent lunge for the boy -- who evades him and dashes off. The author looks at a note-card and rambles a bit, searching for his place:

AUTHOR
Over your lifetime. I can't tell you how many times. Somebody comes up to me.
(back on track)
To him who has often told the tales of others, many tales will be told.

The boy returns, the gun now tucked under his belt, and sits, immediately comfortable, on the author's lap with the old man's arms wrapped around his shoulders. The conflict seems never to have existed. They both look into the camera as the author concludes:

AUTHOR
The incidents that follow were described to me exactly as I present them here, and in a wholly unexpected way.

EXT. MOUNTAIN RANGE. DAY

The late sixties. A stunning view from a rusty, iron-lattice terrace suspended over a deep crevasse, green and lush, alongside a high cascade. The author continues in voice-over as the camera glides along a cracked path through a plot of untamed edelweiss and buttercups:

AUTHOR (V.O.)
A number of years ago, while suffering from a mild case of "Scribe's Fever" (a form of neurasthenia common among the intelligentsia of that time) I had decided to spend the month of August in the spa town of Nebelsbad below the Alpine Sudetenwaltz -- and had taken up rooms in the Grand Budapest --

The camera comes to a stop as it reveals a sprawling nineteenth-century hotel and baths situated on a wide plateau. There is a deep, formidable staircase up to a regal entrance. There is a promenade above and a glass-panelled conservatory below. A rickety funicular groans as it slowly climbs its hillside tracks. The grass needs cutting, the roof needs patching, and more or less every surface of the building needs a coat of paint.

                    AUTHOR (V.O.)
          -- a picturesque, elaborate, and once
          widely-celebrated establishment. I expect
          some of you will know it. It was off-
          season and, by that time, decidedly out-
          of-fashion; and it had already begun its
          descent into shabbiness and eventual
          demolition.

MONTAGE:

The nine other guests of the hotel each observed from a
respectful distance: a frail student; a fat businessman;
a burly hiker with a St. Bernard; a schoolteacher with
her hair in a bun; a doctor; a lawyer; an actor; and so
on.

                    AUTHOR (V.O.)
          What few guests we were had quickly come
          to recognize one another by sight as the
          only living souls residing in the vast
          establishment -- although I do not
          believe any acquaintance among our number
          had proceeded beyond the polite nods we
          exchanged as we passed in the Palm Court
          and the Arabian Baths and onboard the
          Colonnade Funicular. We were a very
          reserved group, it seemed -- and, without
          exception, solitary.

CUT TO:

An enormous, half-abandoned dining room. There are two
hundred tables and fifty chandeliers. The ten guests
sit, each on his or her own, at their separate tables,
widely-spaced across the giant restaurant. A waiter
carries a tray a great distance to the schoolteacher and
serves her a plate of peas.

INT. LOBBY. EVENING

There are faded couches, fraying armchairs, and coffee
tables with new, plastic tops. The carpets are
threadbare, and the lighting in each area is either too
dim or too bright. A concierge with a crooked nose
smokes a cigarette as he lingers behind his desk. He is
M. Jean.

(NOTE: the staff of the hotel in both the relevant time-
periods wear similar versions of the same purple uniform
-- while the public spaces reflect a cycle of "regime
changes".)

On the wall behind M. Jean, there is a beautiful,
Flemish painting of a pale, young boy holding a piece of
golden fruit. This is "Boy with Apple". A patch of water-

THE VILLAS AT

M O N T E V E R D I

TUSCANY

1 A.

STAG'S LEAP w/ BRIDGE
& ELEVATOR. (MAN ENTERS & DESCENDS.)

DOLLY TO:

1 B.

PINK
HOTEL w/ FUNICULAR ASCENDING
& NEBELSBAD PASTEL
FACADES BELOW.

2,

TIGHTER -- FUNICULAR
ARRIVES.

3 A.

COURTYARD FACADE,
w/ GLASS AWNING.

TILT DOWN TO:

3 D.

ENTRANCE w/ EMPTY
CAFÉ TABLES, ONLY ONE
GUEST. (HIKER w/ SAINT
BERNARD.)

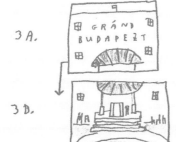

4,

ONLY ONE GUEST AMONG
EMPTY BALCONIES.

THE VILLAS AT

MONTEVERDI

TUSCANY

newspapers table

5. NEWSPAPER ROOM w/ VIEW & ONLY ONE GUEST. (FAT BUSINESSMAN)

6. EMPTY WICKER CHAIRS, OLD WOMAN PLAYS SOLITAIRE.

7. PALM COURT, ONE GUEST, (LIKE A ROUSSEAU) KNITTING. WOMAN.

8. ARABIAN BATHS, ONE SWIMMER. (w/TEA.)

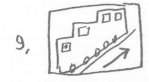

9. DOLLY w/FUNICULAR, ONE GUEST.

10. COLONNADE, ONE GUEST. (TEACHER PAINTING.)

Selected images from the more detailed "animatic" version of the storyboards for the sequence where the Author describes the hotel in 1968.

kind of made up, in some mishmash. I relate him to different kinds of tribes in different ways. But we were essentially looking for an Arab. We looked in Lebanon and Israel, and also in North Africa. We'd also looked in France and England and America.

Do you feel a sense of culture clash between Europe and the Middle East in the movie?

Maybe so?

I'm thinking particularly of those scenes with F. Murray Abraham as the older Zero, when he's one of the richest men in Europe, telling this young white Englishman his story. There's a sense in which, by the 1960s, the balance of power has shifted. None of that stuff is front and center in the movie, but it seems to be a subtext.

You're reading all that into it, anyway, from when you first meet the guy.

The other thing is, you know, Zweig was a Jew, and I think that probably comes into play, in a way. There is no Holocaust in this movie. It's not just that the story is taking place before that event was conceived; it just doesn't exist in our story. But I want to suggest it's still present somehow, maybe.

The sense of imminent, terrible violence.

Zweig's books were banned and burned. He was one of the most popular writers in the world, at that time—certainly he must have been the most popular

writer in Germany. And the next thing you know, his presence was erased. Some aspect of that is, for me, sort of—I don't even know what you'd call it, but it's something I do think about in relation to the story, and it's what I had in mind in relation to the story, even though it's not really dealt with directly in any way. Have you read *Eichmann in Jerusalem*?

Yes. Hannah Arendt. "The banality of evil."

So you already know that it's not entirely or even *mainly* about the arrest and trial of Adolf Eichmann. A significant part of the essay is about how each country in Europe responded to the demands of the Nazis—to give them their Jews, to deport them and kill them, and so on—and how all that played out differently for different peoples, different populations, different governments. Whether they were governments that were being obliterated or not, they all responded individually. Something about her study and analysis of Europe at that time was part of what made me want to do this story. I kept going back to this big essay of hers.

So anyway, all that by way of saying: We ended up choosing a kid from Anaheim.

[MATT LAUGHS.]

And his parents are from Guatemala. His brother gave a very good audition. Then came Tony, who also gave a great audition and looks a lot like his brother, but younger, and I thought: This is the guy.

TOP, THIS PAGE AND OPPOSITE: Still-frames from the film showing the slow, left-to-right pan that takes viewers from Stag's Leap to the hotel itself. Everything in this shot is a miniature or a digital matte painting, composited during post-production. As executed by production designer Adam Stockhausen and his team, this and many other outdoor panoramas aim for a more figurative than photo-realistic feeling, in the manner of 1930s and '40s movies.

BELOW OPPOSITE: Still-frames of young Zero, played by Tony Revolori, and young Salieri in Milos Forman's multiple Oscar-winner *Amadeus* (1984), adapted from the play by Peter Shaffer.

BELOW LEFT: Still-frames of old Salieri from *Amadeus* (1984), played by F. Murray Abraham, with a prosthetic assist by the makeup wizard Dick Smith, who died in 2014. Smith, who was given an Academy Honorary Award in 2012, also aged Dustin Hoffman in *Little Big Man*, Max von Sydow in *The Exorcist*, and David Bowie in *The Hunger*, and created gore effects for *Taxi Driver* and other classics.

BOTTOM RIGHT: A still-frame from *The Grand Budapest Hotel* showing old Zero (Abraham, again).

** The filmmaker is referring to author and illustrator Juman Malouf, his girlfriend, to whom he dedicated *Moonrise Kingdom*.

All these characters are supposed to be from some place called Zubrowka, which is like some mixture of Hungary and Poland and Czechoslovakia, or something. But they speak like Jeff Goldblum and Edward Norton. There's a Hollywood tradition of that, I guess. Whatever language they're meant to be speaking, it's American. We had all these different people around the world audition for Tony's part, and I realized that I wanted actors who could make this dialogue funny, and they needed to have a very easy rapport with the English language. The character of Serge is played by Mathieu Amalric, and he's French. At least we've got somebody in the movie who actually has a Continental European accent.

I really wanted to have Mathieu in the movie. We also had a chance to have Léa Seydoux, who is really quite a spectacular actress, in the cast. We didn't give her much to work with in our movie, but she's always very good, and she makes it into something.

There is a sense of history in this story, for all the major characters. That's not necessarily true for the characters in your other movies. The characters in your other movies have their own personal histories, and their own family histories, that they carry around with them. But in *Grand Budapest*, there is more of a sense of carrying the world's history, history with a capital *H*, around inside of you as well; a sense of the eternal cycles of things. In this fantasy version of Europe, as in the real Europe, you know that if war is happening, this is not the first time that war has ever happened in Europe, and that it may not be the first time war has happened in Europe in your lifetime.

It's a world in which you can be traveling by train, and suddenly the train might be stopped and boarded, and soldiers will get on and demand to see your papers. Gustave is outraged but not surprised. His reaction suggests that this is a part of life there. I somehow got that sense that maybe, even as a kid, he encountered something like this, in a different form?

Right.

Zero seems to have that kind of tragic knowledge as well, and he's a much younger man than Gustave. You've got that scene where Gustave is up in Zero's face, and Zero suddenly drops this bit of information that members of his family were tortured and killed.

We kind of buried that one. We used that because, at one point, I thought I would like to—well, you know, Juman** is from Lebanon. What Zero is talking about, in an oblique way, I think that kind of comes from part of her family's story. The reason I wanted Zero to be from that part of the world is because I live with Juman. Her part of the world has become a part of my life. Anyway, I thought maybe we would save this bit of crucial information in the story for this moment when Gustave goes off the rails.

Zero takes Gustave down a peg. And Gustave's reaction is funny.

"I apologize on behalf of the hotel."

Why did you name the character Zero?

I guess I was thinking of Zero Mostel.

So there's a tribute aspect. But the name is, symbolically, pretty loaded. It suggests that he's starting from nothing—that he's a blank slate, or that he's made himself into a blank slate. He's a young man in the process of inventing or reinventing himself. There may even be some dialogue to that effect, right?

He gives us his work history, the list of places where he's been employed. As a Skillet Scrubber and as a Mop and Broom Boy.

    I think Gustave and Zero may have that in common.*** We have no idea where Gustave comes from, you know, and even Zero says it at one point: "He never told me where he came from. I never asked who his family had been."

This movie is probably the closest thing to an out-and-out farce that you've ever attempted. Yet there's a melancholic sensibility overall, especially when Zero takes over as the narrator. Brutality is everywhere. And binding it all together are stories of older men picturing their younger selves.

I don't feel the movie quite as a zany thing. I was hoping it would be more of a sad comedy. But with a ski chase.

This not-too-zany film also features Willem Dafoe punching people in the face, an activity he seems to be good at. I've been a fan of his for quite a long time, and this is one of my favorite Dafoe performances: an amazing, almost entirely physical performance.

I love Willem. I saw him in this Robert Wilson production with Mikhail Baryshnikov not too long ago.**** He's really unique, Willem, because he's not in any way simply a movie actor. He brings his experience with the Wooster Group and with all kinds of avant-garde theater, with Richard Foreman and so on, to anything he's in. He mixes disciplines, like dance and mime and, kind of, sculpture. Willem is using all of that stuff in the Robert Wilson thing. He dances just as well as Baryshnikov in it. Willem is just a *great* dancer. You know, you *expect* Baryshnikov to dance divinely. It's an exciting thing to see.

    Anyway, in our movie, Willem doesn't speak much. It's just his physicality, and I feel like he gave us everything. It's quite something just to watch him *walk*. He created something for us.

I hadn't thought of Willem Dafoe in quite those terms, but I can see that. There is something very gestural or dance-like about him, and that's part of what makes him a memorable actor. He cuts a very imposing figure, and he does a lot with his body. It is his gesture that is the poster of *Platoon*: that iconic image of Sergeant Elias raising his arms up. And of course, *The Last Temptation of Christ*—you don't get much more physical of a performance than that.

He was a great Jesus.

PREVIOUS OVERLEAF: A digital matte painting and a miniature were composited to create the hotel exterior in 1968, after Communism has allowed the place to decay. "It was off-season and, by that time, decidedly out-of-fashion," says the Author in his introductory voice-over, "and it had already begun its descent into shabbiness and eventual demolition."

LEFT: Adrien Brody and Tony Revolori rehearse fisticuffs.

BELOW LEFT: Still-frame from the scene in *The Grand Budapest Hotel* wherein Gustave, informed for the first time of the hardship that his protégé has endured, realizes how insensitive he's been, and apologizes "on behalf of the hotel."

BELOW RIGHT: Publicity photo of Zero Moustafa's near-namesake, actor Zero Mostel, in costume for the 1964 Broadway production of *Fiddler on the Roof*, in which he starred as Tevye.

OPPOSITE: Tony Revolori as Zero, standing in front of a green screen, Mendl's box in hand.

*** Ralph Fiennes invented a personal history for M. Gustave. The director discusses it later in this chapter, and Fiennes talks about it in an interview on page 75.
**** The director is referring to *The Old Woman*, a stage production directed by Robert Wilson and adapted by Darryl Pinckney.

The parts that you've cast him in have showcased a different aspect of his talent than we saw in the 1980s and 1990s, when he had his breakthrough. They're generally bigger, they're more theatrical, they're more stylized, and they're funny. He's almost a purely comic, poignant character in *The Life Aquatic*, and, even though it's animated, you can still feel Willem Dafoe in that rat in *Fantastic Mr. Fox*. He's really hamming it up as this rat—like he's a bad guy in a Sergio Leone film or something, but *jazzy*. In this film, he's a purely malevolent presence, yet there's something very elegant about him. Self-actualized. Like this is what he was put on earth to do: kill people and be evil.

Willem is kind of a classic. And Adrien Brody, another classic. He and Willem had a very good chemistry. You can feel it even when they're just sitting beside each other. I felt like there was some dark bond. Like they were connected.

You know, Willem and Tilda Swinton are both people who love to act, who just love to do this. But they aren't really *just* actors. They're more performance artists. They're interested in any variety of performing, really.

When you say people like Willem Dafoe and Tilda Swinton aren't *just* actors, what do you mean?

They've both done a lot of performing outside of movies and outside of, I guess you'd say, the "normal" theater. Tilda has done numerous performance pieces that appear in museums or in other contexts, completely different kinds of staged work that may not exactly involve scripts or even characters. And Willem has done more avant-garde theater. They're both people who turn up with collaborators whom you don't necessarily think of first, in relation to actors.

In our movie, Willem and Tilda are both playing characters and continuing their personal tradition of making things, outside of playing roles, if that makes any sense. Tilda, I think, would be interested in being aged, just as an experience. I feel like she'd be into doing that even it weren't for a movie.

Having somebody artificially age her, and then just walking down the street?

Or just sitting in a chair somewhere. And Willem's role—well, Kabuki is not exactly the tradition a performance like that comes out of, but it's not necessarily too far afield of it, either. I'm talking about the challenge of playing a character that's about movement and expression, and not about the words, or even necessarily *actions*.

Certain kinds of actors almost seem to have a nineteenth- or even eighteenth-century idea of what it means to be an actor. You get the sense that they might be acrobats, or maybe they would've joined the circus, if it were a different time and place.
You use Tilda Swinton in that way—a primordially "actor-ly" way—in *Moonrise Kingdom* and in this film. In *Moonrise Kingdom*, she's almost more of a presence than a person, like a fairy-tale troublemaker. When I think about her in that movie, I think about her in relation to the space around her, because of the clothes she wears—their color, their texture—the way she enters a room, the expressions on her face.

I guess in that one, the name of her character is an institution: Social Services. I think both that character and her character in this newer movie are meant to be real people, and human characters. But at the same time, you could say they're something else,

ABOVE: **Willem Dafoe as the assassin J. G. Jopling.**

WILLEM DAFOE
THE "GESTURAL INTELLIGENCE" SERIES

WILLEM DAFOE (b. 1955), who has worked with Wes Anderson three times, is a great American leading man with the eccentricity, versatility, and chiseled, old-world features of a 1930s character actor. Here are a few of his signature roles.

TO LIVE AND DIE IN L.A.

After many years of giving striking performances in underappreciated features (including Kathryn Bigelow's debut, the 1981 existential biker drama *The Loveless*), Dafoe broke out in a villainous role as the decadent, super-competent counterfeiter Eric Masters. This performance cemented Dafoe's skill at playing violent antagonists; he tapped into it again in *Wild at Heart* (1990), *Speed 2: Cruise Control* (1997), and as the Green Goblin in Sam Raimi's *Spider-Man* (2002).

PLATOON

Oliver Stone's Best Picture–winning drama, based on his own experiences as an infantryman in Vietnam, cast Dafoe in an Oscar-nominated role as the angelic Sgt. Elias, essentially a lethal stoner Jesus, as in sync with nature and the cosmos as Natty Bumppo in *The Last of the Mohicans*. Elias's arms-rising pose became the movie's poster image. Dafoe returned to the battlefield in *Born on the Fourth of July*, *Flight of the Intruder*, *Off Limits*, and *Clear and Present Danger*.

THE LAST TEMPTATION OF CHRIST

Director Martin Scorsese's passion project, an adaptation of Nikos Kazantzakis's novel about the life and death of Jesus, filled the title role with Dafoe, then fresh off his acclaimed performance as the Christ-like Elias in *Platoon*. Combining intellectual authority, sensitivity, and beatific grace, Dafoe made a historical character often portrayed as dull and passive come alive with contradictions. His emotional transparency makes a philosophical conundrum seem achingly real.

LIGHT SLEEPER

Filmmaker Paul Schrader envisioned this drama about an aging Manhattan drug dealer (Dafoe) as the third of a series of films about men who live by night; the first two were Martin Scorsese's *Taxi Driver* (1976) and Schrader's own *American Gigolo* (1980). Dafoe's character, John LeTour, is a reformed drug addict who never got over his failed marriage (to Dana Delany) and is troubled by a string of murders that seem to parallel his regular route; Dafoe incarnates LeTour as both a workaday supplier of narcotics and, perhaps, an emblem of failed 1960s Utopianism.

SHADOW OF THE VAMPIRE

Dafoe got his second Oscar nomination playing actor Max Schreck in filmmaker E. Elias Merhige's loopy cinephile fantasy about the shooting of the German Expressionist touchstone *Nosferatu*; the conceit is that while director F. W. Murnau (John Malkovich) fusses and frets and gets lost in his own private torments, unbeknownst to him, he's got a real vampire in front of his camera. Dafoe's work here might be the culmination of his Kabuki tendencies—even his small gestures are delightfully extreme.

THE LIFE AQUATIC WITH STEVE ZISSOU

Dafoe's first performance in a Wes Anderson film taps his rarely showcased comedic chops. His Klaus is a wounded man-child who resents being taken for granted by his boss, hero, and father figure, Steve Zissou (Bill Murray). Dafoe lets us watch the comic rage build up in Klaus but makes sure that when the character finally blows his stack, we're never alarmed, just sympathetic to his all-too-human insecurities. He just wants to be appreciated.

TILDA SWINTON
THE "INHABITER" SERIES

The London-born **TILDA SWINTON** (b. 1960) is one of the most versatile film actresses of the modern era, easing from lavish mainstream blockbusters to art-house fare and back again. Here are a few of her signature roles.

1992

ORLANDO

Sally Potter's visually rich, structurally ambitious adaptation of Virginia Woolf's novel stars Swinton as an androgynous young nobleman who's promised a tract of land by Queen Elizabeth on her deathbed, spends two centuries isolated in his castle, journeys to Constantinople as British ambassador to the Turks, and is then mysteriously transformed into a woman overnight, depriving her of property rights and plunging her into a legal battle lasting two more centuries.

2005

THE CHRONICLES OF NARNIA: THE LION, THE WITCH AND THE WARDROBE

The live-action incarnation of C. S. Lewis's *Snow Queen*—reprised in the 2010 sequel, *The Voyage of the Dawn Treader*—is so frightening that it gave the author of this book a nightmare. As portrayed by Swinton, she seems to be fueled by the adrenaline rush that comes from tormenting the weak and bringing her equals to heel. Swinton gives her a terrifying opacity: You know she's hatching plans that she won't reveal until they've been properly marinated in rottenness.

2007

MICHAEL CLAYTON

In this film by writer-director Tony Gilroy, Swinton won a Best Supporting Actress Oscar opposite the film's star, George Clooney. Swinton plays Karen Crowder, the general counsel for a law firm who discovers that one of the firm's lawyers (Tom Wilkinson) is in possession of a memo proving that a client knowingly manufactured carcinogenic weed killers, and plans to make the knowledge public. It's a classic "fixer" role, but Swinton's unself-conscious efficiency makes it surprising, even after you know what Karen is capable of.

2012

MOONRISE KINGDOM

Swinton's supporting performance in this comedy from Wes Anderson certifies her ability to do a lot with comparatively little screen time. She's featured in just a few minutes of the film's ninety-eight-minutes, has little (mostly expository) dialogue, and is defined mainly by the menacing way she cuts through screen space.

2013

ONLY LOVERS LEFT ALIVE

The vampires in Jim Jarmusch's supernatural drama are remnants of a pre-analog, almost pre-technological past, but they look like Tom Hiddleston and Tilda Swinton, and sometimes they drink blood and lustily bare their fangs. Hiddleston is the doom-and-gloom musician contemplating suicide; Swinton is the more reasonable partner, pulling him back from the brink.

2014

SNOWPIERCER

Bong Joon-ho's post-apocalyptic science-fiction film is a class parable about a high-speed train bearing a microcosm of humanity through frozen tundra. Swinton plays Mason, the ostentatiously bewigged mouthpiece of the ruling class, spouting sub–Ayn Randian blather about the importance of knowing one's place and staying in it.

too—somehow I connect that back to the way Tilda and Willem relate to their other work.

Do you remember the first time you noticed Tilda Swinton?

We were at Sundance when *Orlando* played there, so I went to the opening of that movie, and there she was.

She had a dazzling impact on this whole little town that week. She couldn't be more different from one character to the next. She's done a lot of Jim Jarmusch and all of Derek Jarman. What's your favorite Tilda Swinton movie?

It's hard to choose, but right now I'm partial to *Only Lovers Left Alive*. She's sweet, paradoxically enough, considering that she's playing a vampire. She'll be a voice of reason for a while, and then she'll go feast on blood.

She's a wonderful vampire.

She's also somebody who naturally draws people to her without seeming as though she's trying to draw people. I've been in the same room with her a few times, and it always happens. She's a magnet.

That's just charisma, I guess.

Jeff Goldblum: also charismatic, though it's a different wavelength. He was always interesting and always respected, but I feel like recently he's entered the pantheon in some way.

ABOVE: Tilda Swinton as Madame D.

RIGHT: Swinton and camera crew prepare Gustave's angle on their breakfast conversation.

There was a certain moment when Jeff became a big star, probably when he did *The Fly*.

That's one of the greatest performances I've seen anybody give in anything. It might be among the great lead performances in a

horror film, up there with the best of Boris Karloff and Christopher Lee. Almost thirty years on, I still can't stop talking about his performance in that movie.

There aren't so many people who you can hand pages and pages and pages of legal text and say, "Entertain us with this." But, of course, Jeff can do it. When he's preparing, you hear him practicing all the time. He rehearses like he's doing a play, and that's great. I love that.

As Deputy Vilmos Kovacs,***** he uses his hands in the most amazingly distinctive ways. I wasn't surprised when I learned he was a pianist. His hands do a lot, I think, to make all that legalese a bit more dynamic. You see that during the reading of the will. There are actually three performances going on in every scene with Jeff Goldblum, and two of them are by his hands.

Jeff just has great dramatic instincts. He makes things compelling. In every scene he does, he's not just thinking, "Can I make this sound more natural?" He's thinking, "Can I make this sound more *exciting*?" He finds where the drama is.

He was not in a whole lot of Robert Altman movies—*Nashville* was the first, nearly forty years ago—and yet somehow I think of him as an Altman actor.

I do, too. And I think Altman thought of him in that way.
    I didn't know Altman very well, but he and his wife, Katherine, and I had a conversation once, many years ago, about Jeff, and he talked about him like he was a part of his ongoing stock company. They also talked about Bud Cort in a similar way. Bud

Cort's only in two of Altman's movies, *M*A*S*H* and *Brewster McCloud*, and Jeff's only in two: *Nashville* and *Beyond Therapy*. But maybe Jeff thinks of himself that way, too, in some way: as an Altman actor.

He does more with less in *Nashville*. He doesn't even have dialogue in that. He's just a presence in the background—gesturing, existing. He's even doing magic at one point.

I'm sure Altman saw it and said, "Let's weave that into it. Whatever Jeff's doing over here, let's film it, and we'll have another ingredient." He's probably in *The Player,* too, actually.

You've used Jeff Goldblum in a couple of movies now, and it's interesting that in both of them, he seems incredibly confident to the point of arrogance, but then you bring him down a notch, and we discover new shadings. There are moments of sweetness and vulnerability in *The Life Aquatic* toward the end; Alistair Hennessey and Steve Zissou even have a moment, and it feels real because you can feel warmth between him and Bill Murray.
    And in *The Grand Budapest Hotel*, of course, he carries himself with such tranquil confidence; then comes the stalking sequence at the museum. There's a fear in his eyes that's unsettling, because you've never seen it until now. You get the feeling this is the first time in a really long time that Kovacs doesn't feel like, "Eh, I've got it all under control." And it's his last moment on earth.

Jeff's a great one to work with. He's very fun to have around, super-focused, and a very gentle presence on a movie set—and he's always *on* it.

You mean physically on the set?

Right.

ABOVE: Anderson and Goldblum between takes of the will scene.

***** "Vilmos Kovacs" combines the first and last names of two great American cinematographers, both of whom were born and raised in Hungary: Vilmos Zsigmond (b. 1930) and László Kovács (1933–2007).

JEFF GOLDBLUM
THE "DRAWING THE EYE" SERIES

JEFF GOLDBLUM (b. 1952) is an intuitive and eccentric American actor whose lanky physique and quicksilver mind initially locked him into light comic parts. He eventually broke out into leading roles in comedies and dramas that showcased darker shadings. A small sampling can be found below.

1975

NASHVILLE

Maverick dramatist Robert Altman was famous for treating his actors as a sort of floating repertory company, often casting for look and personality more so than track records, and sometimes throwing performers into his films just because he liked their style. Jeff Goldblum had that sort of role in *Nashville*, playing a quasi-mystical seventies hippie-freak magician type whose main purpose was to draw the eye.

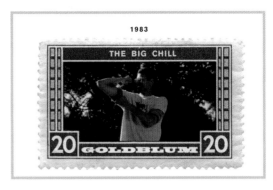

1983

THE BIG CHILL

Goldblum's by then well-established credentials as a sixties-style counterculture oddball were well used by writer-director Lawrence Kasdan, who cast him as one of the "sellout" members of a group of thirty-something hippies-turned-yuppies reuniting after a friend's suicide. His self-loathing *People* magazine writer gets many of the film's biggest laugh lines, including his admission that the publication's first rule is, "Never write anything longer than the average person can read during the average crap."

1986

THE FLY

Goldblum's performance as inventor Seth Brundle in David Cronenberg's remake of *The Fly* (1958) was the first major feature to cast the actor as both a brilliant visionary and a romantic leading man (opposite his then significant other, Geena Davis). Goldblum's ability to make us sense the man inside the increasingly revolting monster makeup rivaled the best of Boris Karloff and Lon Chaney. It's one of the great science-fiction films—and great tragedies—of the 1980s.

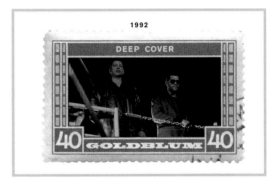

1992

DEEP COVER

As gangsters' attorney David Jason, opposite undercover cop John Hull (Laurence Fishburne), Goldblum gave a performance that channeled Scorsese-style homicidal peevishness. The character's partly improvised dialogue is filled with lines that blend macho posturing and self-deprecation: "A man has two things in this world: His word and his balls. Or is that three things?"

1993–1997

JURASSIC PARK–THE LOST WORLD: JURASSIC PARK

In Steven Spielberg's dinosaur adventures, Goldblum returned to sci-fi again—a genre in which he was always comfortable; see also *Independence Day* (1996) and *Hideaway* (1995). His performance as the brilliant and flirtatious chaos theoretician Ian Malcolm in the first movie was such a crowd-pleaser that the director cast him as the lead in the sequel.

2004

THE LIFE AQUATIC WITH STEVE ZISSOU

As Alistair Hennessey in Wes Anderson's fourth movie, Goldblum played the slick, corporatized, next-generation version of Bill Murray's Cousteau-like explorer Steve Zissou, turning unctuous narcissism into comic fuel, and revealing unexpectedly sweet shadings near the film's end.

OPPOSITE: Three still-frames from *The Grand Budapest Hotel*, from the moment on the carousel when we see Agatha (Saoirse Ronan) through the eyes of the love-struck Zero (Tony Revolori). These shallow-focus images come from a director more often associated with wide-angled lenses and considerable depth of field. The long lens blurs the carousel lights swirling in the background, creating an almost halo-like effect, as if stars are swirling around Agatha's head. The shot faintly echoes the final-reel, brightly colored close-ups of Dr. David Bowman traveling in the "space vortex," from Stanley Kubrick's *2001: A Space Odyssey* (1968).

ABOVE: Tony Revolori and Saoirse Ronan.

OVERLEAF: The Society of the Crossed Keys: Bill Murray as M. Ivan of the Excelsior Palace, Wally Wolodarsky as M. Georges of Chateau Luxe, Waris Ahluwalia as M. Dino of the Palazzo Principessa, Fisher Stevens as M. Robin of L'Hôtel Côte du Cap, Bob Balaban as M. Martin of the Ritz Imperial.

***** The mutual friend who inspired the character of M. Gustave.

I've heard that's something you like—for actors to stay on the set between setups.

He and Willem both stayed on the set during *Life Aquatic*. They didn't want to leave the set in between setups. They stick around. Why does anybody need to leave? I mean, maybe somebody needs to go put on a different costume, or have their lunch or something, but really, in general, I feel like it's better to stay with the scene.

Saoirse Ronan: She doesn't have this storied history of some of the other actors we're talking about.

She's one of those people who, if you see her in a few movies, you think, "Oh, this one can do anything."

We'd only met each other briefly, just one day, when Saoirse arrived in the middle of the shoot. The first scene she did was the shootout in the hotel. Her first day of shooting was the climactic sequence of the movie.

And I said, "So, you've come out of this elevator, and now these guys are going to try and follow you, and he wants to kill you, and so on" and then instantly: There she was. She turned it on: terrified. It wasn't one of those things where there was any adjustment. She just knew the script, and then she knew how to get herself exactly to the right place.

Somehow, very young people who've worked a lot, in my experience, are like acting computers, in a good way: They just know how to do it. It's like you're speaking a foreign language, but they're fluent already.

Speaking of people who know the language: The Society of the Crossed Keys sequence gives you an opportunity to do kind of a roll call of people who have appeared in Wes Anderson films.

We've got Bob Balaban, and we've got Bill Murray, and we've got Wally Wolodarsky, and we've got the one who's newest, Fisher Stevens. I've been friends with Fisher for many years, and not only are Fisher and I friends, Fisher and Ralph are old friends, too, and Fisher and Edward Norton are old friends.

Ralph Fiennes is very funny in this movie. I have seen him be funny before, in certain scenes of certain movies, but "funny" is perhaps not the first word you think of when you think of Ralph Fiennes. He first came to the world's attention as a dramatic actor in films like *Schindler's List* and *Quiz Show*, and he's been very intense, at times romantically dark, in lead roles: *The English Patient*, *The End of the Affair*. And a whole generation now knows him as He-Who-Must-Not-Be-Named in the Harry Potter films. Did you envision Ralph Fiennes as Gustave when you wrote this, and, if so, was there anything in his filmography that made you think that he was the right actor for, basically, a light comic lead role?

I don't necessarily see too much of a distinction between somebody who's able to be funny and somebody who's just able to be good. He's obviously one of these spectacular talents. I knew Ralph a little bit already, so when we were writing it, I was thinking of the real person,****** but from the very beginning of working on the story, Ralph was the person I thought ought to play it.

You know, there's another thing: People who act in movies aren't necessarily that comfortable with paragraphs and paragraphs of dialogue. They aren't necessarily people who are ready to give speeches in a long take without a cut. That isn't necessarily the way movies are done, and that isn't the way movie roles are generally written. I've never had a character who talks as much as M. Gustave. Well, none of that was going to be a problem for Ralph.

PART 4:
THE SOCIETY of the CROSSED KEYS

RALPH FIENNES

THE "TROUBLED GRACE" SERIES

RALPH FIENNES (b. 1962) is a dashing English actor, often cast in slightly reticent and mysterious leading man parts. But his range is considerable, as the selection below demonstrates.

1993

SCHINDLER'S LIST

Fiennes's breakthrough performance in Steven Spielberg's Holocaust drama cast him as Amon Goeth, a murderous, exploitive, yet strangely pitiful concentration camp commander who snipes at prisoners from his balcony. The head cold that the character is sniffling through in his first scene was real—one of many examples of Fiennes's ability to take what other actors might think of as inconveniences and make them work for the character.

1994

QUIZ SHOW

Director Robert Redford, a specialist in portraying WASP delusion, cast Fiennes as Charles Van Doren, the Columbia University professor who became a wealthy winner on rigged network quiz shows in the 1950s. Fiennes captured the mix of vanity and self-loathing that prevented the character from coming clean, as well as the upper-class entitlement that undercut his eventual apology.

1996

THE ENGLISH PATIENT

Fiennes's performance as Count László de Almásy in Anthony Minghella's time-shifting historical drama saw the actor easing into opaque epic-hero mode, à la Peter O'Toole in *Lawrence of Arabia*. He plays the present-day scenes in heavy burn makeup, but in the flashbacks he's handsome and elegant, and reveals the neediness in a character who initially presents as aloof.

1999

THE END OF THE AFFAIR

Neil Jordan's adaptation of Graham Greene's novel was perhaps Fiennes's most purely sensual role in the 1990s: an account of the doomed romance between Maurice Bendrix (Fiennes) and his former mistress, a married woman named Sarah Miles (Julianne Moore). By turns intensely sad and alarmingly possessive, Fiennes's Maurice is one of the actor's subtlest performances.

2002

SPIDER

David Cronenberg's adaptation of Patrick McGrath's novel cast Fiennes as a disturbed loner whose illness pushes him back into a memory cave where he relives childhood traumas. This is an intense, claustrophobic drama, at times nearly a one-man show, which Fiennes is often watching and reenacting as past dramas replay themselves; as such, it's a master class in how to act with the eyes and body.

2005–2011

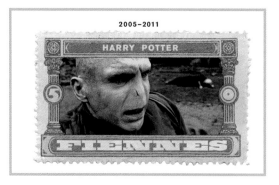

**HARRY POTTER AND THE GOBLET OF FIRE–
HARRY POTTER AND THE DEATHLY HALLOWS: PART 2**

Best nose-less villain performance of all time, for sure—and a great fantasy bad guy, no matter whom you stack Fiennes up against. The Darth Vader of the aughts. Imperious, confident, utterly terrifying. For another bad-guy performance on a different wavelength, see the 2002 version of Thomas Harris's *Red Dragon*, costarring Fiennes as the psychotic Francis Dolarhyde, aka "The Tooth Fairy."

He also has some of that 1930s "European" quality that we talked about. He brings a bit of George Sanders to certain scenes of his. When things turn madcap, we may think of Rex Harrison in *Unfaithfully Yours*, and Alec Guinness in some of the Ealing comedies. It's not quite screwball, that style of performance, but there's a touch of it, I think.

A lot of it's fast dialogue, and that's kind of an old-fashioned thing, but I don't even know what I'd compare Ralph's performance in this movie to. In the end, he doesn't remind me of anybody. He's such a forceful presence. He brings all his energy into every scene.

I always pictured him as coming from a Laurence Olivier sort of tradition, but it's not really quite that. He's more like a Method actor. He wants to do it from the inside out, and he wants to *feel* it. He wants to *be* the guy. I've never had anyone who was like that, to that degree. I've always wanted to work with somebody very "Method"—somebody who's going to kind of demand things.

I've worked with Harvey Keitel before, and we had Harvey again on this movie, and Harvey does that. Harvey requires certain kinds of attention and insists on an extraordinary level of preparation, a level that some actors don't even *think* to do. I loved Harvey doing that sort of thing when we did *Moonrise Kingdom*. He did it here, too. On this movie, Harvey doesn't have a huge role, but he took his fellow inmates and went and stayed for forty-eight hours in the prison we shot in. He and the other actors lived there, and they figured out their whole backstory together, and we rehearsed over there. By the time we were shooting the scenes, they had a whole relationship. Ralph comes from something like that tradition.

The total immersion school.

It's the Russian way. Not that they do it in Russia, but you know what I mean.

Going back to gestures: There are lots of what you might call "anchor points" for performances—little recurring bits of business, such as the way that Gustave is always saying "darling." And the way that the character walks is important: his gait. Gustave does actually seem to have steel in his spine.

Do these character touches tend to be things you that talked about with the actors ahead of time, or do the actors work them out on their own?

Well, the "darlings" are just in the script. But I don't think Ralph necessarily says to himself, "How am I going to walk?" I think he's working more with, "How do I feel?" and "How do I think?" And then it moves on from there to "What am I wearing?" and "Why am I wearing it this way, and not that way?"******* and "How does all that make me move, and how does that make me stand, and *who am I*?"

Speaking of process—in many of your films, you are extraordinarily concerned with process, with procedure, with tradition. *Rushmore* is the first film where those aspects really jump out: The hero defines himself by his association with this academy that has a storied history. One often gets the sense, when watching your films, that there is a particular world that you've created, and that there is a particular way within that world in which things are done.

That becomes incredibly important in this film, because, like Rushmore Academy, and like the *Belafonte* in *The Life Aquatic*, the Grand Budapest Hotel is a place with a storied history. Certain things are done there, at a certain time, in a certain manner.

That's the source of a lot of the comedy between your two main characters. You've got this one early exchange between Gustave and Zero that's an example of what I'm talking about. He tells Zero, "Run to the cathedral of Santa Maria Christiana in Brucknerplatz. Buy one of the plain, half-length candles and take back four Klubecks in change. Light it in the sacristy, say a brief rosary, then go to Mendl's and get me a Courtesan au Chocolat."

"If there's any money left, give it to the crippled shoeshine boy."

You can see a bit of that mentoring thing in Zweig.******** It's definitely there in *Confusion*. And in *Beware of Pity*, there's this younger man who's being told a story by an older man.

In our movie, the mentoring thing is largely there because our friend is like that in real life. He mentors, kind of automatically, more or less anybody he gets to know.*********

"Our friend" being the guy you modeled Gustave on?

Yes.

So you met this man through Hugo Guinness?

I met him through Hugo, yes.

Can you tell me about him?

We've never said his name.

Why not?

I just feel like it's better not to. He's an old friend, a very old friend of Hugo's, and now he's been friends with me for at least fifteen years. He's not a hotel concierge, but he would be—and he would be the first to claim this—one of the great hotel concierges on the planet, if he so chose.

Why would he be one of the greats?

Everything that makes a good concierge, he knows how to do. He also—in the same vein—already knows all the concierges of all the hotels. He will sit and chat with somebody at the desk of a hotel for an hour and come out with all kinds of gossip. He's been on the circuit for a long time. And there are lots of lines in the movie that come directly from him.

Can you give me an example?

Well, like when Zero says, "She was eighty-four." And he says, "I've had older." That's him. The "darlings" come from him. Really, we just tried to write his voice.

That's how the poetry ended up in the screenplay. The real-life inspiration for Gustave recites poetry. It's kind of his . . . well, I don't know if I'd say *habit*, but it's one of his techniques for getting from A to B: There may be a poem along the way.

Did you write all of Gustave's poems?

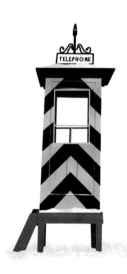

PREVIOUS OVERLEAF: Ralph Fiennes as M. Gustave, saying a fond farewell to Madame D.

******* For more about the effect of period clothes on an actor's performance, see page 74 of the interview with Ralph Fiennes.
******** Alexandre Desplat, who composed the score for *The Grand Budapest Hotel*, says on page 135 that "education" is a theme in *Fantastic Mr. Fox, Moonrise Kingdom,* and *The Grand Budapest Hotel*.
********* For more about Stefan Zweig's work as the inspiration for *The Grand Budapest Hotel*, see Act 3, which begins on page 175, as well as Ali Arikan's essay "Worlds of Yesterday," which begins on page 207.

ABOVE: Police-blotter-type photo of Jeff Goldblum's Deputy Kovacs after his murder by Willem Dafoe's Jopling.

OPPOSITE: Flashbulb-lit, Weegee-style tabloid crime-scene photo of Tilda Swinton as Madame D. Versions of this image are seen twice in the film. The first is when Zero shows Gustave the newspaper story detailing the old woman's death. The second is Zero's flashback account of his conversation with Kovacs regarding the murder and the will.

──────────────

✳✳✳✳✳✳✳✳✳✳ The latter assertion is proved true in the film's prison-break sequence: A fearsome inmate to whom Gustave has shown kindness strangles a prisoner who was threatening to foil the concierge's escape.

I should say, there are really no poems in the movie, just snippets of poems.

That one fragment he recites when he's hanging from his fingernails by the edge of the cliff almost sounds like he's about to launch into Tennyson's "The Charge of the Light Brigade."

I think he wants to go out in a blaze of glory.

When Gustave says, "Rudeness is merely the expression of fear. People *fear* they won't get what they want. The most dreadful and unattractive person only needs to be *loved*—and they will open up like a flower." Is that just a line from your friend, something that he said that you liked and decided to use in the movie?✳✳✳✳✳✳✳✳✳✳

No, that was a line from Hugo, I believe.

Do you personally believe in that sentiment?

I would say: It depends.
There are plenty of times when somebody is rude because they're scared or uncomfortable. They're agitated, and they're worried that they're not being treated properly, or they're rude because they think they're standing up for themselves or against some kind of injustice, and later they might step back and realize, "That guy was drunk; he wasn't really trying to show me up."
It certainly is a good bit of instruction for somebody who's going to work in a hotel, because they're going to have to deal with all kinds of demands and emotions.
You know, Ralph had a very funny idea for Gustave. At one point, we were having a conversation about the character, and then Ralph did Gustave for me, at five different stages of life.

Spontaneously?

Ralph's very good at that sort of thing. On a movie like this, everything is all written, and he's learning the text, you know, and doing it. It's a bit like a play. But Ralph can also just make up dialogue spontaneously, at will. In fact, we shot all these montages where he's talking to these old women, and when he's on trial—things like that. There was nothing written. Unfortunately, there's no room in the movie for us to be able to see all of that, but it was good writing he did on the spot.
At one point, spontaneously, he did for me what he saw as Gustave's story. It involved a transition from a sort of a Dickens Cockney street urchin to a kind of East Londoner, saying: "Hold on, you're not going to want that one, sir, I think." And he followed Gustave through a series of improvisations that showed the evolution of his learning and his education, and the affectation and the development and the refinement of his accent.
I guess that's what probably happened to somebody like Noël Coward or Cary Grant.

It's the movie in microcosm. People transform themselves even as the countries that created them are being transformed.

I like that.

AN
INTERVIEW
WITH

PROPER EXPLORING:

AN INTERVIEW WITH RALPH FIENNES

 Veteran actor and director **RALPH FIENNES***'s career is explored in some detail in Act 1 of this book (see page 55). His role as M. Gustave in* The Grand Budapest Hotel *marks his first collaboration with Wes Anderson.*

MATT ZOLLER SEITZ: *When you are working with a filmmaker who is known for his meticulous preparation, someone who has a vision of the entire film in his head, maps out all of the shots with animatics, and has a good deal of it planned out ahead of time, where does the actor fit in?*

RALPH FIENNES: On a Wes Anderson film, you come knowing what you're in for; a lot of the actors knew exactly what to expect. All you have to do is look at his movies to know that his is the most meticulous style, and that you're just going to have to be up for it. You're agreeing to be a part of his style, and his style is very visually precise, with shots that are very composed.

Wes also has a fine ear for his own dialogue—for his rhythm and his pitch and his tone. And he was clear with me that this movie was inspired in part by 1930s comedies, specifically by directors such as Ernst Lubitsch and Billy Wilder. There's a very particular, sort of rapid-fire delivery of dialogue in those sorts of films. It's real, it's natural, but it's got a slightly heightened quality that has to do with its rhythm and speed, and its delivery for comic effect.

So I knew going in that this wasn't going to be a behaviorist, "feel it," slightly improvised sort of film. I knew it was going to be formal and exact. And I confess that early on, I was worried about obstacles. I was wondering, "Can I just find my way into this? What's the most instinctively natural way to do this?"

Then I realized that this approach wasn't going to work. And here I should say that I was happy to see the storyboards—the little animatics that Wes had worked out. They were very helpful. They let me understand the way *he* was approaching it.

When you're working for Wes Anderson, is there any room for making up dialogue, for pressing for a completely different architecture for a scene? I ask because, as you know, some directors are not only up for that, but they work that way in movie after movie. Mike Leigh even has a phrase to describe it: "Growing a film."

No, it's not like that. But I want to say that it would be a mistake to give the impression that Wes is somehow dictatorial. He isn't. Once you start shooting, he's very generous with the number of takes. He sincerely wants his actors to explore—within the confines of the frame, the compositions, and what the camera is doing—many, many variations. I liked that. I thought it was properly creative.

OPPOSITE   Tony Revolori, Ralph Fiennes, and Wes Anderson rehearsing the sequence in which M. Gustave and young Zero walk through the lobby of the hotel, encountering guests and employees along the way.

When I interviewed Wes for the last book, I asked him about improvisa-
tion, and about the idea of working with actors to develop dialogue and
develop characters. He said his feeling was, anything that wasn't dia-
logue or a plot point, he considered an improvisation by the actors.

I don't remember Wes ever being excited if I improvised even a little bit while doing a take, but yes, he's right: There are ways of finding all kinds of variations within a given script. Once I accepted the style of the piece, I enjoyed the whole experience. It was fulfilling.

So the constraints you feared you'd feel—those never materialized?

Oh, it felt like maybe once or twice there'd be a camera move that I worried was designed in such a way that it would undermine the scene—so that the scene couldn't flow—because it was overly dependent on the actors hitting certain marks.

Most of the time, it was fine. There was one scene—a very well-written scene, a very cool piece of writing on Wes's part—where I felt that the camera, or the organization of the camera, was a bit of a straitjacket, but I think Wes saw that as well. I felt that it was overcomplicating and slightly getting in the way of a very good scene. I said I thought perhaps the camera needed to be more still and let the scene play out between Tony and me. And that's what, in the end, happened. Wes made it very simple for us.

What do you, as an actor, as a performer, have to pay attention to when
you're performing in a film like this one? Do you pay more careful
attention to what you do with your body, to the specifics of movement?
How, in practical terms, does working on this film differ from working
on a film like, say, The English Patient, *or* The End of the Affair, *or*
something like that—something that's more slowed down and, perhaps,
naturalistic, or that aspires to be?

Wes didn't ask for a specific style of acting. He is not saying that you have to act in a different way than you're used to or comfortable with. He wants what you bring, as an actor, but he wants you to put it through the conduit of his own vision. And so you do that, and sort of find yourself becoming part of that world.

I really think that, with Wes, it's best to keep it simple. There is a quality of delivery that he tends to like. It's not overly fussy. I think he is instinctively drawn to an almost deadpan delivery of lines. That deadpan has a lot to do with the comic effect of his lines on-screen. But the comic effect also has to do with naturalness. Wes loves it very pure, you know? I think the overly behaviorist, palsied, broken-up, "let me think how I say these lines" kind of delivery is really not what he prefers. I think he'd be appalled if you did that—if you brought in all the little tics and mannerisms of so-called naturalistic acting while delivering his dialogue. I don't think that sort of acting particularly interests him, or I should say, I don't think it fits the kinds of films he likes to make. I think he likes kind of extreme delivery of text, but delivery that is also totally—well, not natural, exactly. Totally unfussy. And clean.

And I should also say this: There was a speed element. Throughout, Wes kept saying, "Faster, faster, faster."

Is there such a thing as too fast? Did you ever worry about that?

Ralph Fiennes in the scene in which M. Gustave is questioned by police in connection with Madame D.'s murder: He hesitates for a moment, says "She's been murdered . . . and you think I did it?" and then flees. This is a locked-down wide shot filmed with a very wide-angle lens. Every part of the screen space, from foreground to background, is in focus. We might not think about the logistics as we're watching this moment, but they're trickier than they might appear. There are a lot of people grouped closely in the foreground, blocked so that the actors don't obscure one another too much and we can always see the star. The other actors in the scene had to preserve the audience's sight lines throughout, giving Gustave space to do his thing, but without seeming as though they're keeping the sight lines open. When Gustave flees from foreground to background and up the stairs, the cluster of foreground actors opens up a bit, clearing space for us to watch the concierge's retreat without obstruction.

Sometimes I worried it would be too fast, but once I actually saw the results, I realized he was right.

How, as a performer, do you account for all the narration in the movie? The interplay of voice-over, dialogue, and camera movement is very precise. Wes told me a little bit about the different ways that he had adjusted to the actors on set, trying to incorporate the voice-over into their performances, knowing there might have to be a pause here or there to leave space for a line of narration.

I was never aware of that, to be honest. I mean, I never felt that I was being asked to dance around a voice-over that would come later.

Do things like that fall under the heading of "Part of the Job?"

Well, actors like different kinds of challenges. One director might be asking you to "Find it from within yourself," you know, and then on another film you find yourself with a director who could not be more different; I mean in the specific way in which Wes is allowing elements and improvisation to occur, and the sort of modesty that he likes in performances. He really wants the performances to be rooted in who the actors are.

Anthony Minghella, the director of *The English Patient,* which you mentioned, was very different. He wanted a different sort of collaboration. He had written the screenplay, and he didn't necessarily want you to add words or change the script. But he did ask the actors to take what he had written, and then take it a page further, in the way they interpreted it, in the way it was spoken. Anthony Minghella liked being surprised by readings of lines that he had written that he never thought would occur.

Whereas I'd say Wes has a strong sense of how the lines should be, and he is often leading you toward that. With some directors, that can become a bit claustrophobic, but with Wes—because he's so intelligent, and often because what he has heard in his head, or rather, how he imagines the line should be spoken, is often cool—he's got a fine ear for his own dialogue.

Everything about Gustave is distinctive. His walk is distinctive, his posture, the way he tilts his head, the slight quaver in his voice when you sense he's about to lose control. All of these things, I wonder: How instinctive are they? And how much are they the product of preparation? Did you come into the production saying, "Once I get there, I'm going to do this," or "He's going to walk this way," or "He's going to move this way," or is it just something that evolves naturally and you can't even describe it?

I think it's really important—*really* important—to stress that, in any situation you have where Wes is not entirely settled on an approach, he wants your input. He wants your help shaping the character. If there were aspects of the character that he wasn't sure about, I'd say, "Well, Wes, what is it?"

What sorts of discussions did you have about shaping the character?

OPPOSITE TOP   Ralph Fiennes and Saoirse Ronan.
OPPOSITE BOTTOM   Still-frame showing M. Gustave backstage, as it were, sans the uniform that so often visually defines him.

If I remember correctly, I said something to him like, "Wes, there's a spectrum about the way Gustave can be played. High camp, hyper, sort of crazy, or very naturalistically." It ended up being somewhere in the middle. I think that in most of the takes that he ended up using, he went for the slightly more understated bits.

But when you were shooting, you were playing Gustave at various points along this "farce spectrum?"

While we were shooting, we definitely pushed the interpretation in all kinds of ways. I should stress here that Wes has designed a tightly organized structure. But within that, he knows the structure can only fly if there's an organic quality—if the imaginative journey is able to develop organically. He's worked with enough smart people to know that he can't totally take over every element of a performance. And I don't think he wants that! But once he's created his script, he's got his structure, he knows the shots—within that, he absolutely knows the actors have to breathe life into it, through their physicality that emerges during shooting.

And of course he has ideas in the moment. "How 'bout we try this?" "How 'bout we try that?" "What happens if you do this?" And I love that. That's proper exploring, for a director to talk like that, I think.

How does one prepare for a part like Gustave H. physically, or in terms of envisioning the character? You can read him on the page and get a sense of what sort of person he is, but then you have to bring him to life in front of the cameras. You have to incarnate him on film. How does that process work?

That's the sort of question that's really hard to answer, because all these things are so instinctive. You know, you try on a coat, you talk to Milena Canonero about how a shoe should fit, or . . . a thing just appears. You practice in circles through a scene. You're being allowed to play around and feel what is right. It all comes from feeding an instinct. There isn't any sort of fine method that I can describe, except once you start to get in the mind-set and imagine what you're wearing, there's a lot of, "What's Gustave about?"

What is Gustave about?

He's a concierge, so his allotment in life is to present himself to the world in a certain way that anticipates what people expect, or what the hotel's guests expect. There's a charm. In that job, you've got to be clean, and you've got to be precise, and you've got to have an engaging way of acting.

What role do costumes and props play in aiding the creation of a performance? Years ago, when I was on the set of Deadwood, *I interviewed the actor Stephen Tobolowsky, and I asked him, "How do you get into the mind-set of a nineteenth-century character?" and he said, "Look at what I'm wearing. The second I put these clothes on, I'm halfway there." Do you feel that there's some truth to that? Do the clothes, the shoes, and so forth help you get halfway there or, perhaps, some percentage of the way there?*

Still-frames from *The Grand Budapest Hotel* capture a moment from the breakfast conversation between M. Gustave (Ralph Fiennes) and Madame D. (Tilda Swinton). The scene lasts only about a minute, but the actors' performances have to convey the essence of an entire relationship between two characters who have known each other for decades—one of whom is about to die.

Sure, sure, of course. You might be tightly buttoned in vests or waistcoats. You know, there's a certain way you'd have to want to hold yourself, but . . . you know, you look at yourself. There's often a degree of the individual inside the clothes.

I did a period film recently. We shot it, and you're looking at photographs of the people from that era to prepare. People's physicality mines all the factors you listed. To be asked to wear this formal clothing, that has an effect.

But at the same time, you know, people from another time, their bodies are like our bodies. I don't know that nineteenth-century people's physicality, in essence, is necessarily all that different from ours. Literature from every era is full of descriptions of people trying to present themselves to the world in a certain way, a way that they think will impress. And yet you often feel, while reading someone like Dickens, that there are still people who behave naturally, people who just have a "natural-ness" and ease in the way they interact with other people.

It's a fascinating area, this one. When we want to adopt or want to create another world, or maybe a past world, we have to ask, "Were people different?" In some ways, perhaps, but I think bodies function the same, under the clothes. People have back pains. People have digestive problems. They have headaches. It's the same body. They may have this idea they're so totally different from people who lived before them, but how much variation in behavior has humanity known? A bit, to some extent maybe—but then maybe not, you know?

It's complicated.

It is. And we're talking about this in the context of filmmaking. It all depends so much on what the film is asking, what the characters are asking, what the director is asking. Does the character strike an attitude, or present himself to the world in a certain way? It would be interesting to pull up a bunch of actors, do an experiment, and say, "Right, read this. Play this scene in jeans and T-shirts and your own clothes. And then put on these Victorian clothes, do the scene again, and don't change anything. Just remember how it felt in the jeans and a T-shirt. And then see what happens." That would be interesting, I think, to do that, and then see to what degree, despite that, people's true selves would change, or not change.

That's fascinating. I wonder if the actors who did that kind of experiment might somehow come across as imperceptibly more modern once they put on the period clothes?

Ah, but what does that word *mean*, you see? *Modern?* I mean, we think of ourselves as more modern, yes, but we don't know for a fact that our consciousness today is really all that different from the consciousness of someone from another time. I think clothes affect people, for sure—who they are, their sense of themselves—but in some fundamental way, they might not. I suppose what I'm saying is that when we do period films, there is a temptation to think that over time, the essence of humanity changes, but I don't know if it necessarily does, or if it does, to what degree.

All right. I've said enough!

One more question, then. Wes told me that you had imagined a whole history for Gustave H., detailing how he more or less invented the man that you see before you when you're watching The Grand Budapest Hotel. *That dovetails rather nicely with the Wes Anderson universe, as it were, which is filled with characters who kind of create these personas for themselves, often in response to a personal trauma in their history. Can you share any of Gustave's story with us?*

I imagined M. Gustave coming from quite a poor background in England. I imagined his parents being very poor, and his father dying when he was young. But his father sent him on errands. His father was maybe a shoemaker, I think. And then he was asked to deliver shoes to a wealthy client, who lived in a hotel.

Suddenly, on his own, he saw another world and became . . . well, after his father's death, I think he had a job as the lowest of the low at a grand hotel. Certain wealthy clients liked him and took him aboard. Then he started a new life in a French hotel. And from then on, he sort of traced his own persona as he grew up through these European hotels, working his way up. Wes's idea was: Well, maybe that was how he finally came to be out on his own, living equitably.

Ralph Fiennes: a touch-up at the hand of makeup artist Frances Hannon; a light reading at the hand of cinematographer Bob Yeoman.

they wear
what they are:
the grand
budapest hotel
and the art
of movie
costumes

christopher
laverty

1 *Indiana Jones and the Temple of Doom* (1984)
2 *A Clockwork Orange* (1971)
3 *Gone With the Wind* (1939)
4 *Breakfast at Tiffany's* (1961)
5 *Marie Antoinette* (2006)
6 *Saturday Night Fever* (1977)
7 *Drive* (2011)
8 *Blade Runner* (1982)

they wear what they are:
the grand budapest hotel and the art of movie costumes

CHRISTOPHER LAVERTY

We glean so much from what a person wears on-screen. The clothes serve many aesthetic masters: character, narrative progression, period accuracy, and spectacle. They can also determine how a film is remembered in the public consciousness; the most vivid costumes may, in memory, come to stand for the film itself. Scarlett O'Hara's velvet-curtain gown. The droogs (costumed by Milena Canonero) in white, with black hats and codpieces. Indiana Jones's leather jacket, fedora, and bullwhip. Like the costumes in *The Grand Budapest Hotel*, these can be scrutinized and obsessed over or duly noted in context: You're under no obligation to fixate on particular details, but should you choose to, the details may disclose a larger purpose.

Anderson often chooses to uniform his creations. Sometimes the uniforms signify specific jobs: the Lawn Wranglers in *Bottle Rocket*, the crew of the *Belafonte* in *The Life Aquatic with Steve Zissou*. Other times the uniforms are self-created, signifying characters' views of themselves, or the world's view of them. They wear clothes as armor, as subtext, or, crucially, as a visual bait-and-switch. When the armor cracks or is discarded, we notice. We can read their interiors by studying their exteriors. They wear what they are.

1 *Moonrise Kingdom* (2012)
2 *Bottle Rocket* (1996)
3 *The Royal Tenenbaums* (2001)
4 *The Life Aquatic with Steve Zissou* (2004)

On first glance, Agatha is just a typical pastry girl wearing a candy-colored, pistachio-green dress, a peach cable-knit sweater, and thick wool socks. As the story unfolds, she acquires a motif that marks her as one of the film's most important characters: a porcelain Society of the Crossed Keys pendant. We gather that this emblem is normally only worn by concierges who've been inducted into the prestigious guild. Because of her resourcefulness, Gustave considers Agatha worthy of the accolade. As an old man, the still-grieving Zero wears the pendant as a connection to his lost love.

When Gustave tumbles from symbol of luxurious tradition to disgraced criminal, he trades his tailored suit for a striped prison uniform with too-short sleeves and half-mast trousers grazing the ankles (above a pair of clunking *sabots*). He seems to accept this little indignity, not to mention the bigger ones, with relative good cheer; but we may wonder what the departed Madame D., in her Klimt-esque velvet coat, would have made of her dapper lover at this point. The old lady's finery represents hotel culture at its zenith: an age of parties and champagne, four-poster beds and foie gras.

Production sketches by Juman Malouf
1 Still-frame of Agatha (Saoirse Ronan) in Mendl's uniform.
2 Saoirse Ronan, with cinematographer Robert Yeoman in background.
3 The Society of the Crossed Keys pendant.
4 Gustave in concierge uniform.
5 Gustave in prison garb.
6 Madame D. in Klimt coat, with Gustave in uniform.

J opling's knee-length leather coat: a stable, unswerving silhouette, just as much about function as form. Resembling a World War II–era *Kradmantel*, this is, in essence, a motorcycle dispatch rider's coat designed to keep the wearer warm and dry. A near-parody of the archetypal baddie in black, Jopling nevertheless calls up mythological associations that make laughter stick in the throat. Nosferatu-pointed teeth. Skull knuckledusters. A hidden "drunk pocket" in his coat that houses a gun, a flask, and an ice pick (where a map should be). Yet even his nastiest bits of violence don't quite shatter the comic tone.

K een-eyed viewers may have spotted the half-belt on the rear of the brothers' jackets (a nod to the classic Norfolk suit) in the director's fifth film, *The Darjeeling Limited*. The two characters of the old Author and the young Author wear their own full versions of the Norfolk in *The Grand Budapest Hotel*. From the Victorian era right up to the 1920s, the Norfolk was considered a sporting garment. Spotting a Norfolk on-screen, and outside of a country environment, can imply that we're seeing a well-traveled gent, someone away from his natural habitat—a man like our scribe, whose precious hours with Zero transformed his life.

Production sketches by Juman Malouf
1 Willem Dafoe as the assassin J. G. Jopling.
2 Dafoe in black leather coat.
3 Jude Law in Norfolk suit.
4 Tom Wilkinson in Norfolk suit.

AN INTERVIEW WITH

THE
GRAND BUDAPEST HOTEL

Madame D

Costume Designer
Milena Canonero

Production sketch of Madame D.

THE WES ANDERSON STYLE:

AN INTERVIEW WITH MILENA CANONERO

MILENA CANONERO *grew up in Genoa, Italy, before moving to England to finish her studies. Canonero's film career started with Stanley Kubrick when she designed the costumes for three of his films:* A Clockwork Orange *(1971),* Barry Lyndon *(1975, for which she won the first of her three Academy Awards), and* The Shining *(1980). She has worked with Alan Parker (*Midnight Express, *1978), Hugh Hudson (*Chariots of Fire, *1981, for which she won her second Oscar), Francis Ford Coppola (*The Cotton Club, *1984;* The Godfather: Part III, *1990), Sydney Pollock (*Out of Africa, *1985), Louis Malle (*Damage, *1992), Warren Beatty (*Dick Tracy, *1990;* Bulworth, *1998), Julie Taymor (*Titus, *1999), Roman Polanski (*Carnage, *2011), and Manoel de Oliveira (*Belle toujours, *2006). Her work with Sofia Coppola on* Marie Antoinette *(2006) brought Canonero her third Oscar. She has collaborated with Wes Anderson on* The Life Aquatic with Steve Zissou *(2004),* The Darjeeling Limited *(2007), and* The Grand Budapest Hotel *(2014).*

MATT ZOLLER SEITZ: *Were you familiar with Wes Anderson's films before you started work on* The Life Aquatic with Steve Zissou? *What did you think of his movies as visual statements?*

> **MILENA CANONERO:** I had seen his movies and how his work had evolved into a sophisticated, highly personal cinematic style. Wes is not only a film director, but an author. Like a great painter's, his work is very identifiable, and unique to him. His visionary world is very inspiring; I completely submerge myself into it.

What is it like to work with him on a day-to-day level?

> Wes is particular about details, and so am I. He is very specific, and yet he also leaves you a lot of space. He wants input and ideas. The "look" of the characters, when not specified in the script, evolved over the course of much discussion. I have continuous exchanges with Wes via e-mail, his favorite medium lately, but he is also very available in person, even when he's under the pressure of a film shoot.
>
> I work closely with the production designer and the cinematographer, so that everything comes together as a whole—especially in the overall color palette of the movie. Colors have their own music, and Wes cares a lot that they are the right notes.

How did Wes describe the world of this film to you? Did he have any specific or general suggestions for how he wanted the clothes to look?

> He told me he wanted to set the movie in an invented northern European Teutonic country, sometime in the 1930s, and for the opening sequence in the 1960s, he wanted Eastern European tones. Most of the story would take place in a luxurious mountain hotel resort and the surrounding area. Of course, this being a Wes Anderson movie, the title had nothing to do with the city of Budapest. Therefore, the look could be inventive, with historical innuendos, but at the same time accurate. This story is told through memories and therefore we could develop the look that was able to freeze the image in your mind.
>
> Wes's references of Austrian and German writers, artists of the pre–Second World War period, were a good guideline, but also I looked at the work of August

THE
GRAND BUDAPEST HOTEL

M. Gustave

Costume Designer
Milena Canonero

THE
GRAND BUDAPEST HOTEL

Zero

Costume Designer
Milena Canonero

THE
GRAND BUDAPEST HOTEL

Young Writer

Costume Designer
Milena Canonero

THE
GRAND BUDAPEST HOTEL

Mr. Moustafa

Costume Designer
Milena Canonero

Production sketches by *The Grand Budapest Hotel*'s costume department, a mix of illustration and Photoshop.

Sander, a great German photographer of the thirties, as well as at old movies and other sources. Of course, during the creative process, the final look of each character evolved. For instance, at the beginning, Ralph Fiennes's character, M. Gustave, was supposed to be quite blond, with hair like the dyed blond hair of the very old ladies he goes to bed with. But then it seemed more suitable that he would have more realistic auburn hair, with golden highlights.

Were the clothes entirely original, or did you use some vintage items?

We made most of the clothes in our workshop in Görlitz. Some were made at Theater-kunst in Berlin, and all of the uniforms were made at Krzysztof's costume workshop, Hero Collection, in Poland. I also rented and bought vintage clothes for the extras in the crowd scenes. One of the vintage shops we used in Berlin is called Mimi. Great shop.

How do you work out ideas for costumes before they're sewn? Do you draw rough versions of them in a sketchbook and then have somebody do more elaborate illustrations when the ideas have settled a bit?

On the other two movies I did with Wes, *The Life Aquatic* and *The Darjeeling Limited*, I applied traditional sketching methods to design the look of the characters. On this one, our illustrators used both Photoshop and traditional sketching to incorporate Wes's and my own ideas. With Photoshop we could get very close to the actors' likenesses, and then easily do variations and send them to Wes via e-mail. The actors were very pleased because they could relate easily to how their character would look. Having worked on two of Wes's other movies, I had already worked with some of his "ensemble" actors and it was interesting to change them again to these other characters. Wes had decided that all the men in the movie would have moustaches or beards, save for Jopling and the nasty sergeant in the train. I loved this idea, and it is curious that hardly anyone notices this detail—but it gives a style to the men's looks.

What are some of the materials that you used most often when designing the costumes for this film? Were there particular materials that you considered "workhorse" materials—ones that you perhaps used more often than others?

The purple and mauve facecloth, which is a very densely woven wool used for military uniforms. I wanted to avoid being too classical and using typical subdued colors for the hotel uniforms. I showed Wes the purple and mauve facecloth from an old swatch book from a company called Hainsworth in London. Wes was immediately taken by those colors, which worked beautifully with the set. Then the nightmare began, because I could not find the volume of fabric in that shade anymore, and time wasn't on our side! But just in the nick of time, we discovered a German company, Mehler, who came to our rescue with an identical fabric, as well as so many of the other great colors that I needed for the movie.

What influences did you bring to bear on the hotel staff's uniforms?

I used the cut and style of real uniforms of that period, and also many photos of high-end luxury hotel staff.

Can you describe the look of Ralph Fiennes's character, M. Gustave? What did you hope to convey about the character based on his clothing?

M. Gustave, from the top of his hair to the tip of his shoes, had to give us a sense of perfection and control. He had to be able to move with elegance and freedom. Even when the world he knows collapses, he still maintains his sense of style. This is not at all difficult when you're working with an accomplished actor like Ralph. It was delicious to watch him perform, and he is a great person to work with.

What are Tilda Swinton's clothes made of?

Silk velvet, for both the dress and the coat. Then I had it hand-painted with design patterns inspired by the paintings of Gustav Klimt.

Tilda's character, Madame D., is eighty-four years old. We had to age her, and a great team from London did that beautifully. Wes described her as a great eccentric beauty and an art collector, belonging outside the fashion of her present time. Therefore I designed the clothes in a retro style, like that of the early twenties. Wes liked that. She just went for this look with incredible ease and so much humor.

Fendi, with whom we had a relationship, contributed by making Madame D.'s muff for us, as well as the black diamond mink fur trimmings on her cape and hat. Fendi also made the gray Astrakhan fur overcoat I designed for Edward Norton, and they gave us all the furs I wanted for the movie. Nowadays, movies need the generous input of patrons from the fashion world to help with our costume budgets.

Can you tell me a little bit about the look of Willem Dafoe's character, the assassin Jopling?

The design of Jopling's leather coat was based on the coats of 1930s military dispatch riders. Our tailor made the toile, and we sent it to Prada, who generously manufactured the coat for us. When we got it back from them, we lined it with a red super-fine wool, and constructed the inside of the front lapel to contain the weapons arsenal as Wes had described it in his script.

We made gauntlets gloves, but these were never used, as Wes liked to see the beautiful knuckle-dusters that Waris Ahluwalia had designed and made specially for us, with a skeleton head for each finger. Waris, an actor who has appeared in several of Wes's movies and here plays one of the concierges, is also a terrific jeweler.

How would you describe the director's own sense of style, as he appears in daily life?

The Wes Anderson style.

(ABOVE) Manhattan-based jeweler and frequent Wes Anderson cast member Waris Ahluwalia designed both the lapel pins for the Society of the Crossed Keys and Jopling's brass-knuckle skulls.

(TOP LEFT) Production sketches of Agatha, (TOP RIGHT) Milena Canonero on set, (BOTTOM LEFT) Early treatment for Dmitri, (BOTTOM RIGHT) Madame D.'s three daughters (in mourning).

The Snow-globe Version

MY SECOND CONVERSATION WITH WES ANDERSON took place in December 2013. He was staying at a hotel in Munich, putting the finishing touches on *The Grand Budapest Hotel*. I was in New York City, doing the critic's usual year-end work of writing Top 10 lists and Year in Review–type pieces.

In the weeks since we last spoke, I had visited a bookstore in the West Village, emptied them of every Stefan Zweig book they carried, and was voraciously reading his work.

I was also able to watch *The Grand Budapest Hotel* a second time. I studied the movie's production design and became fascinated by the relationship between the imaginary geography of the film and the real geography of locations and sets. I wondered how fact becomes fancy. What were the steps?

More striking still was the way that *The Grand Budapest Hotel* seemed a substantially different film on second viewing. While it felt mostly light and playful the first time I saw it, it acquired a solidity during my second screening—moments of pain and sadness stood out in sharper relief. I even found myself slightly dreading the impending violence and death during the sweeter sections. My own melancholy synced up with that of the film's narrators, who love telling yarns but remain ruefully aware of how things will end, not just for Gustave and Agatha, but for them, and for everyone.

When I spoke to the director again, he indulged my curiosity, left his hotel room, cell phone in hand, and walked around the neighborhood. We talked about the practical realities of movie magic: location scouting, props, special effects. We also detoured to discuss the film's score, by Alexandre Desplat. In the background of Wes's end of the conversation, I could hear traffic and chirping birds.

The

5,069–Word

Interview

OPPOSITE: Photochrom image of Jelení skok (Stag's Leap) in Karlovy Vary. This statue, known as socha Kamzika, was re-created in miniature in slightly different form by the film's production design team.

BELOW: Wes Anderson at the spa in Görlitz where the movie's bath sequences were shot.

✻ According to the Library of Congress, "The Photochrom Print Collection has almost 6,000 views of Europe and the Middle East, and 500 views of North America. Published primarily from the 1890s to the 1910s, these prints were created by the Photoglob Company in Zürich, Switzerland, and the Detroit Publishing Company in Michigan. The richly colored images look like photographs but are actually ink-based photolithographs, usually 6.5 x 9 inches."

MATT ZOLLER SEITZ: In *The Grand Budapest Hotel*, you've created an entire world. It's not just a building or an imaginary country. It goes beyond that. It's very detailed.

At the same time, even though the movie isn't set in real Europe or in actual history—as we discussed in our first interview—there is a sense of reality, historical and geographical reality, that somehow seeps through anyway. What's the relationship between this imagined Europe and the real Europe where you shot the movie?

WES ANDERSON: It's funny. I talked to a couple of people recently—one Russian and one Lithuanian journalist—and they were pointing out particular little things we sort of picked up on that they are very familiar with, because that's their part of their world; things that seem like fantasy to us, but that are actually quite familiar to them. Strange little things.

For instance: When you travel around that part of the world, any time you're in an old building, you see these tall, ceramic wood-burning stoves of a particular

variety, and they're in every single room—in *every single* room you go in, in all the abandoned buildings that we visited. This is the world capital of abandoned buildings. Behind the Iron Curtain, or what used to be behind the Iron Curtain, there are so many places that remain sort of untouched, places where what was done to them in 1950 was so thin and simple, it really doesn't cover up the turn-of-the-century place underneath. The one thing that remains in all of them is these wood-burning stoves. I mean, these *big* wood-burners. They're so heavy and cemented—they can't be moved. Nobody can steal them. Even our art department said, "We can't move this thing."

Did I ever tell you about these photochrom images? Did I ever mention those to you?

No, tell me.

If you go on the Library of Congress's website and look up their photochrom collection, you'll see them.✻ The photochrom collection includes all these commercially produced pictures showing views of Europe around the turn of the century. They're black-and-white photographs that have been colorized. What you see when you look at these pictures are landscapes and cityscapes, from all over the world. No portraits. Just places. Views from streets, and views from paths and trails and buildings and rooms and so on. A huge number of them are from the Austro-Hungarian Empire and Prussia.

These pictures were a great inspiration for *The Grand Budapest Hotel*. Many of the old hotels in these photographs still exist as buildings. But none of them exist as the places they once were.

So there are buildings in these pictures that were once hotels but are not hotels anymore?

Well, some of these places *are* still hotels. But they're nothing like the hotels that they were back then. They've been changed so many times over the years. I had all these old hotels that I researched and was interested in. Often the exterior of the building was still there, and sometimes the corridors and the

staircases were still there, and there were other things that were still there. But the surfaces and the rooms, and the way the rooms are furnished—what you see today are remnants of the way those hotels used to be run, all these different versions of what people thought, over the years, was the right way to do it.

What do you mean?

I mean that whatever people thought was the right way to do things changed, depending on what period they were in.

Can you give me an example of how the "right way" to do things changed over time?

Well, a big one is, Communism appears at a certain point. And the architectural impact of Communism—of the Communist period—on these places is particularly interesting.

That's what we tried to represent with our hotel. In the 1930s part of the movie, we tried to show the way these grand hotels were back when people would go there and stay for a minimum of a month. People would go for a season and stay there, and people would go back to the same place, year after year. And the staffs of those hotels were consistent. It was just a completely different sort of experience.

But in the Jude Law–Murray Abraham part of the story that's supposed to be set during Communism, we see that the hotel has been changed in a way that goes along with the change in ideology. That came from us traveling all over Eastern Europe. All the details of what Communism does to the architecture, which are not in the script, came out of our travels, and from looking at things, and researching, in an effort to figure out how we were going to bring our story to life.

There is a sense, in those 1960s scenes, of not merely decay, but perhaps neglect. As if beauty were no longer a priority.

The hotel is not a fancy place for rich people anymore. It's much more "democratic."

Tell me about your travels through Eastern Europe to gather ideas for the production. Did you travel before writing the script? After writing it?

Before and after. I'd already been to some places that are relevant to our story. I've been to Vienna many times. I love Vienna. And I've been here, to Munich, many times, and to Berlin.

But immediately after we showed *Moonrise Kingdom* in Cannes, we went to some places in Italy, towns with old thermal baths that sort of relate to our story. We went to Budapest, we traveled around Hungary, we went to the Czech Republic. And we went to Karlovy Vary, which used to be Carlsbad, and also to the place that used to be called Marienbad. All of those places, but especially Karlovy Vary, became very important as we were putting this movie together. The town we call Nebelsbad in our film is some version of Karlovy Vary.

And then we went traveling all over Germany, because we figured out at a certain point that Germany was probably the best place to work, for financial reasons and crew reasons and organizational reasons. We traveled quite a lot around Germany, driving. We ended up finding this department store that we made into our hotel, a department store in Görlitz. Once I'd found that, I searched around the town, and I thought it might be a great place to make the movie.

Where is Görlitz?

Half of Görlitz is in Germany—what would have been East Germany—and half of it is in Poland. It's on the Neisse River. So we worked in Germany and also a little bit in Poland. The department store is twenty-five minutes from the Czech Republic, and we did some shooting there, too. But most of our work was in Saxony, that little area of Germany.

BELOW LEFT: Photocrom image showing the Hotel Schafberg in Upper Austria, near the Austro-Hungarian border.

BELOW RIGHT: *Morning in the Riesengebirge*, an 1810 painting by Caspar David Friedrich that captures the dawn light on Dresden-area hills, which the painter loved to climb. Friedrich is a key influence on *The Grand Budapest Hotel*'s landscapes and production design. His innovation was to present landscapes not as mere backgrounds for human subjects, but as spiritually or allegorically imbued objects worth contemplating for their own sake, and for the way in which they revealed humanity's relationship to nature.

OPPOSITE: Three still-frames showing a series of inserts from *The Grand Budapest Hotel*. The framed "paintings" are actually photochroms.

So the physical production was fairly geographically confined?

One thing I've learned over the years is that I prefer to work in an efficient way, and part of that is, I really don't like traveling a long distance. I mean, I don't mind traveling a long distance so that I can *stay* there while I make a movie. And I don't mind if there are some crucial things that require travel during a shoot—like, we have to go from here to there for a short time, to do one thing or another.

But what I don't like is making people travel an hour every day, day after day. I like to be able to travel ten minutes to get where I need to be. I want everybody, especially the cast, to get right to work.

What's it like scouting locations for the movie? You're moving from place to place, looking for something but not knowing exactly what you're looking for?

When you go looking around in that part of Germany—when you go behind what was once the Iron Curtain—you find that there are still a lot of abandoned buildings, and that a lot of the things that ordinarily would have been changed have, instead, not been touched. That works to your advantage when you're doing a period picture.

We had these golf carts sent to Görlitz, and I just traveled around with our cinematographer Bob Yeoman and our production designer Adam Stockhausen. Once Bob and Adam got there, we all started looking aggressively for anything we could find. And more and more, the things that we needed just sort of appeared, very close by.

We found thermal baths at Chemnitz, not so far from Dresden—that was a pretty good location, and it wasn't too heavily renovated. At that point, we were still contemplating going to the thermal baths we had found in Italy, or to another amazing one, which is at the Hotel Gellért in Budapest, to do our thermal bath scenes with Murray and Jude. Those scenes are a small part of the movie, but you have to have the thermal baths in there, because that's what the town in the movie is all about. You go for the waters.

One day, from our golf cart, we saw these tall brick smokestacks. We didn't know what they were. Well, what they were was the exhaust from an abandoned thermal baths that was just right there in

the middle of a row of townhouses. We searched and searched, and then there it was, right in front of us.

Can you give me an example of a place that seemed perfect on first glance but actually needed a lot of help, as it were, to become the place you needed for the movie?

This movie was a complicated puzzle, because the places that I envisioned just didn't really exist anywhere. So our approach was, "Let's just create it, through whatever methods we have available." There's a real hotel in Karlovy Vary called the Grand-hotel Pupp. I knew about it from an old photocrom picture. To me, *that* was the place.

Well, I went to the Pupp. I found out that the Pupp still looks like that old picture from the outside, but it had things added to it. It had parking lots, and the angle I wanted to show didn't exist anymore, and the river that runs through the place—it was all different.

Also, the landscape that I had imagined around the hotel—that I had imagined outside the frame of the old photograph—is actually not what I pictured, anyway. So it turned out that I had an imaginary version of the Pupp in my mind, combined with an old version that no longer exists.

Then there's another hotel in Karlovy Vary, the Hotel Bristol Palace. That one has a very interesting exterior, and it's situated up higher in the hills, like I thought our hotel ought to be. And there's another hotel, the Imperial, that has a funicular, and the Belvedere, which has these amazing pine trees behind it. And there's a hotel in Switzerland, the Giessbach, that also has a funicular; it takes you up to the hotel above this lake. In Karlovy Vary, there's a rock with a stag, Stag's Leap, which I first knew about from the 1908 photocrom picture of it. We made our own miniature version of this.

Across the river from this little town called Bad Schandau—which, like our town in the movie, is also an old spa town—there is a village that's up on top of high cliffs, on top of the plateau. A ninety-five-foot Eiffel Tower–period elevator runs up along the side of the cliffs. And so we took that exact elevator and made a miniature of it. That's the elevator that goes up to our miniature version of Stag's Leap.

What was the inspiration for the look of the landscapes?

OPPOSITE ABOVE: The 1932 exterior of the Grand Budapest Hotel is a facade built by the film's art department in front of the exterior of the Görlitz ballroom (the Stadthalle). Note the visible separation between the facade's "entrance" to the hotel and the existing structure behind it.

OPPOSITE BELOW: The 1968 facade (later significantly altered in post-production).

ABOVE: A Mendl's delivery truck parked outside of the 1932 facade, after the ZigZag takeover.

I was interested in these paintings by this German painter, Caspar David Friedrich.** We made our own version of these Friedrich paintings, and we made the backdrop for the hotel based on Friedrich, who is also the inspiration for the big painting that's in the dining room of the hotel.

Let's talk about the totality of the production design, then—the way your crew merged special effects and real locations to create the world of this film.

This is one of those situations where you say, "Well, I'm more interested in the thing that we can invent, the thing that's not trying to be completely realistic, the thing that's more a representation." Rather than trying to figure out a way to digitally composite all of these photorealistic things, which I think can limit your scope, I like to do something that's a painting *and* a miniature—and very clearly, that's what a lot of the stuff in the movie is: a painting or a miniature. That is *exactly* the world that I would like for the audience to be in. We can create whatever mood we want, and go further than any reality is going to let us.

The key locations that we see many times in the film—the baths, the entrance to the hotel, the hotel lobby, that sort of atrium area where the shoot-out happens, the exterior of the hotel—when we're seeing these places in the movie, what are we actually seeing? Are we seeing real locations with some embellishments added during shooting? Are we seeing sets? Are we seeing miniatures? Are we seeing some sort of compositing? Can you give us a sense of how it all fits together?

Almost every location in the movie is a real place, with us building some kind of set inside of it.

For instance, you know the interior of the hotel, the lobby that goes all the way up to that atrium? The atrium is just the top of the department store

lobby; it's got that stained glass window, with these vaulted staircases—that's all part of a real department store. But we built all of the interior walls of it—not the staircases, and not the railings, and not the skylights, stained glass, and all that stuff, but the walls just beyond the edge of the atrium: That's our set. We went to where all the clothes and all the department store goods would be, and we put in walls with doors. Those doors are the "hotel rooms." We built the back of the edges of the ground floor, and then we put in the carpets.

We also built the 1960s lobby inside of that space. A little bit of the real building shows through the 1960s lobby. The staircase—where the concierge desk and everything is—that's the same, and the columns that hold the place up are the same.

So the interior of the hotel is a set, but it's a set that's been created within existing architecture. It's much bigger than anything we could have just built, and it's grander, and it's kind of *real*. You know there's a *real* thing there.***

What about the dining hall where old Zero and the young Author eat? Is that in another part of the department store that you used for the main lobby?

No. That's a ballroom in Görlitz, which I think was built around the same time as the department store—a great, big, huge ballroom that we made into our big dining room.**** And in the parking lot outside of that, we just built a facade of the entrance of the hotel.

So all these interiors that seem to have such a sense of history— you're saying those were sets layered on top of actual locations?

Sets. You know, plywood.

Can you give me an example of a set that was made to seem bigger, or different, through miniatures, or backgrounds created in a computer?

You know the scene where Agatha goes out the window, and she's hanging from that ledge—I don't know what you call it—a vertical section, it's five stories high or something?

Yes.

That's probably only twelve feet wide. Everything that you see beyond it, on the sides, we added in from our miniature. We made a miniature hotel, and we shot matching angles of the miniature hotel to go with the shots of the actors hanging on. So in that scene, what you're looking at is partly a full-scale set, but the image is filled in on the sides with our miniature. Of course, that still means Saoirse is actually hanging off a five-story scaffolding, but we didn't build the rest of it on the sides. In the old days, they would paint it on glass, as you know.

To work that way, I'd imagine that you have to have a pretty good idea of what your shots are going to be when you arrive on set.

Well, the more you already know going in—the more you know about how you're probably going to do

LEFT: Jeff Goldblum in costume as Deputy Kovacs, viewed from the reverse side of a "doorway" built by the set department.

OPPOSITE TOP: Storyboard of Agatha hanging from a window ledge.

OPPOSITE MIDDLE LEFT: Un-composited, raw footage of the same shot.

OPPOSITE MIDDLE RIGHT: Still-frame from the finished film, composited with miniature elements to complete the hotel, plus digitally created snowy cobblestones.

OPPOSITE BELOW: Tony Revolori as Zero and Saoirse Ronan as Agatha hang from a section of the hotel exterior set, with camera and sound equipment visible.

OVERLEAF LEFT-HAND PAGE: Clockwise from top: Concept illustrations for the miniature version of the hotel as it would be seen in wide shots; two production photos showing the miniature hotel under construction by the movie's miniatures department.

OVERLEAF RIGHT-HAND PAGE: Clockwise from top: Two images showing the completed miniature version of the hotel, in front of a green screen into which tree-covered mountains will be added digitally in post-production; still-frame from the finished movie showing the complete hotel, with every element in place.

** See caption, page 102.
*** In a 2014 interview with *The Independent*, *The Grand Budapest Hotel* producer Jeremy Dawson said of the Görlitzer Warenhaus: "It had beautiful bones."
**** The ballroom where old Zero relates his story to the young Author is a performance space inside the Stadthalle, the old city hall on Reichenberger Straße near the city park. It was built in 1910 and had gone unused for many years when *The Grand Budapest Hotel*'s crew arrived. Painter Michael Lenz did the mural on the wall at the back of the room in the style of Caspar David Friedrich, a primary influence on the film's look.

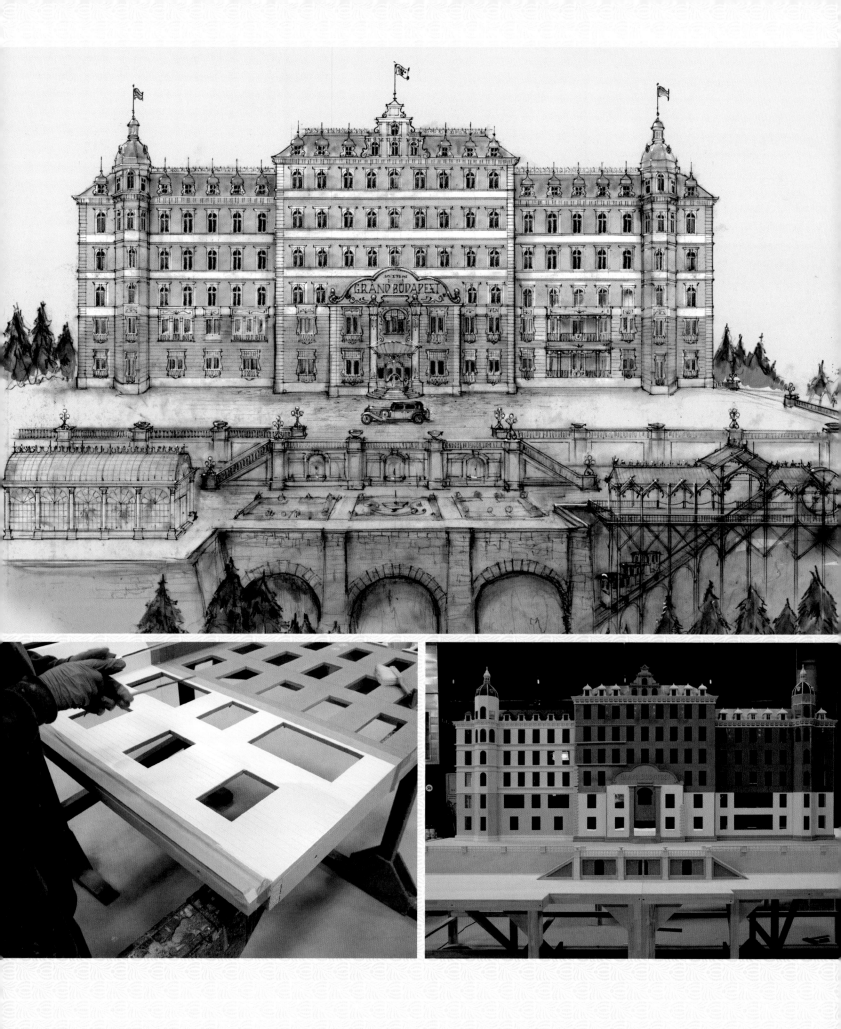

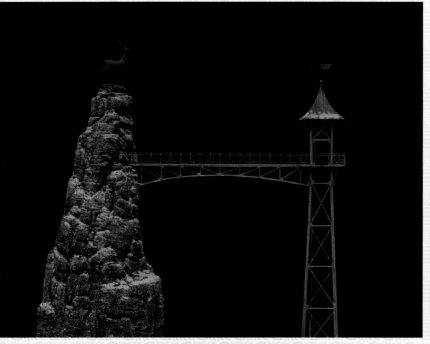

ABOVE: First row, from left: The Stag's Leap miniature after the green-screen backdrop has been digitally stripped out, but before it has been composited into the final frame; a still-frame from the finished film. Second row, from left: The miniature funicular being shot by a camera on dolly tracks (note that, even though the funicular moves diagonally in the film, this tracking shot is lateral, for convenience's sake); the funicular, closer to the angle at which it is seen in *The Grand Budapest Hotel*.

OPPOSITE TOP: Concept art, plus blueprints, for the observatory at Gabelmeister's Peak, which was suggested by a real observatory, the Sphinx Observatory in Switzerland.

MIDDLE ROW, FROM LEFT: The miniature Gabelmeister's Peak observatory in front of a green screen; the observatory as it appears in the finished film, with snowy background added in post-production.

BOTTOM ROW, FROM LEFT: The cable car miniature in front of a green screen; the cable car as it appears in *The Grand Budapest Hotel*.

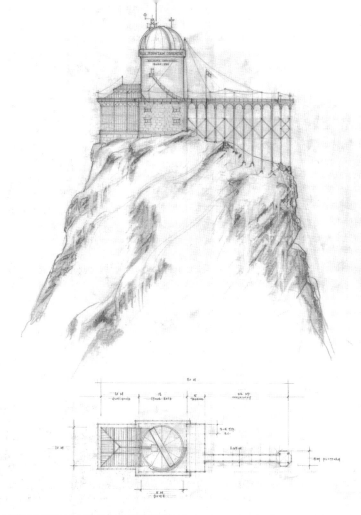

it—the less you have to deal with the whole thing not working right later.

There is only so much leeway to how well-executed the digital stuff, the compositing and everything, can be. If you have a plan going in, you can instead say, "We have this exact thing that we built that goes here, and we know that these other things that we built somewhere else will go around it," and then you can concentrate on making it all better.

You also have, by virtue of the sorts of movies you're known for making, a kind of an "out." By that I mean, you're not always trying to fool somebody into thinking that a rather fantastical image actually *exists*.

When you're looking at the ski chase near the end of the movie, for instance, you're not seeing something that we're supposed to interpret as a *realistic* ski chase. In fact, there is an old-movie quality to some of the rear projection in that sequence, and to the way the people move. It kind of turns into an old Walt Disney cartoon, like Goofy on the Matterhorn.

It is definitely a whole series of old-movie techniques.

We had found these Victorian snow portraits—do you know about these? People used to have their picture taken around the holidays in these little sets, with fake snow, and they'd create these very beautiful images, almost like snow globes, that people would pose in. We were kind of hoping we could have that sort of feeling—something antique.

There's a scene in the Max Ophüls adaptation of Stefan Zweig's *Letter from an Unknown Woman*—

Yes, from 1948. With the great Joan Fontaine.

Yes, Joan Fontaine, who just died! Well, remember that scene when they go on the train, but it's not a train—it's just a ride? And there's that scroll of a landscape that goes by? You pay something, and you can sit in this little train car; it's kind of an Expo-type diversion thing. Well, we wanted the ski chase to have that kind of feeling.

Of course, I hope that when you see it in the movie, it also feels like a ski chase, where you're *with* the characters. I don't want you to be laughing *at* it. I want it to feel like you're with them on the ride. But we have definitely gone, in some respects, in the opposite direction from a James Bond ski chase.

About the trains: Were all of the train scenes in *Grand Budapest* done on actual trains?

Well, we did go on a train to shoot some steam engine stuff. We got a train for a day, and we went around the southern part of Saxony. We went around on this tourist train that still runs. But all the stuff in the train compartments we built inside.

OPPOSITE ABOVE: The tree-lined snowy stretch through which Zero, M. Gustave, and Jopling race in the film's climax is actually a miniature, shot in front of green screens, merged during post-production with background elements and actors.

OPPOSITE BELOW: From the finished film, a shot from the vantage point of Zero and M. Gustave racing after Jopling.

RIGHT: A still-frame from Max Ophüls's 1948 film, *Letter from an Unknown Woman*, an adaptation of the Stefan Zweig story, starring Joan Fontaine and Louis Jourdan.

"Inside," meaning the "interiors of the trains were actually sets"?

Right. You remember that room in the movie where F. Murray Abraham and Jude Law go—that great big dining room where they're having their conversation? We built the train inside of that place.

So you had a green screen and you put the background in digitally?

No, we built the set in there. It's a pretty big set, because it's got a corridor attached to it. And then, outside the windows, we just blew them out.*****

But then we also did this thing where—in scenes where you need to see the actors in the foreground of the shot and then, through the window, some stuff going by outside the train, like soldiers or something—we'd physically take a hunk of the wall out of the set we'd built, bring it out to the location, mount it on a dolly, and the actors sat there next to it. For that one shot in the sequence, the dolly *becomes* the train.

So you've got the actors actually sitting on the dolly pretending they're on a train?

Pretending they're sitting in a train compartment. It was just for one shot in each of those scenes.

Often a film is filled with little tricks, cobbled together. And like we were talking about earlier, when a movie is all storyboarded out ahead of time, it's not so hard to figure out your game plan.

Would it have been easier to put a green screen beyond the window for that train shot, and add the stuff you see through the window later?

I don't know about "easier." Green screen would have been *another* way to do that train shot. But remember, even if you're doing the train stuff with a green screen, somebody's still got to go out there and shoot the soldiers that you're supposed to see through the window of the train when it's moving, or whatever it is that you're supposed to be seeing through the window. You have to shoot that part anyway.

So when you shoot a scene using a green screen, you have to create two shots that have to be put together in post-production. But if you do it the way you did the train-window shots in *The Grand Budapest Hotel*, it's just one shot. You've eliminated a step.

Right. And also, it's a little more reassuring.

How do you mean?

I can just do it right there and know that it works. Any time I *don't* have to use a green screen or digital, I prefer not to. With a green screen, you never know when something's going to be a little wonky, and every now and then you'll feel, "Why is this not looking right?" But when you do it all *in* the camera, you don't really feel that, and you can always spruce it up visually later, digitally.

I mean, we do tons of digital stuff in this movie. But it tends to be a matter of putting together things

ABOVE: Wes Anderson directs Ralph Fiennes looking through the window of a "train," actually a window frame mounted on a plywood platform attached to a dolly on rails.

OPPOSITE: The sequence in *The Grand Budapest Hotel* in which the train bearing Zero and M. Gustave is stopped in a barley field by government troops. The left column consists of storyboards from the animatic; the right column includes corresponding still-frames from the finished film.

***** Cinematographer Robert Yeoman explains: "By 'blown out,' Wes means that we placed large white silks out the train window on the set that I backlit, so that the background was extremely overexposed and would essentially 'white out.' As the background in the film was essentially a snowy field, this seemed appropriate."

Why are we stopping at a barley field?

M. GUSTAVE
Well, hello there, chaps.

19 October
Closing of the Frontier

that we've already shot. It's compositing. We don't do a whole lot of shots—or any?—where what you see on-screen actually originated in a computer.

Let's talk about the score, by Alexandre Desplat, who scored your previous two movies.

Alexandre and I have an interesting way of working, which is that Alexandre does long musical sketches. Then I work with the music editor and arrange the sketches to picture. Then I go back to Alexandre, and we think together while he refines the music. And it sort of goes back and forth between the composer and the music-editing department, and back to the composer, and back to the editing department. This system works well for us.

Often, when you see orchestras recording film scores, everyone's there at the same time in the studio, performing together, while a screen shows a rough cut and one person conducts. Was that the way you did it on *The Grand Budapest Hotel*?

No. We did it that way on *Fantastic Mr. Fox*: The orchestra was all together, and Alexandre conducted it. But on *Moonrise* and this movie, Alexandre wasn't able to be there with us for the recordings, because he had to go compose the score for another movie. When we were recording the scores for *Moonrise* and *Grand Budapest*, we had orchestrators Alexandre recommended and who also became our conductors. Conrad Pope did that on *Moonrise*, and Mark Graham on *Grand Budapest Hotel*. They were both great.

You know, I didn't want to record the full orchestra all at once for this movie; we really *couldn't* do that without Alexandre present, anyway. We did it the same way we did it on *Moonrise Kingdom*, and we made it work, because we've developed a very efficient way of working.

We recorded all the balalaikas, which were a big part of the score—this whole orchestra of balalaikas—outside of Paris. And we recorded the pipe organs in a church near Hampstead, near Golders Green. Then we recorded most of the other instruments—the cimbalom, and all the brass and the woodwinds, and so on—in a place called AIR Studios in St. John's Wood. Alexandre had written the percussion parts, and we brought those to Paul Clarvis, who's just a great all-around percussion person, and he went off on his own and re-recorded all the percussion work separately, and then we re-edited what Paul did.

I would imagine that recording that way—in that "modular" way—gives you greater latitude. It's like you have layers of music. I'm imagining that there may be a moment where you're cutting the movie and you listen to the score in a scene and realize, "You know, maybe we don't need *quite* so many instruments for this scene; it's overwhelming things."
And because you haven't recorded an entire forty-piece orchestra all at the same time, you can peel things back a layer at a time, until you get that music cue down to the size you want, or the tone you want.

Right. Because we recorded the score completely split out in pieces, we could just focus on one thing at a time. It also gives us the ability to rearrange and

reshape afterward. Because we have all the parts split out, we can edit the music any way we want.

On *Moonrise Kingdom*, so much of the movie was set to the music that we were able to do a sort of storyboard sketch version of it; there was music with that version. This new movie, on the other hand, we couldn't do that way. This was a case where the entire score really was made after the movie was done shooting, and when we were editing the movie, and so on—which, as you know, can be kind of a humongous undertaking.

What sorts of discussions did you have about instrumentation?

Alexandre and I talked about Gregorian chants before we even shot the movie. We'd also talked for a long time about balalaikas and cimbaloms. We even had this one instrument we liked called an alpenhorn, which was used to communicate from one mountain to another, and we managed to use that a little bit, too.

And then we have this yodeling that Alexandre didn't do—music that we just licensed. That came from a Werner Herzog movie, *Heart of Glass*.

There's yodeling from a Werner Herzog movie mixed into the score?

Well—you know, maybe in the end we didn't use an *exact* one from *Heart of Glass*—we might have used another. But if it's not yodeling that comes directly from *Heart of Glass*, it's yodeling that's very much like it. It's yodeling from the northern part of Switzerland. I think it's medieval or something. It's called Zäuerli.

We should probably mention your music supervisor, Randall Poster, here, because when you say something like, "Hey, there's yodeling in this Werner Herzog film that I want to use—can you track it down?" he's the guy who does that, right?

He's really the producer of the music-making part of the movie, and everything to do with music. He comes to the cutting room regularly and stays involved. Then, at a certain point, we do everything together. Once we get into the music, he's there for me, and we figure out what we want to do. We're just together, and we go wherever in the world we need to go. If you're recording in London, you probably have a person there who knows who all the musicians and technicians are, and keeps track of all the Union stuff and their hours and how much it's going to cost, and negotiates with the players, like, "We don't want two sessions; let's do a session and a half." But when you're looking for a Hungarian cimbalom player, that's a little more particular, and that's the kind of person that Randy would go track down himself.

This movie has a very dense score. It's an old-movie score. There are a lot of motifs and little jokes in it. There are also things that I would characterize as embellishments, places where the music takes the comedy on-screen to another level, through music.
For example, in the stretch of action on Gabelmeister's Peak, there's a moment when Gustave and Zero transfer from one cable car to another. When the first cable car stops, you hear it squeaking. It's squeaking in time to the music. Then the second cable car stops, and it's also squeaking in time to the music. And

OPPOSITE: Ralph Fiennes in a moment of repose, taken during the shooting of M. Gustave's final scene in *The Grand Budapest Hotel*.

then when they go into the monastery, the Gregorian chants are timed to coincide with the score that's already in progress.

The Gregorian chants and that sort of stuff, though—I feel like that was pretty much planned in the script. The clanking of the cable cars we did later, after the score was recorded, during editing. What happened was, the squeaking cable cars—almost by chance—was lining up to the music.

So it was a case of your asking the post-production people, "Can you slow the clanking of the cable cars on-screen a little bit, so that it syncs up with the score?"

It's a bit choreographed.

And then you get to the ski chase, and Desplat hits some very James Bond-ian notes.

He brings in the French horns a little bit more.

It's almost like he becomes John Barry for a second.****

We had *On Her Majesty's Secret Service* in mind for that sequence. The whole concept of the ski chase comes from *On Her Majesty's Secret Service*. We're just doing the snow-globe version.

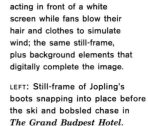

ABOVE: Ralph Fiennes as M. Gustave and Tony Revolori as Zero in the ski chase sequence, acting in front of a white screen while fans blow their hair and clothes to simulate wind; the same still-frame, plus background elements that digitally complete the image.

LEFT: Still-frame of Jopling's boots snapping into place before the ski and bobsled chase in *The Grand Budpest Hotel*.

LEFT BELOW: Still-frame from the start of the ski chase sequence from the 1969 James Bond film *On Her Majesty's Secret Service*, directed by Peter R. Hunt.

OPPOSITE: Still-frames from the climactic bobsled chase sequence in *On Her Majesty's Secret Service*, a key inspiration for both director Wes Anderson and composer Alexandre Desplat.

****** John Barry (1933–2011) scored eighty-six feature films and wrote themes or incidental music for twenty-four TV programs, winning Academy Awards for *Born Free* (1966), *The Lion in Winter* (1968), *Out of Africa* (1985), and *Dances with Wolves* (1990). But he's perhaps still best known for scoring eleven James Bond movies, stretching from 1962's *Dr. No* through 1987's *The Living Daylights*.

the music
of the
grand
budapest
hotel:
a place,
its people, and
their story

olivia
collette

THE GRAND BUDAPEST HOTEL

Concert Score

2M1
"Daylight Express to Lutz - pt1 "

Music by
Alexandre Desplat

Matches stereo mixes:
2M1A-SF-Daylight Express to Lutz-pt1-Cut34-2.00.08.00-2108b
2M1B-SF-Daylight Express to Lutz-pt2-Cut34-2.01.33.15-2108b

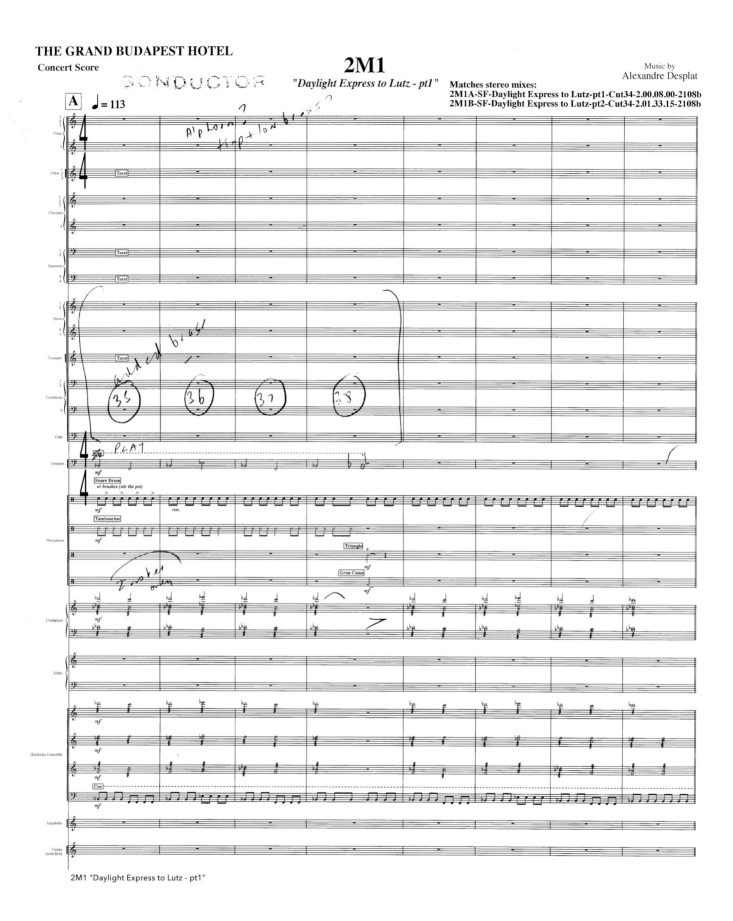

2M1 "Daylight Express to Lutz - pt1"

the music of *the grand budapest hotel:*

a place, its people, and their story

OLIVIA COLLETTE

an
introduction

What made me feel as though *The Grand Budapest Hotel*'s score had an Eastern European folk vibe? It was a combination of things: the pace. The style. And a prevalent instrument—one I couldn't immediately recognize. It sounded like a slightly out-of-tune piano or harpsichord. I couldn't tell if the keys were being struck or plucked. Looking at composer Alexandre Desplat's instrumentation, I learned that the sound I couldn't quite place was produced by the cimbalom, and I thought: *Yes, of course; how appropriate.* Classical composers have often scored for the cimbalom, usually to lend a folkloric feel to a given piece. Film composers often use it as shorthand for foreignness, European division. The sound of the instrument is at once mysterious and charming; the cimbalom's curiously out-of-tune quality, coupled with the difficulty of telling how the notes are played, enhances those traits.

The cimbalom is a hammered dulcimer. Picture the exposed soundboard of a piano laid flat, then placed on four legs, like a xylophone. The player is armed with two leather-covered hammers to strike the strings, but the instrument can also be plucked, so that its notes can be clipped or sustained. What makes the cimbalom sound out of tune is the fact that it's

a hassle to tune to begin with. Since replacements are hard to find, the board's strings might have to be drawn from multiple sources, made under many different conditions, to varying standards of quality.

I'm delving into the construction of the cimbalom because I want to emphasize how much this gritty instrument contrasts with the crisp, polished music we've come to expect from commercial movies, even Wes Anderson's. The sound of the cimbalom has an obvious physicality; it sounds handmade because it is handmade. Anderson's films are also handmade, to the extent that it's possible to work that way in an increasingly digital, virtual era.

On top of that, although Desplat uses regular orchestras comprised of real musicians playing real instruments, his score for *The Grand Budapest Hotel* doesn't have a conventional Hollywood string section consisting of violins, violas, cellos, and double basses. Instead, he favors portable folksy instruments, such as guitars, mandolins, balalaikas (a triangular, three-stringed guitar from Russia), and the very international zither (the zither sounds like a sitar, in name and in noise; it's a kind of neckless lute that has so many strings, I'm surprised Jimmy Page didn't play it exclusively).

In combining classical and folkloric sounds, Desplat also invokes the very essence of the word "Budapest." Today, it's the capital of Hungary. Previously, it was the second capital, along with Vienna, of the Austro-Hungarian Empire, a Central European entity that was (and remains) the spot

on the map where East meets West. So from the score's very first note—which, incidentally, is yodeled—we hear something that clambers atop a craggy peak and cries, "Europe!"

Well, maybe not "Europe," per se; more like a fancy, hybridized version of Europe. Desplat's quirky instrumentation and compositions do more than root us in Zubrowka, the fictional European country where *The Grand Budapest Hotel* takes place. They reinforce a specific kind of fictional narrative. By veering into folk territory and then spending the next couple of hours getting lost there, the *Grand Budapest Hotel* score substantiates the story's tall-tale proportions. There are lavish properties—the hotel, the monastery—built on remote, inconvenient hilltops. There are exaggerated villains (Dmitri Desgoffe und Taxis and J. G. Jopling), an audacious orphan (Zero), a lovable trickster hero (M. Gustave), feisty females (Madame D. and Agatha) and uncanny sideways references to actual history (ZZ: the ZigZag Division). There's only one pastry chef in all of Upper Nebelsbad, but his sweet, stacked concoctions are the best you'll have this side of the Alpine Sudetenwaltz.

So how does the music add to the lore?

Consider the dreamy introduction to M. Gustave. It's punctuated by two clear elements: the tremolo and the celesta.

The tremolo is a single note or chord played repetitively. There is no flamenco without the tremolo. Nor a Dick Dale, for that matter.

Score detail, with still-frames from Gustave's introduction.

With its name suggesting the heavens, the celesta's chiming sound has often been used to express otherworldliness. It's what makes the "Dance of the Sugar Plum Fairy" one of the most memorable pieces from Tchaikovsky's *The Nutcracker*. It's why John Williams's *Harry Potter* theme is so eerie and bizarre.

In his introductory scene, M. Gustave is in his element, coordinating an impeccable table setting for his upcoming visit with Madame D. While he does, the tremolos, supplied by Desplat's alternative string section, are the perfect stand-in for an angelic chorus, swathing M. Gustave in resplendence. Meantime, the celesta chirps around the scales, sprinkling the man with the pixie dust of myth.

M. Gustave isn't strictly his own free-standing person in *The Grand Budapest Hotel*; he's reconciled through Zero's nostalgic, venerating lens. Since the story is actually being told to us by the Author, who's retelling Zero's account, there are, as in all folk tales, several levels of unmitigated idolatry here. The music that accompanies M. Gustave's intro carries all of that baggage and more. The concierge is lightly mythologized from the instant that that close-up of his handsome face gives way to a wide shot of him striding through the hotel suite with the whirling buzz of Desplat's music seeming to bear him forward.

The overture doesn't resolve, in that it doesn't end on the note your innate musical expectations are waiting for it to end on. It stops, just one measure short of the resolution. In fact,

M. Gustave's overture is interrupted by his meeting with Madame D., and while that scene has its own cimbalom-heavy theme, it's set up in silence.

What does it mean when a composer cuts off a music cue like that? What does it do to you as you're watching the scene? It leaves you hanging. This seems like a small touch, but in retrospect, it's the first instance of a storytelling motif expressed through music, as well as the screenwriting. Gustave is always left hanging. He's promised a painting and then made to think he won't ever claim it; he's sent to prison and worries that he'll never get out; once he's escaped, he participates in an elaborate scheme to return to the hotel and reclaim *Boy with Apple*. Right before that comical climax, the movie literalizes this idea by having M. Gustave hang from a cliff. The music accompanying what he thinks is his final recitation is also cut short, this time by Zero shoving the murderous Jopling into the abyss and saving our hero from death.

This is an example of something Desplat talks about in an interview with Matt Zoller Seitz (p. 138): Wes Anderson likes to stop both his scores and his source music abruptly, often in unexpected or jarring places. It doesn't seem much of a stretch to infer that all of those odd intrusions of silence in *The Grand Budapest Hotel* foreshadow M. Gustave's eventual and sudden death at the hands of army officials.

Other characters also get their musical due, courtesy of Desplat's intricate and playful compositions. On the fouler end of the spectrum, Dmitri

and Jopling tend to be associated with the deep and heavy church organ and, on a couple of occasions, a Hammond organ, which is really just the at-home version of the former. The church organ's funereal sound befits a couple of murderous characters. It lends a comical gravitas to the despicable pair, since the instrument itself is so commonly associated with the sober, ominous experience of its religious setting: One is most likely to hear it in church, the place where births, marriages, and deaths are commemorated. When played in a house of worship, an acoustic space that echoes relentlessly, the church organ produces a sustained sound. It is in every sense a commanding instrument, telling churchgoers when to rise, kneel, sing along, and leave.

Desplat identifies both Dmitri and Jopling with the organ; they're purely authoritarian characters, creatures of pure will. The organ is there when Dmitri confronts M. Gustave after the reading of Madame D.'s last will and testament. It opens and closes Jopling's interrogation of Serge X.'s sister. It fills the negative space leading up to the murder of Vilmos Kovacs. It signals Dmitri's slow stride down the hotel's hallway when he realizes Agatha has the painting. It even comes in on the tail end of Madame D.'s theme, which we hear at the hotel and again at her funeral, subtly confirming that her son and his accomplice were somehow involved in her death.

Speaking of Madame D., there are some similarities between her theme and Zero's. The melody varies slightly,

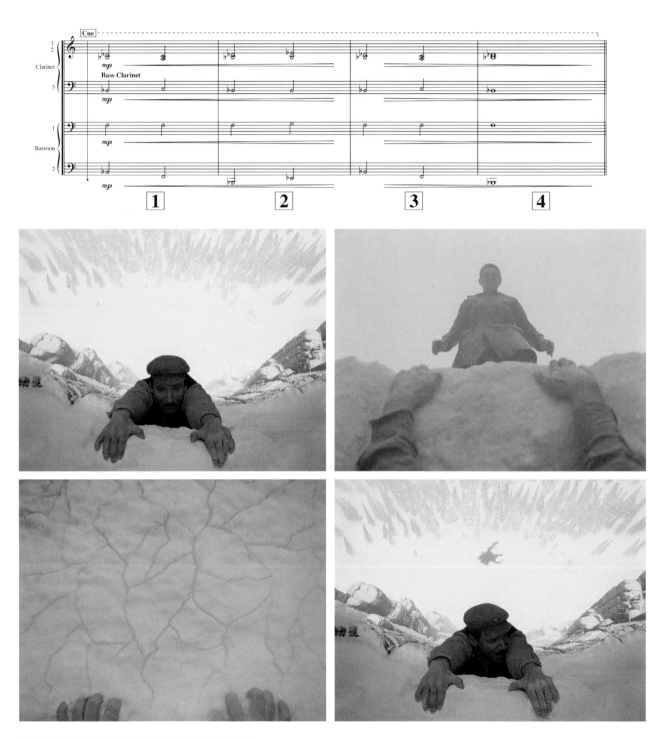

Still-frames from the literal cliff-hanger scene, with score detail.

Conductor note: 2 bars/6 beats cut from previous version

but the rhythm is nearly identical, and both rely heavily on the cimbalom. The main difference is that Zero's theme is in a major key, which we tend to link to pleasantness and positivity, while Madame D.'s is in a minor key, hinting at her demise.

Zero's theme and Madame D.'s also glancingly mirror each other. Both characters own the hotel at different points in its history, and Gustave is the person who connects them. Both the old woman and the young man are fond of Gustave, and in some sense protected by him. Their themes are backed by the alternative string section, with the odd chirp of the celesta thrown in. It's the bit of music that sounds the most like Eastern European folk, and it has little support from the conventional orchestral instruments. Since both characters are, in some way, analogous to the chimerical hotel, the music tells us that Zero and Madame D. are entwined in its legend.

beyond the background

When theater directors started commissioning composers to create scores for their play productions, it was called "incidental music." The term implies that music is not inherent to the thing it's scoring; it's just sort of happening at the same time.

I'm bringing this up because music is integral to Wes Anderson's dramatic ecosystems. It's never something that sort of "happens" in the background while the story is being told in the foreground, nor is it content merely to comment upon the action. It's one of the tools Anderson needs to *tell* his stories. It actively participates in them, enforcing or subverting our initial impressions, lulling us into complacency before springing a surprise, and often foreshadowing twists that, in retrospect, we should have seen coming.

Music is also a "tone corrective." It can be the light touch that offsets the movie's most dreadful moments, enveloping terrible events with sweetness and compassion, and then urging us to move on. The resulting tone can be serious and silly at the same time.

No surprise, then, that Desplat cites frequent Alfred Hitchcock collaborator Bernard Herrmann and cartoon composer Carl Stalling as influences: both specialized, among other things, in helping audiences frame darkness and cruelty in ways that made them palatable, or at least bearable. Desplat belongs in this tradition, not just because of his sense of composition and orchestration, but because all of his scores are recognizable as his own, even when they collaborate humbly and enthusiastically with the director's vision.

A Bernard Herrmann score belongs with the movie it's in and cannot really exist anywhere else. Even when the iconic screechy theme from *Psycho* is used in TV or another film, it never

becomes glorified source music, because it always makes you think of *Psycho*. Any use of any part of that score, no matter what the context, must therefore be considered an homage. Same thing with a Carl Stalling score: It always mirrors the motion of the picture it's in. Even out of its *Looney Tunes* or *Merrie Melodies* context, you can visualize what the music was illustrating. The conveyor-belt theme, maybe Stalling's most famous piece, cannot be used anywhere else and just blend in, because it will always make you think of cartoon animals scampering around conveyor belts, trying not to get squashed.

Herrmann and Stalling collide in *The Grand Budapest Hotel*, in a tune that recurs throughout the movie. It's a tiny, repeated, eight-measure leitmotif that's first introduced to us when Zero and M. Gustave head to Lutz for Madame D.'s funeral. It reappears when they return, and once again when the pair meet an endless string of "Are you Monsieur Gustave of the Grand Budapest Hotel in Nebelsbad?" at the hilltop monastery. It also infuses bits of the rest of the score at various moments.

The theme tends to occur when the story is literally moving forward, either by train or by toboggan. It's consistently backed by a jazzy snare drum, and the only thing that changes is the instrumentation of those eight measures.

In *The Grand Budapest Hotel*'s monastery scene, you notice that each time the leitmotif plays, it's adapted to the on-screen action. Here's a breakdown:

ABOVE: Score detail and still-frame of Jopling in the reading-of-the-will scene.

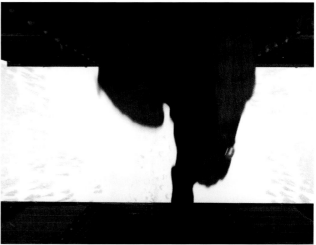

1
zero and m. gustave climb aboard the cable car

We hear sparse orchestral instruments, the bass balalaikas on tremolo duty, and bass vocals singing the melody in *ahs*, hearkening the echoes you might hear from such a summit.

2
zero and m. gustave switch cable cars

The church organ comes in, as well as the rest of the balalaikas and the zither. They've *almost* arrived at their destination, and the music builds to that.

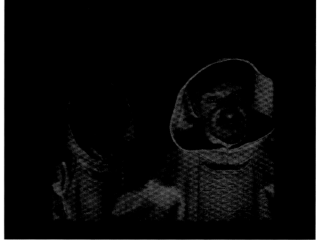

5
zero and m. gustave disguised as monks

What especially marks this passage is the way the leitmotif was taken over by Kyrie Eleison chanting, first by a full male choir, then by a single tenor voice. Zero and M. Gustave suddenly find themselves in a chorus. The music seamlessly transports us to both a place and a mood.

6
in the confessional

Zero and M. Gustave finally meet Serge X., who tries to tell them everything he couldn't at Madame D.'s funeral. A single church organ plays the leitmotif in this part. It might sound like it's underlining solemnity, but as the theme shifts from single notes to slightly dissonant chords, it's actually warning us of Jopling's presence. In fact, when Zero and M. Gustave discover Serge's dead body and see Jopling in the distance, the moment is crashed by sudden organ chords that are otherwise unrelated to the leitmotif.

3
the cable car takes them to gabelmeister's peak

More orchestral instruments jump in, and the celesta and cimbalom make their entrance, marking Zero and M. Gustave's imminent arrival at a sacred place. The male choir is now singing rhythmic *oom-pahs*, in a bit of foreshadowing.

4
in the gabelmeister's peak courtyard

The alternative string section plays a staccatoed sequence, replicating Zero and M. Gustave's quick steps in a manner that evokes Carl Stalling.

7
toboggan chase

Enter the full orchestra, vocal *oom-pahs*, and even a church bell for eight measures, the most clear auditory indication that we've arrived at the apex of this scene. Then, for the next four measures, a Hammond organ overrides the score as Jopling skis ahead. Immediately after, the brass section takes over, accentuating the majesty of their surroundings, as brass sections do. When they land on a bobsled half-pipe, a fast-moving cimbalom solo characterizes the perilous, winding track.

8
is this it?

M. Gustave hangs from the edge of a cliff, while grave, quasi-funereal flutes and recorders play the leitmotif as he recites what he believes is his last poem. The music doesn't resolve, and M. Gustave's recitative is interjected by Zero pushing Jopling off the cliff.

AN INTERVIEW WITH

Alexandre Desplat

Alexandre Desplat at a soundboard, supervising the recording of the score for the 2011 film *Extremely Loud & Incredibly Close*.

INTIMATE SOUND:

AN INTERVIEW WITH ALEXANDRE DESPLAT

 Paris-born composer, conductor, and musician **ALEXANDRE DESPLAT** *has scored more than 150 films and television programs. One of the most sought-after film scorers of the modern era, he has been nominated for dozens of awards, including six Oscars. Desplat is a chameleon, adapting his tender, at times mournful romanticism to serve projects as temperamentally different as* The Curious Case of Benjamin Button *(2008), both parts of* Harry Potter and the Deathly Hallows *(2010, 2011), and* Godzilla *(2014), as well as* Girl with a Pearl Earring *(2003),* Syriana *(2005),* The King's Speech *(2010),* The Tree of Life *(2011),* Extremely Loud & Incredibly Close *(2011),* Argo *(2012), and* Zero Dark Thirty *(2012). Desplat provided the scores for Wes Anderson's* Fantastic Mr. Fox *(2009),* Moonrise Kingdom *(2012), and* The Grand Budapest Hotel *(2014).*

MATT ZOLLER SEITZ: *Can you tell me a little bit about the process by which you conceive of themes and melodies for a film score? Is it something that's worked out with the director ahead of time? Or do you go off by yourself and work for a bit, and then show the director what you've come up with? How does this work, exactly, and where does it all start?*

ALEXANDRE DESPLAT: When you're called to work on a project, there are many ways that you can start.

You receive a script—or not. Sometimes, the movie's already shot, and you've just been shown the first cut, and then you have to start. Sometimes, you are hired to work on the film very far ahead of time, and your brain is kind of dreaming slowly. Other times, you have only two weeks to write a score, and you just have to dive into the pool, and you have to find the key quickly to what the film is going for.

The main questions are, "What am I here for? What is the movie calling for? What can I bring to the movie that is not yet there on the screen?"

And that's where I start. After that, it's knocking things around with a director and trying to figure out an instrumentation: a lineup of instruments that will emphasize this, or that.

What sorts of things can a score emphasize?

It could emphasize the emotions. The pace. The scope. It could emphasize whatever specific thing the movie requires at that exact stage of the editing.

After the movie is finally done being shot and it's being put together, you find yourself in a moment when you can really understand what the movie is. Before that, it's all just paper and ink. It is the combination of moving images and sound, and actors moving within the frame, and the exchange of my point-of-view with the point-of-view of the director, that brings me into a collaboration that will become the score.

What's the first step in starting to devise a movie score? Do you work out themes on a piano, generally?

You say "themes," but you know, some movies I've done have no themes, because they don't deserve to have a theme, or they can't stand having a theme, because the director can't stand to have a melody in his film, or because something about the movie just rejects it. Composing is a global sensation. It's not about themes. It's not just about naming a melody.

What is it about, then?

Asking such things as: "In this scene, do I need three or a hundred notes?" And thinking about instrumentation, and asking, "What can the film inspire in terms of all these elements, and how I can tailor something that will have all these elements and be, at the same time, a piece of music, and truly belong to a film?" And that process is a mental process, an intellectual process.

I own an upright piano, but I'm not a pianist. I can find an idea, or a color, or a combination of sounds on my Vespa or on a plane. It's not just by sitting at a piano or playing flute or guitar or keyboards that I can find my way through the film. It's a mental thing. There is a lot of thinking before you do anything. If you look at my sketchbooks—and I have many when I start a project—you'll see it's filled with fragments that have not yet become something. You look in them, and sometimes you will see two bars, a chord, or the hint of a melody that is not yet developed and that I might just drop very early on and move on to another one. So it's a very, very, very complex combination of things.

It almost sounds as if you're describing portraiture—as if your role is to create, through music, a portrait of the film.

Yes, a portrait. Or an impressionistic landscape, or whatever sort of canvas you want to think about. You know? The sky is over there. If the painting is a Vermeer, there's the light coming from the left, through the window. There are two characters in the frame, and there's something in the corner; there's a still life. In a still life, you have all the elements: the light, the table. But you still want to try and make the table look unique.

A score is not just a bunch of notes played together; it's many, many other things, because a movie is a long journey. It's an hour-and-a-half journey—sometimes two hours, sometimes more—in which the score of the movie has to flow, or to feel "flow-less" and be completely interwoven with not only the story line but with what you see on-screen.

Sometimes, I have to find a key. Sometimes, I find the key by going back to the story line. Sometimes, I find it by talking about the story line with the director. Other times, it's by thinking about the psychology of the characters that I can find my way through the movie. When I do it that way, it's like I'm trying to be almost like another actor in the film—to be part of it, and be completely involved with what is on-screen and not just stay out of it, with distance.

How is a Wes Anderson score different from scores that you might compose for other directors?

Well, Wes has a world of his own, which I call "Wes's World," and it belongs only to him. There are no movies like Wes Anderson's movies. I can't think of any! Yes, you can notice some reference, homage, or influence. You can tell that he's watched François Truffaut and Ernst Lubitsch and many, many, many masters of cinema, just as I did when I listened to the masters of music. This is the normal procedure for artists. But Wes invented a tone, a world that is peculiar and inspired and melancholic—and at the same time filled with farce and with moments of extreme ecstasy. It is a very special world. Musically, of course, I want to reflect all of the emotions that I just mentioned. A touch of melancholy, a lot of fun, but at the same time, it's never heavy. Comedy can't be heavy.

Olivia Collette said she would describe Wes's films as having "an ethereal childlike quality coupled with a light, springy step," and that the music for his films often has a bit of that quality, too. Would you agree with that description?

Definitely. The childlike element is something I could have mentioned, especially in the three films that I have done with Wes. It's there in *Mr. Fox*, because of the nature of the puppets, and in *Moonrise Kingdom*, because of these very young adults—if not older teenagers, because to me they seem really like teenage protagonists. And it's there in this film, because the heart of it is Zero is being educated by Gustave H.

There is education, funnily enough, in all three movies I've scored for Wes. Education is a recurring theme, and you can definitely use that musically; it's something you can refer to. *Moonrise Kingdom* and *The Grand Budapest Hotel* both have movie score sounds that have recurred since *Mr. Fox*.

You're speaking now of the tone of a movie score, or the size of it.

Yes. On *Mr. Fox*, at first there was this idea of doing a big, bright, cartoonish, Carl Stalling type of score, in the spirit of the most incredible, beautiful, classical cartoon music that I loved from the fifties and sixties. And then I felt that because the puppets were tiny characters, a score like that might overwhelm them. So I suggested that we instead reduce to a minimal sound, and that meant having only very small instruments—if we used orchestral devices, we would use only one of each kind of instrument. We had a string quintet instead of a full orchestra of strings, and one of each kind of brass, and one flute. And a lot of the instruments we used were physically small: glockenspiels, tambourines, bells. These all create a very intimate sound.

When we recorded the score for *Moonrise*, there were echoes of those methods we used on *Mr. Fox*.

The score for Fantastic Mr. Fox, *then, was the starting point for a certain method of working with Wes, which you developed further on the next two films?*

Yes. The way we did the *Mr. Fox* score became the first layer of DNA for us. There are aspects from that score that we returned to. We used choir in *Mr. Fox*, and we used choir again in *Moonrise*, and then again in *The Grand Budapest Hotel*.

But on top of this first layer of DNA, you add other layers—layers after layers. On *The Grand Budapest Hotel*, we've added cimbaloms and zithers, but there again, we've used tinkling sounds and choir as before.

You also want to find ways to distinguish the characters through music. There are many characters in the film, and I worked very deliberately with Wes to have distinctive themes and motifs expressed for each of them, with very distinctive sounds—for example, the cimbaloms and zithers used to play M. Gustave's and Zero's themes.

I remember an e-mail from Wes at the beginning of the process. He said, "I've just written a new story, would you like to have fun using monk voices and cimbaloms and zithers and yodels?" I said, "Of course, it's great!" But this was all coming on top of the first layers that we had developed on the two previous movies.

You've mentioned the words "building" and "layers" a lot. It seems to me that you're not just adding conceptual layers as you work on each new movie; you're also layering elements within each movie. In some cases, you hear the layering happening within a sequence.

For example, in The Grand Budapest Hotel *score, you have a repeated, eight-measure leitmotif that we first hear when Gustave and Zero are on the train, traveling to the reading of the will. It reappears at different points in the story, including the long action sequence where they go to Gabelmeister's Peak. The way you weave variations of that leitmotif throughout the score reminded me of something you might hear in a score for an old Hollywood movie.*

That's true. When we get into the core of the story and the danger and adventure, that's where that theme you mentioned comes in again, and it's not as bouncy as the first time you hear it. It's more even. We knew we could use that theme in many different ways: slow, fast, sung by the monks, played by various instruments, played by the balalaikas in tremolo. I guess it was almost a counterbalance to the bouncy, gentle theme that opens the film with Zero and Gustave.

Is it too much to suggest that the quieter, more intimate themes suggest the private life, and that the more propulsive one I've just described suggests the public life, or history? There's a quality of inevitability to the way you build it up at the end and make it more heavy and ominous.

Yes. We could say that in this film, History—with a big *H*—is an omnipresent element we can't deny, which is why I mentioned Lubitsch before. If you know your movie history, you know that a few movies, like *To Be or Not to Be* or *Ninotchka*, managed to mix comedy and the big-*H* of history, where the drama becomes a comedy. It's sort of a way of being light without bringing pathos into the big-*H* history.

There is a hybrid aspect to the score that is fascinating. You've got some Eastern European folk, symphony-orchestra classical, including an almost "movie-score" kind of classical, and there's jazz, classic, and modern themes with some folk phrasing. . . . How do you decide how to measure all of these things out? Is it an intuitive process, where you're just thinking about the scene or moment? Or is there a larger plan or pattern?

There's a lot of intuition in what I do, because you have to not only understand the story line, you have to be able to feel what is given to you on-screen: what the actors are doing, what the lines are, what's happening offscreen, what you can anticipate or prepare the audience for. It is a very strange process, because you can't really say that there is always a clear decision. You just have to make a decision at some point about using this instrument over that one. We built this instrumentation together, with instruments that I know very well, because I've used them a lot, because I've always loved using odd instruments in my scores, for various reasons.

I've always loved to mix orchestral sounds with ethnic sounds, and with jazz influences or Brazilian bossa nova influences—but without everyone seeing it, because I'm not doing a Brazilian movie taking place in Rio, by the beach. So instead of having guitar play the rhythm, it'll be the strings. Or there might be a melody that sounds like a bossa nova, but what is playing underneath is brass, maybe something a bit rough. Nobody can tell it's influenced by bossa nova—but I know.

So it's all these things. I'm half Greek, and I've been hearing and listening to Balkan and Middle Eastern music since I was born. I've used the cimbalom in many scores of mine. It's maybe not as prominent in other movies as it is in *The Grand Budapest Hotel*, but even in *Argo* and *Zero Dark Thirty* and other scores, I've used instruments just because I love to use them, and because they're part of my musical heritage.

You have, in many of the tracks on many of your scores, instruments that sound, shall we say, less than perfect. By that I mean they don't sound like they've been overproduced in a studio. In a lot of cases, it almost sounds as if you've sought out old instruments, maybe even instruments that are a little bit beat-up—particularly for The Grand Budapest Hotel. *It's as if you're not looking for a mechanical cleanliness or perfection, but character.*

Exactly. We were not trying, on this score, to make something pristine or crystal clear. It had to have a bit of mud under the shoes, you know, like the characters have when they're running away. We needed to feel that.

But we also wanted to feel some elegance. That's why I love Gypsy music from Hungary or Romania, or Django Reinhardt: There's an elegance to the way they play. Gypsies, real Gypsies, are very smart with their clothing, the way they dress, and they play with elegance. They don't play as Mozart would have, but they bring something else to the music: a charm and a panache that matches very well with what Wes was after.

The Grand Budapest Hotel *score uses some elements of Eastern European and Russian folk music, right down to the choice of instruments.*

There are balalaikas all along, actually. There's a balalaika group, with many balalaikas playing—balalaikas of all sizes, from the tiny one to the bass one. That's a sound that Wes liked very much when we first started writing the music. He and I could feel that there was a quality to the sound of several balalaikas playing in tremolo very softly that was very beautiful, and at the same time very wide, opening a wide soundscape. That sound would also open the landscape, visually, and make the picture even larger to complement it. The music makes you feel as though something is opening up because of these wide, light, almost cloud-like vibrations of the balalaikas.

At the same time, there's another influence, which has always been there—in my organic way of thinking about music for films—and that is Bernard Herrmann.

First of all, I think he invented the method of using short motifs in films. He also invented how to place music at a certain spot.

That's another thing that is very important in Wes's movies: where and how to start and stop the music. You may notice that music in a Wes Anderson film is not wall-to-wall. It starts sometimes very strangely and ends very abruptly. This technique is one that designs the sound and the music, and that gives an energy, a pace, a rhythm to the film, which is different from what many other directors would do. When we work together, we pay a lot of attention to these breaks and sudden starts, and how many instruments, and which sound.

I talked to him about the sequence where Zero and Gustave go to Gabelmeister's Peak and pose as monks. There's a cable-car scene leading up to that. The movie integrates the chanting of the monks and the squeaking of the cable cars right into the score. That's almost a Carl Stalling sort of touch.

Yes, and I guess it was inspired by the way Wes directed it, and the way he uses sound, but it also came out of my first experience on *Mr. Fox*.

When I watched *The Grand Budapest Hotel* for the first time, I felt as if he had reshot *Mr. Fox* and all his previous movies, and transformed them into one object. To me, *The Grand Budapest Hotel* is his first of many masterpieces to come, because it has all the elements Wes has been playing with for a few films already. I think this film opens a new chapter in Wes's artistic life, as it did in mine.

How so?

We've put together all these layers during the last four or five years when we have worked together, and they have kind of been glued into a very specific style in this film. Even more so, maybe, than before.

I have a lot of fun with Wes, I must say. Ours is a very real, very close collaboration. We very often burst out in laughter just thinking of what we're trying to achieve.

Desplat conducting the Hollywood Studio Symphony at Sony Scoring Stage in Los Angeles, recording music for 2014's *Godzilla*.

a grand
stage: the
production
design of
the grand
budapest
hotel

steven
boone

a grand stage: the production design of

the grand budapest hotel

STEVEN BOONE

Meticulously designed with colorful, dandyish flourishes, a Wes Anderson film is often described as a dollhouse or a confection. This rep might lend the impression that Anderson's work is mostly set-bound, wall-to-wall artifice. In fact, the writer-director strives for a balance between stylization (art direction of toy-like form and function; special effects from the L. B. Abbott "wire, tape, and rubber band" school) and realism (psychologically grounded performances; use of preexisting locations). This balance is what gives the films their distinct tension. In *The Grand Budapest Hotel*, such dualistic struggle also describes Europe in the era of industrialization, expansion, war, and genocide: the cultivated grace of places such as Vienna, Paris, London, and Berlin falling under the shadow of the world wars' systematic barbarism.

What helps these opposing forces blend instead of clash is the soft, bright, pale-to-warm light that cinematographer Robert Yeoman bathes them in. While Adam Stockhausen's production design draws heavily from Edmund Goulding's *Grand Hotel*, along with 1930s and '40s classics by Ernst Lubitsch (*Trouble in Paradise*, *The Shop Around the Corner*), Rouben Mamoulian (*Love Me Tonight*), and Alfred Hitchcock (*The Lady Vanishes*, *The 39 Steps*), Yeoman only rarely borrows their intensely directional, hard-shadow lighting styles. In Anderson's world, color usually takes the lead, not black-and-white tonalities. Strictly in terms of palette, his full-color early twentieth century offers a nostalgia possibly more accurate to the memories of those who lived through

the period than to those whose world war romanticism comes only from black-and-white movies. Soft and bright is the glamour lighting that life often gives us to work with, thrown from lamp shades or bouncing off cream-colored walls. This is the romantic realism that two of Anderson's major influences, François Truffaut and Louis Malle, brought to the screen via New Wave cinematographers Henri Decaë and Raoul Coutard. The light invites us to take in settings as extensions of character, and as eccentric personalities in their own right.

The Grand Budapest Hotel (in real life, a department store), as presented in 1932, is an environment of pinks and pastels imagined in the art nouveau style that master concierge/gigolo M. Gustave clings to, but which was already expiring when he entered the business as a young lobby boy. The 1930s explosion of modernism is nowhere on his radar. The hotel, as we see it, is Gustave's enduring elitist toy box, done up in the colors of his youth. In this space, his vulgarity, refinement, cynicism, and high ideals get a grand stage. It makes sense that every exterior view of the place is a 1:18 scale model by Simon Weisse.

The film's frenetic second act kicks off at the Grand Budapest's evil twin, an estate called Schloss Lutz (played by Saxony's Castle Hainewalde for the exteriors; Schloss Waldenburg for the interiors). Where the Grand Budapest's warm tones and plush textures radiate accommodation and luxury, the brooding, hardwood arrogance of Schloss Lutz asserts oppressive wealth. Its labyrinthine chambers could have easily accommodated Universal Pictures' Dr. Frankenstein or Nazi officers (the lat-

ter of which Castle Hainewalde actually did, in 1933). Its cold heart is the trophy room, where the will of Gustave's elderly lover, Madame Desgoffe und Taxis, is read. The space isn't so much decorated as *littered* with the preserved heads, antlers, and torsos of conquered beasts. The room is otherwise packed, shoulder to shoulder, with "loved ones" dressed for a funeral but vulturing the executor Kovacs (done up like an owlish professor of mortuary science) as if listening for lottery numbers. Patches of deep green and gold on the walls hardly relieve the general sensation of being trapped in a crypt. One look at Madame D.'s son, Dmitri, in a raven-black sheath of a coat to match his severe mustache and locks, and we know for whom the room speaks.

At least Schloss Lutz admits some warmth, from straining candlelight and the basic browns of wood surfaces. No such luck when we get to Checkpoint 19, where Gustave is imprisoned (framed) for murder. This crumbling blue-gray box is where the grittier corners of Gustave's soul come to light. He's no mere dandy; he's a survivor—of what all, God only knows. As Max Ophüls might note, all the high-class puffery that the Grand Budapest represents is supported by a society's untold toil and violence—to none of which, the movie implies in devastating visual asides, Gustave is a stranger. Given to vulgar outbursts back in his Euro-resort element, Gustave rigorously maintains his Grand Budapest courtliness in prison. Is his refinement inherited? Or is his crudeness learned? In one comic highlight, he treats his fellow inmates to a box of Mendl's pastries, a luxury item on par with

OPPOSITE: A stack of Mendl's boxes in the props department, awaiting shipment to the set.

truffles or caviar. The convicts, in their concentration-camp grays, framed by the blunt stone walls, huddle in awe over a pyramid of sugary pastels that might as well be a scale model of the Grand Budapest itself. This is production design as sublime character building and social commentary.

Anderson's use of historic locations in this, one of his most brutal films, gives each act of violence a disquieting backdrop. Aside from the downright whimsical climactic shoot-out, where the camera glides laterally between the shooters on the Grand Budapest's upper tiers, the movie's beatings and killings tend to have a dark undertone. Dmitri's henchman, Jopling, wears the mahogany and sable walls of the trophy room like a cape. Later, he stalks

Deputy Kovacs through a mood-lit museum in a sequence modeled after the KGB goon's pursuit of Paul Newman in Hitchcock's muted *Torn Curtain*. For Anderson, violence, loss, and even a particularly harsh emotional slight darken the world, and his settings change to reflect as much—sometimes within a single shot. When elderly Zero remembers his long-gone love, Agatha, the light in the Budapest's dining room fades out as strong sidelight passes over his face.

It's Anderson's early-Truffaut-inspired taste (and Yeoman's flair) for anamorphic cinematography as much as any other visual component that ties together the wildly different settings of *Rushmore*, *The Royal Tenenbaums*, *The Life Aquatic with Steve Zissou*,

and *The Darjeeling Limited*. In *The Grand Budapest Hotel*, he reserves the anamorphic look only for the 1960s scenes, technically appropriate to the widescreen era of James Bond. The wide-aspect ratio also better suits the Communist period's illusion of leveled hierarchies. Of course, Anderson mainly uses the look here as he always has, to enhance the aura of grandiose, wistful reflection that gathers around F. Murray Abraham's character, Zero Moustafa, as he tells his tale (Anamorphic's subtle distortions and oil-paint suppleness in the defocused areas can heighten a set's air of mystery). Though the Grand Budapest has become a submerged relic, its gilded grandeur buried under Soviet-style utilitarian drabness, the optics give us something of Moustafa's heavyhearted

ABOVE: The Schloss Lutz's trophy room. The screenplay describes it as a "dark, woody parlor with mounted heads everywhere (lions, tigers, buffalo, antelope, etc.)."
OPPOSITE: The atrium of the Karstadt, the department store in Görlitz, Germany, that production designer Adam Stockhausen disguised and redecorated to create the atrium of the Grand Budapest Hotel.

way of seeing the place. We can almost see the ghosts.

Yet the nadir for Anderson is not darkness (which he presents as an inevitable fact of life), but a world without color and variety—just stark, ugly choices. Black and white. In what we soon learn is the prelude to Gustave's off-screen death, an incident in a train car we've already been primed to associate with militant brutality occurs in monochrome. This is the black-and-white of Chaplin's *The Great Dictator*, Borzage's *The Mortal Storm*, and Spielberg's *Schindler's List*. It's the beginning of a terrible history and the end of Gustave's illusions about civilization.

The final shots of *The Grand Budapest Hotel* gently back us out of a series of narrational portals, as Moustafa concludes his story of Gustave and the Author does the same for his recollection of Moustafa, both with what the former would call "a marvelous grace": Moustafa answers the riddle of why he still clings to this dying, joyless hotel before slow elevator doors close on him like a curtain. The Author then relates that he never revisited Moustafa or the hotel—in a sentence started by the Author's young self as we see him writing in the 1960s lobby, and finished by the Author as an older man, writing from his early-'80s home. Cut to the bookish young girl who has been reading this story all along, on a

bench near a monument to the now-deceased Author. It's a sweet chain of empathy and identification told not in emphatic close-ups, but rather in wide shots of characters dwarfed by their settings, stuck in their moments in time yet reaching for one another through the printed word.

What gives this montage special kick, I suspect, is a brief shot moments before it. It's the final image of Gustave. He is posing for a picture with his hotel staff in the dining room, under a massive landscape painting many would call kitsch. The framing is outrageously top heavy, favoring the painting and making us work for our brief glimpse of Gustave. Watch carefully whenever Anderson gets "sloppy." In this case, he is using set decoration to speak up for his most beloved character, a man of airs, pretensions, flaws, and comical excesses—but also with a heart as big and unavoidable as that painting. This, Anderson is saying, was the life that fascist thugs extinguished in an instant. One of millions, and one in a million.

The vending machine area in the Grand Budapest Hotel's lobby, 1968.
The "broken" and "at own risk" signs testify to Communist-era customer-service issues.

ABOVE   Overhead view of the Grand Budapest Hotel's main lobby.
BELOW   The hotel's Grand Ballroom, where the 1968 sequences in which old Zero and the young Author dine together; it also appears more fleetingly in scenes from the 1930s section of the movie.

KEEPING THE TRAINS RUNNING:

Like so many production designers, **ADAM STOCKHAUSEN** *started out working in the art departments of various features, starting with* Ash Tuesday *(2003) and* Alfie *(2004). He began working with Wes Anderson on 2007's* The Darjeeling Limited, *on which he served as supervising art director. He moved up to production designer on* Moonrise Kingdom *(2013) and served the same function on* The Grand Budapest Hotel *(2014). Stockhausen's work has enlivened some of the more visually inventive American features of recent times, including Charlie Kaufman's directorial debut,* Synecdoche, New York *(2008), which envisioned an endless, all-encompassing play that plumbed the depths of the hero's tortured psyche, and Steve McQueen's* 12 Years a Slave, *a historical drama that won the 2013 Academy Award for Best Picture.*

MATT ZOLLER SEITZ: *What's the difference between a production designer and an art director? I've seen both terms used, and I've never quite understood the distinction.*

ADAM STOCKHAUSEN: It's kind of confusing, because the production designer's job really grew out of art directing, which was the original term for it. "Production designer" is a more recent term that came in as the roles became more specialized.

A production designer is responsible for the physical look of the film—everything except for costumes. That ends up covering a whole lot of different bases. So it's a huge, sprawling kind of position. You're helping to sort out and direct what the locations are going to end up being, figuring out what's a location versus what's a built set, designing and executing the built sets, and overseeing set decoration and props.

All that comes under the umbrella of what the art department does on the film, and so the production designer is the primary interface between the art department and the director. You, the production designer, are the communicator, making sure that the wishes of the director are being executed properly, on a full scale. You're taking all this input from all these different people: the set decorator, the prop master, the construction people, the painters—all the different people working on all the different aspects of this film.

The art director provides the primary communication from the production designer to everybody else, as the tree builds out. So when a painter or a carpenter has a question about a specific thing, that question goes to the art director.

So the production designer is thinking more about the big picture, and the art director is thinking about the particulars of how everybody's going to realize the big picture?

In a way, yes. There's a level of discussion about what things should look like and how they should function for the camera. Then there's also a parallel conversation happening about what things cost, and about construction and installation timelines. Those two halves of the discussion need to happen simultaneously. The budget resides primarily with the art director. So the art director is really the key person letting the production designer know what's required to execute things. The question "Can we do this?" is asked a thousand times a day, and the "this" you're asking about can be pretty much anything you can imagine. And so "How much is this gonna cost?" and "How long is this gonna take?" are answers that you need to have at your fingertips.

Are there different kinds of production design for different kinds of movies, or is each one unique? I ask that because when you look at Wes Anderson's films, you'd think they were almost science-fiction movies—the kind of movies where you're creating everything. His movies aren't exactly set in the real world, and yet at the same time, they tend to be shot in real places, and they tend to be very, very physical in the way that they're made. Can you tell me how you reconcile those two aspects of his style?

I think that's a wonderful way to describe it: science fiction. When you're making science fiction, you can never fall back on: "Well, we're just going to shoot this big location the way it is!" You're creating everything, because you're dealing with a fictional world. Wes's films are very similar to that, because although they're tied into reality, and although real locations are often used, nothing is taken for granted in terms of the way it's normally done. So you end up designing the movies frame by frame, shot by shot, through each sequence. Although it's based in reality, it's all created. The process on a science-fiction film is actually kind of similar, where you can't take anything for granted, and you're designing every piece of it.

But in a funny way, what we're doing on Wes's movies is kind of an extreme version of the process on any movie, because you're asking the same questions about what things need to look like, and how to get there, and whether you have to build it or find it, or find it and modify it. That sort of overarching process is sort of the same for each movie. Are you designing 100 percent of the shots, or 75 percent of them, or 50 percent of them?

So for somebody in your job, the question is always some variation of, "How much does the art department have to add or modify?" Obviously, there'll always be adjustments made for lighting and blocking, and maybe you'll say, "Let's move that couch over to the other side of the room so the shot will be balanced"—that sort of thing?

Yes, but on Wes's films, it actually goes a step beyond just moving the couch to the other side of the room. Often, the room itself will need to be modified to fit the way he wants to design a shot, and often, real rooms don't play along with how Wes wants to see them. So you'll use part of a real room, but then you find that the rest of it just doesn't fit, or doesn't match.

Can you give me an example from one of his movies?

One really clear example is the way Wes wanted to see the Bishop house in the opening scene of *Moonrise Kingdom*. No real house could satisfy that, and so the Bishop house had to be fully built, to work with the way he wanted the camera to move. What we did was build physical space around that moving camera, to help explain the house.

There are smaller versions of that shot all the way through *The Grand Budapest Hotel*. For instance, when we're in Madame D.'s estate, Schloss Lutz, and we're down in the kitchen, when Serge has the ice pick and Gustave and Zero are in the room with the little cactus and the glass of water? For that space, we went and found a location that made sense as a kitchen. But then there was a very specific way that Wes wanted to pull sideways across from that window to the door, and then start backing up across the room and end up exiting the room. The space didn't allow for that. We ended up having to build that little room, align the door to it, and line it all up with a complicated platform for the dolly coming back. We had to restructure the room to make that shot possible.

In the last book, Wes told me a story in the Bottle Rocket *chapter that feels like the origin point for the scenario you're describing. At the beginning of that film, when Anthony leaves the mental facility, Wes wanted the camera to track from one room to another, but the space they shot in wasn't actually two rooms: They had one big room, and they built a partition to make it seem like there were two rooms. He told me he did not know you could do something like that until someone suggested it. Once he heard, "Oh, yeah, we can just put a fake wall here where there was no wall before, and turn one room into two," I think he was off to the races.*

[ADAM LAUGHS] Yes. Exactly.

But what you're describing in that kitchen shot from The Grand Budapest Hotel *is something that's much more complex, because what you're talking about is picturing a shot and then changing the world to fit that shot, or that camera movement, on a much higher order of difficulty?*

It's exactly what you were just describing, but the complexity level has gone way, way up. Thinking of the shot and then modifying the physical environment to match it is the polar opposite of filmmaking that says, "We're going

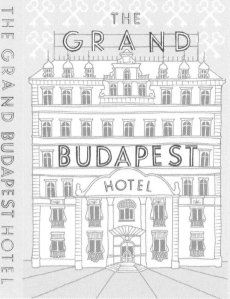

to walk into the space and deal with physical reality the way it is." If you're making that kind of a movie, you might move the couch to the other side of the room, but you're never going to question the physical space in terms of its right to be the way it is—questioning the physical space is a totally different way of thinking about it.

So when you're making movies the way Wes Anderson makes movies, reality becomes fungible through the eye of the camera.

ABOVE The fictional work of fiction meant to be the basis for the story in the film.
BELOW A shot from the film from the point of view of the young woman who visits the bust of the Author, as she regards her treasured copy of his book.

Right. And here's the funny thing: Reality is *always* fungible through the eye of the camera. That's kind of a given on a film. But once you have the nerve to say, "Yes, we know that's a given, and now we're going to *really* have some fun with the actual physical reality"—well, that's really exciting.

Is it fair to say that when you design a movie like Wes's, or perhaps any movie, you're only concerning yourself with what the camera can see?

That's correct.

So what's in front of the camera is created only for that shot, and if you could somehow magically pull the shot back just a little bit—by maybe 20 percent—you'd see a bunch of cables and lights, and people in windbreakers standing around?

You absolutely would, yeah.

Can you give me another example of the alteration of physical space to shoot a shot on Grand Budapest Hotel? *A particular distinctive shot, maybe?*

Here's one I think was especially fun: We were trying to find just the right train stations for two shots. Train stations are tough, because a train station can be a big place, it could be an exterior, and here we're dealing with a period movie, so you have to find a 1920s or 1930s train station, and those don't grow on trees. Plus, the shots take place in the winter, so we have to put snow on everything. On top of all that, you have to get a train! Trains are really expensive, they take a long time to reset, and it's not easy to get them to go where you want them to go.

One of the stations we needed was for a shot in the countryside—the station you see after the jailbreak. The other is the station where the train pulls in at Gabelmeister's Peak. We went around and around and around. We looked at all these different existing train stations, trying to find two stations that we had the right feeling for, and it just wasn't working. We realized it was going to be hugely expensive, and that we were going to be constrained by which trains we were able to get, by what the trains were able to do, and by how much the snow was going to cost to put on the trees.

So Wes came up with these really remarkable solutions for those two sequences. For Gabelmeister's Peak, we took over an abandoned train shed—it was really kind of a rail house sort of thing—and designed the shot so that you only saw the train station through the frame of a doorway of the train as it was pulling into the station. The combination of the movement of the camera and the tiny frame mounted to the dolly through which we see the station suggested the *idea* of the train pulling into the station. The station was actually only seen from that one angle.

So in this shot, the open door of this boxcar became kind of a matte, and the image of the station as the train pulled in created a frame within a frame.

Exactly. With this station, we knew exactly what we were seeing, how we were seeing it, and from what angle, so we were able to line up this shot, which we did through a minivan. I just had to take my guys out there and dress and build a train station for this one view from this one angle.

The shot starts off with a tree covered in snow. We pass one of the ZigZags' tanks, we pull up to the platform with people waiting for their luggage, and then we're at the Gabelmeister's Peak station. When the camera pulls to a stop, you feel like you've pulled into a train station. And we did it without any of the rigamarole of getting a train, dressing a gigantic train station—all that. It's just a one-shot, clear view of this whole alpine train station, and hopefully it says everything it needs to say.

The other train station is the one where Bill Murray's character drops off Zero and Gustave to catch the train to Gabelmeister's Peak. Wes had this idea for a shot where you see a car zoom under a bridge, then appear on top of the bridge, and then Zero and Gustave jump out and catch the train. Well, there was no train station there at all! So we found a spot on a hill that had this great underpass of a road. The trick was how to make that into a station. We came up with a really fun solution of getting two cars, so that one car could be pulling in underneath the bridge, and then, suddenly, the other car could pull in from one side on this bridge up above—all in the same shot.

We had very little room up there on the bridge to play with, so we made a train. But the train wasn't a real train. It was just cardboard and tape. There was nothing much to it.

So it was like a stage train?

It was exactly like a stage train! It was made out of cardboard and sticks and painted black, with smoke coming out the top. We pushed it into the shot on dolly tracks from the right-hand side of the frame. There is no way, in a major motion picture, that you could get away with a shot like that—but I think we pulled it off! I think it worked, and it's fun.

The solution you all came up with is so basic that it reminds me of the sort of tricks that would've been done in a much older film, like that wonderful shot in The Night of the Hunter *where you see Robert Mitchum's character, Reverend Harry Powell, riding up on a ridge. The kids look out a window and see Mitchum on his horse, and he's kind of silhouetted off*

ABOVE   From actor Charles Laughton's only film as director, 1955's *The Night of the Hunter*, a still-frame showing special effects done "in camera," on a soundstage, with a forced-perspective backdrop.

Two still-frames from *The Grand Budapest Hotel* spotlighting two moments where audiences were fooled by simple stagecraft.
ABOVE   Zero and M. Gustave run from a car to a "train" that is actually the wooden facade of an imitation train engine mounted on wheels.
BELOW   Inspector Henckels (Edward Norton) peers into the "boxcar" of a "freight train" arriving at the Gabelmeister's Peak railway station. You're actually seeing the point of view of a camera shooting through a disconnected chunk of wall mounted to a camera dolly on rails. The director talks about this process in Act 2 (see page 114).

in the distance. The whole shot was done "in camera," on a soundstage
with a forced-perspective backdrop, and, apparently, the role of Robert
Mitchum was played by a little person riding a tiny pony.

That's the exact same thing we were trying to do in that bridge shot. Wes
wanted to do it that way because, one, it's an homage, and two, if you can do
the old tricks and really pull them off, there'll be a charm to the shot that can't
be produced any other way.

Isn't there also a kind of liberating quality to the fact that in Wes's
movies, the point is not always just to convince you that something
is real? I mean, in the shots of the trains that you described, we
obviously have to believe that they're real trains, because, otherwise,
it might take us out of the moment. But in something like the shot

ABOVE   Still-frames from Ingmar Bergman's 1963 film, *The Silence*, a drama about two sisters traveling home through a
made-up European country on the brink of war.

TOP   Still-frame showing an overhead view of the Grand Budapest Hotel's lobby, with rug patterns and overall composition hearkening back to Bergman's *The Silence*.

MIDDLE   Signs on the front gate of Madame D.'s estate (LEFT). Deputy Kovacs's unfortunate claim check (RIGHT).

BOTTOM   Design for Mendl's bakery.

of the funicular going up the side of the mountain that leads to the hotel, there's a different kind of feeling. Everything in that shot looks like something out of a pop-up book, so we're not questioning the physical realism of any of it.

It's a delicate balancing act, because the funicular shot is absolutely not supposed to draw you out of the moment or make you aware of its artificiality in a way that's too exacting about the artificiality. The scene I just described with the car on the bridge is simply about a train—about getting dropped off and running to catch a train. It's not about "How cleverly can we do this thing?" or "What can we do to show off our scenery?" or whatnot. It's about the storytelling.

But I think that as you use these techniques with miniatures, and all these other ways of accomplishing complicated camera moves and visuals, you develop a vocabulary that then, once established, is accepted by the audience. So *Grand Budapest* has an overall look to it that you come to accept very quickly as the look of *The Grand Budapest Hotel*. Once you've accepted it, your mind lets go of it. You don't get pulled out of the storytelling, because that *is* the storytelling.

Speaking of storytelling, I'm interested in the role that history plays in this story and how it affects what we see on the screen. Maybe we should put "history" in quotes, because this story is not anything drawn from history books. It's kind of an invented history, but still there's a sense that this proud, probably monarchial country has changed—and will eventually become a Communist satellite state. What do you do physically, with your materials, to communicate that sort of change?

We were trying to make the most of the architecture that was around us. In the town of Görlitz, there's this extraordinary architecture that goes all the way back to the Baroque period. But Görlitz also has this art nouveau look that, back then, would have been the new style—literally The New Style. Supposedly, the construction of the Grand Budapest Hotel happened around the turn of the twentieth century. Our story starts some years later than that, but the hotel would've been basically new at the time. That gave us a way to use this existing, surrounding world to our advantage.

We used an existing shell of a department store, Görlitzer Warenhaus, in Görlitz, to become the hotel. Then we put set dressing on top of that, and props on top of that, to draw out the specifics of the history and of the period, even though, as you say, it's sort of an invented history. Then we started inventing things to layer on top of that: the money—the Klubecks for Zubrowkian currency, for example. From there, the world of the film started to develop a richness and a history of its own that had definite roots in the actual location and history of where we were.

Wes wanted to see the hotel strongly in these two different time periods, and he wanted a complete transformation of it. So on one side of the ledger, we did the miniatures, which is how the audience is able to see the big, wide establishing views of the hotel. We designed and built a miniature of the 1930s starting point of the hotel, and then we built a complete miniature of a radical transformation of it in the 1960s, in the Communist era.

We were in what had been East Germany, shooting this film, so there were examples of Communist-era architecture all around us—and also in Czechoslovakia. There were buildings from that time period that were intact, and also buildings that had been modified in that time period, so you could kind of get comfortable with this style of Brutalist renovation, for lack of a better term. That was the idea: that our hotel had undergone that kind of transformation.

On the other side of the ledger, we had this real, physical scenery in the department store, and we built it out to create a 1930s look. We then built the entire 1960s Communist version of the hotel on top of the older look of the 1930s hotel, in skins and pieces that sat in front of all the 1930s stuff.

We shot the whole thing in reverse—that is, we shot the 1960s scenes, and then we peeled all those layers away, revealing the 1930s version of the hotel that was sitting underneath it, and shot the 1930s scenes.

Wes works a lot with animatics, these semi-animated storyboards that let him kind of "pre-make" the movie before he actually shoots it. Can you tell me what role animatics play in helping to visualize his films?

They're really key. Animatics are, basically, storyboarding taken to the next level, where storyboards are actually cut together into animated sequences. So you get to feel the sense of timing, and you get to feel the film itself, in a *moving* way, as opposed to when you're just looking at storyboarded frames.

That's critically important on a movie like this. We were talking earlier about piecing together sequences from different locations and different sets in a way that makes you feel like it's all one thing. Well, at the beginning of a project, you look at the script, and then, as you start to talk about the different locations, you realize that they're actually incredibly complex sequences made up of different pieces. The animatic becomes your road map through all of that.

Can you give me an example?

The best example I can give is the introduction of the hotel at the very begin-ning of the film, where we open on an elevated platform, we dolly across the landscape, we're introduced to the hotel in a wide view, and then we move in to a closer view of the front of the hotel. That sequence is made up of different miniatures, built sets with extensions, and filmed interior spaces. It's impossible to wrap your head around all of it until you really start to break it down, piece by piece. That happens through the process of storyboarding, and then building the animatic. Once I have the animatic, I can turn around to my whole depart-ment and say, "OK, here's what this is going to be. We need to work on these sets, design these miniatures, and create all of these other component parts."

What would you say were the most difficult challenges on this par-ticular shoot, materially or logistically?

The biggest challenge was the hotel—just building this hotel. It was a really big set, and it took a lot of development time and construction time. We had to build

the 1960s version on top of the 1930s version, and doing that all together was a bit of an undertaking. It took a huge amount of focus and attention. We got it done for the very beginning of the shoot, took a deep breath, and then turned around and went, "Oh God, now there's the other 90 percent of the movie to deal with!"

Then it became a race of sets. We were moving very quickly through the process, and all the sets had to be built out and finished and done. It was a fast-moving shoot. Just trying to stay in front of it was a big trick. The train-station shots I described to you? We had two or three days to build them, and then they show up and shoot a scene for two or three hours, and then you have to have the next thing ready to shoot immediately.

So the big trick is taking the schedule apart and saying, "How do we stay in front? How do we make sure that we always have the next thing ready?" That's always the case on any movie, but this one was especially fast-moving. We sometimes had especially big pieces that we were trying to get ready, so it was more challenging than usual.

What particular films or other sources did you look to for inspiration?

*For a more detailed description of the role photocrom images played in the production of the film, see page 101.
We first looked at photocrom images, which I know Wes has mentioned to you.* There's a huge collection of those at the Library of Congress. They show this slice of Europe that moves far beyond the Eiffel Tower: You see these hotels up on hilltops, and these funicular trains going from the town below up to the hotel, and it's all filtered through the way photocrom shows you the world—with this amazing, distant, faraway look that really fit the film.

Next, we looked at a bunch of different films; the movie has references from all over the place. In particular, there's a sequence in Hitchcock's *Torn Curtain* that we looked at, the one where Paul Newman's character is being followed. He comes out of the hotel, takes a streetcar to a museum, and then tries

ABOVE   M. Gustave's formidable stockpile of his favorite cologne, L'Air de Panache.

to lose this guy who's been following him. That became the museum sequence in our film, where Jopling is pursuing Deputy Kovacs. It's kind of shot-for-shot.

We also looked at the scenes when they're walking around a hotel in Ingmar Bergman's *The Silence*. The hallways in that movie became very important to us. We borrowed from those hallways to create the details of our own hallways. We also looked at *The Life and Death of Colonel Blimp*, *To Be or Not to Be*, and *The Shop Around the Corner*; I love the way that the sets in those films kind of feel like sets but at the same time communicate a specific world.

Beyond just looking at films for inspiration, Wes loves to do a lot of scouting—not necessarily just scouting for places to shoot in, but reference scouting, to get ideas. We went to visit all these spa towns, and in the baths, we saw all kinds of bits and pieces that were exciting and that ended up informing the fictional world we're making. Some of the details were so interesting that we end up trying to go out, get the real things, and put them in the movie. At this one spa we went to, their baths had mud treatments, and there were these amazing rolling mud buckets that looked like rolling trash cans. They were just incredible. We loved them. So we got them! At another place, there were these blue tubs that Wes really loved, so we called the owners and got a couple of them. That's why the tubs in our movie are blue! You look back on it all, and you can pick out where every little piece came from.

I've got to ask you about the Mendl's boxes and the pastries. How were the foodstuffs made, and how was the packaging made? What was the thought behind the design and execution of those elements?

I'm so glad you brought that up, because it allows me to talk about two super-important people on this film. One is Robin Miller, the prop master. He was the point person on working with a baker to develop the pastry, and on going through about eight thousand versions of the "magic" opening box to try to get it right. The other one is Annie Atkins, who was the graphic designer for the film. She did the look of the box itself, and she just did a wonderful job.

In both cases—and, in fact, in every case having to do with anything you might ask about on the film—the process is something like this: First we go, "OK—so there's this Mendl's box. Mendl's needs a graphic. What does a Mendl's box look like? It probably says 'Mendl's,' so we need to design something to say that." Then we'll pull references of different, relevant materials that already exist and that are interesting. You ask things like, "What's the most amazing bakery that you've ever heard of? And what pops into your mind when you think of that?" From there, you can look at questions like, "What were the big kitchens in Paris and Berlin from the turn of the century through 1930? Let's look them up and see what their boxes looked like."

Through the process of doing something like that, you'll look at all of these boxes, and then Wes will come in and say, "I like this one and this one. These are really interesting. I love the way this one has scrollwork on it."

Then Annie—or whoever's doing whatever job, because this process is basically the same, whether you're building scenery or doing all those other designs that Annie was drawing—will take all the different references and synthesize them into something that's new but that also has roots that go down

deep into the reference pictures. That process leads to version after version after version, until finally everybody agrees that we've settled on the right thing.

Before we got to that point with the Mendl's boxes, there were many weeks of walking around with all these different sample boxes, trying to get the ribbons right. It was definitely a "back to the drawing board" kind of project.

Can you tell me how you got that box to open in the way that it opened in the movie?

We used a false tabletop, and then somebody underneath the tabletop pulled on a fishing line to open the box.

When you untied the ribbon, the box needed a little bit of help to pull itself apart and down. The opening of the box has an origami kind of quality, but there's a little push involved. Without the fishing line, two sides of the box would've fallen right away, and the other sides would've slowly tipped over. To give it repeatability and consistency, we had to help it out a little bit.

So a box can't actually do that in real life?

Well a box *can* do that—we didn't try to make it do anything that it couldn't actually do—but we had to figure out a way to make it do it faster, and to do it consistently, all at the same time.

ABOVE   Still-frame from Jacques Becker's 1960 prison film *Le Trou (The Hole)*, based on José Giovanni's same-named 1957 novel. The director says this was the basis for the food-inspection scene in *The Grand Budapest Hotel* (OPPOSITE), though the latter is speedier and funnier.

ABOVE   Carpenter/set dresser Roman Berger portrayed the Parcel Inspector at Checkpoint 19 Criminal Internment Camp, who is ruthlessly efficient at his job, yet seems to have a soft spot for beauty.

At the Algonquin Hotel

OUR THIRD, AND LONGEST, *GRAND BUDAPEST HOTEL* conversation occurred in February 2014. Wes had temporarily relocated to New York City in the run-up to the release of his new film.

OPPOSITE: Wes Anderson directing some of the Lutz Military Policemen on *The Grand Budapest Hotel*'s main set. The man in the purple jacket, playing one of the hotel receptionists, is Georg Rittmannsperger, the owner of the Hotel Börse in Görlitz, where the director and the cast lived during filming. Georg's wife, Sabine Euler, played the Schoolteacher (painter) in the 1968 part of the story.

ABOVE: The pile of "scraps, slips, shreds, slivers, forms, files, postcards, and various bits of lint and loose thread," as described in the screenplay, that constitute the last will and testament of Madame D.

OVERLEAF: Ralph Fiennes, Wes Anderson, and Tony Revolori on location, shooting the scene from the 1932 sequence in which M. Gustave begins mentoring Zero Moustafa.

We met at the Algonquin Hotel. The main order of business was to talk about Stefan Zweig, although we gave ourselves room to digress. Our conversation lasted a little over two hours, starting at a small table in the hotel's main lobby and continuing at another table in an adjacent bar.

By that point, I'd read key works by Zweig, including *Confusion*, *Fear*, "Compulsion," *The Post-Office Girl*, *Beware of Pity*, "A Story Told in Twilight," "The Debt Paid Late," and his memoir, *The World of Yesterday*. A good portion of this conversation centers on Zweig's work: what Wes did and did not take from him, as well as key themes, recurring situations, and storytelling devices, including voice-over narration and how it's used—and, sometimes, abused. As the hour grew late, the conversation veered into nostalgic territory: specifically, memories of Wes's friend and collaborator Kumar Pallana, who had died a few months earlier.

The

8,838–Word

THIRD

Interview

MATT ZOLLER SEITZ: How do you decide which details to include in a script, beyond the plot and dialogue?

WES ANDERSON: I used to put a lot more stuff in my scripts. I used to put in everything I knew. If I had some information about the costumes or details of the set, I would put them in there so that the different departments would have it all in front of them.

And then, after a point, I stopped putting in a lot of that kind of stuff. I started trying to put in only the stuff that helps you along in the story, and that helps you picture a character as a person. And I stopped putting in specific music, unless it's something that's really relevant to the scene, like when the people on-screen are singing a Gregorian chant. I don't name specific songs.

Why? Because the people who own the rights to the song might read the script and go, "Wow, Wes Anderson must really want this. We can charge him a lot"?

Or somebody else gets a hold of the script, and they use that song in another movie before we even get a chance to. You know, with that sort of thing, like with a lot of stuff, it's not a terrible idea to kind of just keep it under your hat a bit.

Also, I don't really like putting camera descriptions in screenplays, because they're boring to read. Every now and then, I will say, "The camera moves to such and such," but I only do that if I think it's the only way for me to express what's happening—that there's no other way for me to describe it. Like, you know that one shot in *The Darjeeling Limited,* the one you called the "dream train" shot, where we're kind of moving through this train car and looking at these people in the compartments? That's something I wouldn't know how to describe without mentioning the camera. You might as well just tell people what the shot is.

You've written a very distinctive kind of narration for this movie. This is not narration that's just sort of helping the story along. It's *active.* And there's a lot of it. Given that you're known as a director

who goes in with a pretty tight blueprint for how you want things to unfold, and that you're blocking shots and devising camera moves that you know are going to interact with the narration in a specific way, how do you make the pieces fit?

Hmmm.

I mean, look at your script: It's not written to industry standard. It reads like literature. And the delineation of what's narration versus what's action—that's somewhat blurrier on the page than it is in the finished film.

Well, like I was saying, the screenplay is written to be read. So that means I'm writing it more like a short story. That's what I always try to do: aim it more toward a reader than toward the people who are going to be making the movie, because I figure I'm going to be there, anyway.

On the set, you mean.

Right.

I mean, I can also go the other way, and describe things differently from the way I'm going to actually shoot them. Sometimes, on the page, I'm describing something a particular way, but I know I'm not actually going to *shoot* it that way once I'm on the set. A lot of times, I write it another way in the script because describing it *exactly* the way I plan to shoot it would take up too much space or just be confusing, and I don't want to subject anybody to that. I want to give people something that's nice to read.

I'm also careful with the punctuation, and *that* certainly doesn't show up in the movie.

If you were writing the narration after the fact, as some directors do, you could just make it fit with the action on-screen; but that's not what you did in this movie. You went onto the set already knowing what the narration would be, right?

Right.

And the narration works with the image precisely. You have scenes where you hear a bit of narration, and then the character will say,

"And then he said to me . . . ", and then the camera will whip-pan to catch a line of dialogue right when a character says it.

How do you do that kind of filmmaking? I mean, in practical terms?

Well, doing that sort of stuff, you know, with Murray and Jude and Jason and everyone—when we were on the set, what would happen is, they would do their part, and then I would say the narration, and then they would continue.

So you were standing offscreen while the actors were performing the scene, reading the narration out loud?

Yes, but then I had one scene—I don't remember exactly where it is—with Ralph, where I was going to do that. We're doing the scene, we're doing take one, and then Ralph says his thing, and I chime in, and this is the way we've always been doing it, and then Ralph looks at me and says, "What are you doing, darling?"

[MATT LAUGHS.]

"Is it meant to be that way? Is there not another way to go about this? Can we not just *imagine* your voice?"

Could you "just imagine," though, and get the timing right?

Ralph is very precise.

There were a couple of other places where I didn't quite leave enough room for this line or that line, though, and I thought: "We're going to have to go into the editing room later and figure out how to do that."

And we did figure it out. Nowadays we have, I guess you could say, digital alternatives. We can slow something down just slightly, imperceptibly, and speed something up a little bit, stuff that we never used to be able to do before.

It's interesting, this sort of narration, because of this "Show, don't tell" thing that they teach you in film school and in screenwriting books—this anti-narration sentiment. In fact, there's a good joke in *Adaptation* about that. It's the Robert McKee seminar when the schmuck screenwriter is sitting out in the audience muttering to himself in voice-over, going "I've sold out, I am worthless . . . " and McKee yells, ". . . and God help you if you use voice-over in your work, my friends! *God help you!*" And, at that point, the voice-over narration on the film ceases and is never heard from again.

I wonder: When do we first hear narration like that, in a movie? Not where it's just there at the beginning to sort of get you into the story, but where it's all the way through? I mean, I can't think of movies in the 1930s where there's narration, but I can think of plenty of movies in the 1940s. Can you name a 1930s movie with the kind of narration we do in our movie?

I can't think of too many. Is that because sound had just come in, and they were so enamored with the novelty of hearing people speak that they didn't feel the need for a lot of voice-over?

Maybe they hadn't thought it up yet. Certainly they were already doing it on newsreels. But you don't see it in Warner Bros. gangster pictures of that period. You don't see it in comedies or Lubitsch-type movies,

or anything like that that I can think of. You don't see it in any of these pre-Code movies. But you see it in film noir, and you see it in some biopics.*

Film noir was the first big flowering of that "active narration" in the American cinema, where you saw a complex, sustained interplay of voice-over text with images. That "noir sophistication" started in the 1940s. *Double Indemnity*, for me, is the peak of that early phase.

But you saw it happening in non-noir as well. Frank Capra played around with this sort of wall-to-wall narration in parts of *It's a Wonderful Life* in 1946—which is a great year for narrated film noir, as well. In the Capra movie, you almost feel like there's a story being told to you after the fact, and there are even a lot of freeze-frames, à la documentaries, or *Goodfellas*. It's like we're watching the movie of George Bailey's life, and the angel and Saint Peter are freezing the image so they can take a second to discuss what's happening.

Another one of my favorites is *All About Eve*, which is so heavily narrated in parts that it's almost like somebody is sitting there reading a story to you. The 1930s, though—I think you're right, that was a protean phase.

I'm mainly going down this road because I'm interested in your thoughts on the "Show, don't tell" edict.

Well, that's the thing that some movies do, where you can tell they're using narration to pretty obviously fix problems in the story. But if you do good writing as part of the narration, and if the narration is a part of the whole *idea* of the movie, that's just a different thing.

If you go to Stanley Kubrick's movies, you see great examples of narration. Kubrick's version of *Lolita* has Humbert Humbert as the voice of the story, or the voice of the movie, really, the same way that he's the voice of the novel, which is written in first person. And then there's *The Killing*, which has this great narration by a narrator who's pretty clearly not personally involved in the story.

Yeah—third-person detached narration, like you're hearing somebody read a crime report, after the fact.

Then there's another variation of that detached third-person narration in *Barry Lyndon*. And then you've got another great first-person narration in *A Clockwork Orange*. There's some first-person narration, written by Michael Herr, in *Full Metal Jacket*. Herr also wrote the narration for *Apocalypse Now*, which is the best voice-over.

It's Raymond Chandler–esque. It turns into *Philip Marlowe Goes to Nam* in certain places. "Charging a man with murder in this place was like handing out speeding tickets at the Indy 500."

The Coen brothers have often done great narration, sometimes in pretty surprising ways. In *The Big Lebowski*, we have a narrator who seems like he's one of those detached narrators, but as it turns out, he's an actual guy, and he appears in the movie. Who knows how he got there, but there he is. And they do sort of the same thing in *The Hudsucker Proxy*, but he's a little more directly involved.

You do a version of that in *Moonrise* as well, where Bob Balaban's "stage manager" character, at first, seems like he's standing outside the story, but then, a few scenes later, he joins it.

Critic and film historian David Bordwell writes:

Matt and Wes are right to say that narration, as we usually think of it, really developed during the 1940s—particularly the idea that narration can move us swiftly among different characters' stories, with the voice-over guiding us overtly or stealthily. The best book about voice-over narration in movies is Sarah Kozloff's *Invisible Storytellers*, and most of her examples of early, heavily narrated movies are from the 1940s. In the 1930s, that sort of narration is rare, I think partly for reasons of syncing up the sound as precisely as necessary. But there are two big exceptions I can think of. One is *The Power and the Glory* (1933), directed by William K. Howard, with a script by Preston Sturges. The other is *Le Roman d'un Tricheur* (1936), by Sacha Guitry, which is available from Criterion as *The Story of a Cheat*.

Going further back, you very occasionally get whole films in the 1920s with "voice-over" narrators, but because there was no synchronized sound, their narration is delivered in the form of intertitles. In a way, *The Cabinet of Dr. Caligari* (1920) has continuous voice-over, via the character of Francis; he's telling us the main tale by way of a framing story (rather like the storytelling in *The Grand Budapest Hotel*). Maybe the most famous example of narration-through-intertitles from that era is 1921's *The Phantom Carriage*, directed by Victor Sjöström, a film that also features stories-within-stories.

But in silent cinema, we don't get the sense of a prolonged narration, at least not in the same way that we can in sound. In silent movies, the pictures always interrupt the narrative.

The fascinating thing is that you don't need to justify voice-over as somebody telling a story to somebody else. It can be pure subjectivity ("I remember . . .") or, nowadays, just talking straight to the audience—for example, the opening of *Jerry Maguire* (1996), or the entirety of *Kiss Kiss Bang Bang* (2005), or any *Dragnet* episode, which picks up from the sort of narration Wes and Matt later describe in Kubrick's *The Killing*. By the time we get to *All About Eve* in 1950, we see and hear a very complex mingling of internal points-of-view, guided by voice-over. (Some of the complexity comes from the studio boss Darryl F. Zanuck's

ABOVE: Wes Anderson directs F. Murray Abraham and Jude Law during the 1968 dinner scene.

forcing the writer–director Joseph L. Mankiewicz to cut whole sections from the movie.)

What's also interesting to me about this question is how the voice-over technique fits with the story-within-story dynamic, which can get very complicated, as in Pier Paolo Pasolini's *Arabian Nights* or the embedded flashbacks of 1940s movies. One thing Wes learned from Zweig is the power of the embedded-story technique—going beyond flashbacks (which can behave like embedded stories) to more autonomous ones, with a new cast of characters at each shift. [1]

[1] To read Bordwell's analysis of Wes Anderson's use of changing aspect ratios in *The Grand Budapest Hotel*, turn to page 235.

✷✷ M. GUSTAVE (V.O.) What is a Lobby Boy? A Lobby Boy is completely invisible, yet always in sight. A Lobby Boy remembers what people hate. A Lobby Boy anticipates the client's needs before the needs are needed. A Lobby Boy, above all, is discreet, to a fault.

Lebowski and *Hudsucker*: Both of those movies have a similar concept when it comes to narration. And *Blood Simple* has something like that, too, doesn't it? Who's doing the voice-over in *Blood Simple*?

That's M. Emmet Walsh's character, Visser. The private detective.

M. Emmet Walsh is narrating the movie himself.

From beyond the grave, presumably.

The *Sunset Boulevard* idea.

You mentioned *Lolita* and *Barry Lyndon* and *The Killing* and other Kubrick movies. Those are all examples of active, dynamic narration. It's not just supplying bits of data that we could have gotten from watching the movie; it's giving you something extra, or something different. In some cases, the narration is sort of telling you how you're supposed to take what you're seeing—clarifying the tone of the movie. In other cases it's going the other way, and complicating your reaction to what's happening on-screen.

Kubrick's adaptation of *Lolita* is an example of the second kind of active voice-over. It would be a very different movie if you didn't hear James Mason reading bits of the novel to you. The sense of humor might get lost, and the whole thing would seem purely tawdry.

I hope I'm remembering this right, but I feel like James Mason's *Lolita* narration was part of what I was thinking of, with this narration in *The Grand Budapest*. I feel like that's why the character is English. I feel like Jude entered my mind when I was thinking of James Mason in *Lolita*.

And I wanted to work with Jude, anyway. I just saw him in *Henry V* here. He was so great in it. He's

also in that Steven Soderbergh movie *Side Effects*. Did you ever see it?

Yes. Quite an underrated film.

Jude was great in it.

Anyway, in *Moonrise Kingdom* we have a narrator who's doing the thing where really it's just, "Here's some information we want you to know—and here's one way to tell it." It's all about getting briskly to the next place in the story.

But in this movie, I was thinking of trying a Stefan Zweig–esque thing, which is: A guy meets somebody who is going to tell the story, and so it begins to unfold itself.

Well, once you have a character who's going to tell you the movie, very likely you're going to be doing narration. And, in this case, we have a few different kind of layers and weird kind of *branches* of narration.

At some point, I think Ralph is even narrating. I think there's a part of it where M. Gustave is giving lessons to Zero, and he's the voice-over during that montage.

Yes, kind of dialogue-as-voice-over. I like to call that "stealth narration." ✷✷

It's fascinating, the effect of all these narrators. It's narration within narration.

I've been thinking a lot about that opening sequence, where this young woman goes to see the statue of the person who wrote the book about the story that you're about to see, which is something that was told to him by somebody else—and you close with the young woman, as well.

The second time I saw the movie, I thought about that final shot again, and I was asking myself, *What are we looking at*

#1 DOUBLE INDEMNITY (1944)

DIRECTOR:
Billy Wilder

SCREENPLAY:
Billy Wilder and Raymond Chandler; adapted from the novel by James M. Cain

NARRATOR:
Walter Neff (Fred MacMurray)

NARRATIVE FUNCTION:
Explain, after the fact, how Neff's plot to help Phyllis Dietrichson (Barbara Stanwyck) murder her husband went awry.

SAMPLE NARRATION:
Walter: It was a hot afternoon, and I can still remember the smell of honeysuckle all along that street. How could I have known that murder can sometimes smell like honeysuckle?

Cine•Star™

#2 IT'S A WONDERFUL LIFE (1946)

DIRECTOR:
Frank Capra

SCREENPLAY:
Frances Goodrich, Albert Hackett, and Frank Capra; additional scenes by Jo Swerling; story by Philip Van Doren Stern

NARRATORS:
Clarence Odbody (Henry Travers), Joseph the Angel (Joseph Granby), and Senior Angel (Moroni Olsen)

NARRATIVE FUNCTION:
Set the stage for Clarence the Angel's intervention in the life of suicidally depressed savings and loan manager George Bailey (James Stewart).

SAMPLE NARRATION:
Clarence: Hey, who's that?
Joseph: That's your problem, George Bailey.
Clarence: A boy?
Joseph: That's him when he was twelve, back in 1919. Something happens here you'll have to remember later on.

Cine•Star™

#3 ALL ABOUT EVE (1950)

DIRECTOR:
Joseph L. Mankiewicz

SCREENPLAY:
Joseph L. Mankiewicz

NARRATORS:
Addison DeWitt (George Sanders) and Karen (Celeste Holm)

NARRATIVE FUNCTION:
Retrospectively comment on the rise of Eve Harrington (Anne Baxter) in the New York theater scene.

SAMPLE NARRATION:
Addison: To those of you who do not read, attend the theater, listen to unsponsored radio programs, or know anything of the world in which you live—it is perhaps necessary to introduce myself. My name is Addison DeWitt. My native habitat is the theater. In it, I toil not, neither do I spin. I am a critic and commentator. I am essential to the theater.

Cine•Star™

#4 SUNSET BOULEVARD (1950)

DIRECTOR:
Billy Wilder

SCREENPLAY:
Charles Brackett, Billy Wilder, and D. M. Marshman Jr.

NARRATOR:
Joe Gillis (William Holden)

NARRATIVE FUNCTION:
Posthumously explain the circumstances by which narrator Joe Gillis ended up floating dead in a swimming pool at a mansion owned by fading star Norma Desmond (Gloria Swanson).

SAMPLE NARRATION:
Joe: Well, this is where you came in, back at that pool again, the one I always wanted. It's dawn now, and they must have photographed me a thousand times. Then they got a couple of pruning hooks from the garden and fished me out . . . ever so gently. Funny, how gentle people get with you once you're dead.

Cine•Star™

#5 THE KILLING (1956)

DIRECTOR:
Stanley Kubrick

SCREENPLAY:
Stanley Kubrick; Jim Thompson (dialogue); adapted from the novel *Clean Break* by Lionel White

NARRATOR:
Narrator (Art Gilmore)

NARRATIVE FUNCTION: Create a sardonic kind of detachment between the thieves planning a racetrack heist, and the cosmos's utter indifference to their passions and plights. Most of it is very dry, and sounds as if it could have been pulled out of a newspaper story or a Hemingway novel.

SAMPLE NARRATION:
Narrator: At exactly 3:45 on that Saturday afternoon in the last week of September, Marvin Unger was, perhaps, the only one among the hundred thousand people at the track who felt no thrill at the running of the fifth race. He was totally disinterested in horse racing and held a lifelong contempt for gambling. Nevertheless, he had a five-dollar win bet on every horse in the fifth race. He knew, of course, that this rather unique system of betting would more than likely result in a loss, but he didn't care. For after all, he thought, what would the loss of twenty or thirty dollars mean in comparison to the vast sum of money ultimately at stake.

Cine·Star™

#6 HIROSHIMA MON AMOUR (1959)

DIRECTOR:
Alain Resnais

SCREENPLAY:
Marguerite Duras

NARRATOR:
Elle (Emmanuelle Riva)

NARRATIVE FUNCTION:
Reflect language's inability to recapture the physical and emotional sensations of powerful events in the past (historical or personal).

SAMPLE NARRATION:
Elle: How could I have known that this city was made to the size of love?
How could I have known that you were made to the size of my body?
You're great. How wonderful. You're great.
How slow all of a sudden.
And how sweet.
More than you can know.
You destroy me.

Cine·Star™

#7 LOLITA (1962)

DIRECTOR:
Stanley Kubrick

SCREENPLAY:
Vladimir Nabokov and Stanley Kubrick (uncredited); adapted from the novel by Vladimir Nabokov

NARRATOR: Professor Humbert Humbert (James Mason)

NARRATIVE FUNCTION:
Help provide a cinematic equivalent of the first-person narration in the novel, which created a tension between the grotesque events described and the narrator's romanticized descriptions of them.

SAMPLE NARRATION:
Humbert: What drives me insane is the twofold nature of this nymphet, a veteran nymphet perhaps, this mixture in my Lolita of tender, dreamy childishness and a kind of eerie vulgarity. I know it is madness to keep this journal, but it gives me a strange thrill to do so. And only a loving wife could decipher my microscopic script.

Cine·Star™

#8 A CLOCKWORK ORANGE (1971)

DIRECTOR:
Stanley Kubrick

SCREENPLAY:
Stanley Kubrick; adapted from the novel by Anthony Burgess

NARRATOR:
Alex (Malcolm McDowell)

NARRATIVE FUNCTION:
Draw the viewer into complicity with the tale's homicidal gangster hero.

SAMPLE NARRATION:
Alex: Suddenly, I viddied what I had to do, and what I had wanted to do, and that was to do myself in; to snuff it, to blast off forever out of this wicked, cruel world. One moment of pain, perhaps, and then sleep, forever and ever and ever.

Cine·Star™

#9   BADLANDS   (1973)

DIRECTOR:
Terrence Malick

SCREENPLAY:
Terrence Malick

NARRATOR:
Holly Sargis (Sissy Spacek)

NARRATIVE FUNCTION:
Add a layer of irony to the story of a bloody rampage by a psychopathic garbageman, Kit Carruthers (Martin Sheen), and his teenage girlfriend. Holly starts out describing the relationship in blinkered romance-novel terms; by the end, she has become more "mature" but never really deals with the horrors she's been party to.

SAMPLE NARRATION:
Holly: We took off at sunset, on a line toward the mountains of Saskatchewan, for Kit a magical land beyond the reach of the law. He needed me now more than ever, but something had come between us. I'd stopped even paying attention to him. Instead, I sat in the car and read a map and spelled out entire sentences with my tongue on the roof of my mouth, where nobody could read them.

Cine-Star™

#10   BARRY LYNDON   (1975)

DIRECTOR:
Stanley Kubrick

SCREENPLAY:
Stanley Kubrick; adapted from the novel by William Makepeace Thackeray

NARRATOR:
Narrator (Michael Hordern)

NARRATIVE FUNCTION: Provide a detached overview of and commentary upon the turmoil and scheming of Thackeray's characters; the narration is third person and drawn directly from the book. The icy detachment of the narration is often slightly at odds with the passion and misery of the characters on-screen.

SAMPLE NARRATION:
Narrator: Gentlemen may talk of the age of chivalry, but remember the ploughmen, poachers, and pickpockets whom they lead. It is with these sad instruments that your great warriors and kings have been doing their murderous work in the world.

Cine-Star™

#11   APOCALYPSE NOW   (1979)

SCREENPLAY:
John Milius and Francis Ford Coppola;* adapted from the novel *Heart of Darkness* by Joseph Conrad

NARRATOR:
Captain Benjamin L. Willard (Martin Sheen)

* Journalist Michael Herr, author of the Vietnam memoir *Dispatches*, wrote Captain Willard's voice-over narration in post-production.

NARRATIVE FUNCTION:
Find a twentieth-century equivalent of Joseph Conrad's *Heart of Darkness*, a story within a story, told to someone else (Willard narrates).

SAMPLE NARRATION:
Willard: They were gonna make me a major for this, and I wasn't even in their fuckin' army anymore. Everybody wanted me to do it, him most of all. I felt like he was up there, waiting for me to take the pain away. He just wanted to go out like a soldier, standing up, not like some poor, wasted, rag-assed renegade. Even the jungle wanted him dead, and that's who he really took his orders from anyway.

Cine-Star™

#12   WINGS OF DESIRE   (1987)

DIRECTOR:
Wim Wenders

SCREENPLAY:
Wim Wenders and Peter Handke, with contributions by Richard Reitinger

NARRATORS:
Too many to count

NARRATIVE FUNCTION: Although there is plenty of straightforward voice-over in this movie, it also contains examples of what could be called "stealth narration": angels eavesdrop and comment on the thoughts of citizens in divided Berlin, their scattered musings and epiphanies creating a poetic tapestry.

SAMPLE NARRATION:
Damiel (Bruno Ganz):
When the child was a child,
it had no opinion about anything,
had no habits,
it often sat cross-legged,
took off running,
had a cowlick in its hair,
and made no faces when photographed.

#13 **GOODFELLAS** (1990)

DIRECTOR:
Martin Scorsese

SCREENPLAY:
Nicholas Pileggi and Martin Scorsese; adapted from the book *Wiseguy* by Nicholas Pileggi

NARRATORS:
Henry Hill (Ray Liotta) and Karen Hill (Lorraine Bracco)

Cine·Star™

NARRATIVE FUNCTION: Mostly an anthropological, nostalgic description of a gangster's life, Hill's narration is eventually revealed to be testimony given to government agents prior to entering witness protection; we find this out when Henry steps out of the witness box during a federal trial and addresses the camera. The jaunty, detached tone of the voice-over is sometimes intriguingly at odds with Henry's shocked on-screen reactions to brutality. *Goodfellas* is mainly narrated by Henry, but his wife, Karen comes in at the halfway mark to give us an alternate perspective. Scorsese's next gangster film, 1995's *Casino*, would feature several narrators.

SAMPLE NARRATION:
Henry: Anything I wanted was a phone call away. Free cars. The keys to a dozen hideout flats all over the city. I bet twenty, thirty grand over a weekend, and then I'd either blow the winnings in a week or go to the sharks to pay back the bookies

---

#14 **THE BIG LEBOWSKI** (1998)

DIRECTOR:
Joel Coen

SCREENPLAY:
Ethan Coen and Joel Coen

NARRATOR:
The Stranger (Sam Elliott)

Cine·Star™

NARRATIVE FUNCTION:
Mythologize the nitwit misadventures of the Dude (Jeff Bridges), on those occasions when the narrator can follow a thought from start to finish. The Stranger is an offscreen voice at the beginning of the film, but materializes on-screen later, without warning, and for no discernible reason, really.

SAMPLE NARRATION:
The Stranger: Sometimes, there's a man, well . . . he's the man for his time and place. He fits right in there. And that's the Dude, in Los Angeles. And even if he's a lazy man—and the Dude was most certainly that. Quite possibly the laziest in Los Angeles County, which would put him in the runnin' for laziest worldwide. But sometimes there's a man . . . sometimes, there's a man. . . . Aw. I lost my train of thought here. But . . . aw hell. I've done introduced him enough.

#15 **ELECTION** (1999)

DIRECTOR:
Alexander Payne

SCREENPLAY:
Alexander Payne and Jim Taylor, adapted from the novel by Tom Perrotta

NARRATORS
Principal Jim McAllister (Matthew Broderick); students Tracy Flick (Reese Witherspoon), Paul Metzler (Chris Klein) and Tammy Metzler (Jessica Campbell)

NARRATIVE FUNCTION:
Convey the conflicting agendas and points-of-view of key players embroiled in a school election scandal. The film's narration appears in discrete snippets within a story full of documentary affectations; the transition from one speaker to another is often heralded by a comically awkward freeze-frame.

SAMPLE NARRATION: Tracy Flick: Dear Lord Jesus: I do not often speak with you and ask for things, but now I really must insist that you help me win the election tomorrow, because I deserve it and Paul Metzler doesn't, as you well know. I realize that it was your divine hand that disqualified Tammy Metzler, and now I'm asking that you go that one last mile and make sure to put me in office where I belong, so that I may carry out your will on earth as it is in heaven. Amen.

#16 **THE NEW WORLD** (2005)

DIRECTOR:
Terrence Malick

SCREENPLAY:
Terrence Malick

NARRATORS:
Pocahontas (Q'orianka Kilcher), Captain Smith (Colin Farrell), John Rolfe (Christian Bale), and others

NARRATIVE FUNCTION: As in *Hiroshima mon amour*, a big influence on Malick, this film's narration captures the surging emotions of characters struggling to make sense of experiences whose complexity is beyond the grasp of language. Malick's style shifted from single to multiple narrators after 1998's *The Thin Red Line*.

SAMPLE NARRATION:
Pocahontas: Mother, where do you live? In the sky? The clouds? The sea? Show me your face. Give me a sign. We rise . . . we rise. Afraid of myself. A god, he seems to me. What else is life but being near you? Do they suspect? Oh, to be given to you. You to me. I will be faithful to you. True. Two no more. One. One. I am . . . I am.

here? It's the key to the movie, I think—the moment that unlocks that Russian-nesting-doll sensation, the story within the story within the story within the story. We're looking at a story that happened to Zero, and that was intensely personal to him—very real, in terms of its facts and its emotions, you know?—but then, it was told and retold, until it eventually became legend. The young woman is holding the book; she's looking up at the statue. I think that, in a strange way, that moment justifies the tone of the film, which is ultimately a couple of inches away from being a fable. You're showing us that process.

But it doesn't feel like a lesson. They're running, they're climbing, they're jumping, they're hiding, they're carrying pastry boxes so that you don't see their faces. It's very madcap, but there's also the constant threat of death hanging over them.

It's a little bit strange, this movie. It's very gently paced, and then, suddenly, it's pretty fast and goes along really, really quickly for the rest of the

movie—but then, just as suddenly, it becomes slow again. Those framing scenes with Murray Abraham and Jude Law are just a whole different movie. I mean, they even have a completely different kind of rhythm.

The movie's also a little bloodier than I expected it to be. I didn't notice during the writing of it how many limbs are getting chopped off, how many knives and guns are being used. But when we actually looked at the whole thing in Paris, we invited a friend who brought his daughter there, and she kept covering her eyes. And we thought, "This is too violent for Lily!" I hadn't really thought of it that way. I thought the bloody stuff was kind of supposed to just be funny. If you've got some screaming woman's head lifted up by the hair, I can see now why that might be disturbing, but I can't say that at the time I expected it to be gravely serious.

It's bloody, but in the way that *Evil Dead II* is bloody. You're not supposed to look at it and go, "Oh, the humanity." It harks back to that sort of Roald Dahl sense of humor that you teased out in *Fantastic Mr. Fox.* You're not supposed to be horrified when you see Mr. Fox's tail being worn as a necktie; it's just a little sick joke.

I like what you said when we talked about that movie in *The Wes Anderson Collection:* that it was Roald Dahl's idea to shoot Fox's tail off, but that your movie added the touch of turning it into a necktie. "That basically defines the collaboration."

Yes.

Which brings us to Stefan Zweig. Let's define that collaboration, such as it is. Do you remember the first time that you read Stefan Zweig's work?

ABOVE: The statue of the Author in Old Lutz Cemetery in the film's prologue.

BELOW LEFT: A caricature of Stefan Zweig by Hugo Guinness, the co-author of the screen story for *The Grand Budapest Hotel.*

BELOW RIGHT: A bust of Stefan Zweig, located in the Jardin du Luxembourg, Paris, France.

OPPOSITE: Three still-frames from *The Grand Budapest Hotel.* (TOP) The catalog page that Dmitri is looking at when he realizes that *Boy with Apple* has been stolen from its usual spot above the fireplace in the study at Schloss Lutz. (MIDDLE) *Two Lesbians Masturbating,* the painting's replacement, was commissioned for the film from Rich Pellegrino, who had previously produced Wes Anderson–themed fan art. (BOTTOM) M. Gustave (Ray Fiennes) models himself on *Boy with Apple* ("See the resemblance?").

Lot 117

"Boy With Apple"

JOHANNES VAN HOYTL THE YOUNGER
(1613-December 1669)

Van Hoytl, native son of the Murkish Low-lands, worked his bright pigments in slowest solitude. Remarked especially for his light and shade; and his attraction to the lustrous and the velvety. Extremely unprolific and therefore a financial failure, he nevertheless produced perhaps a dozen of the finest portraits of the period.

A RARE AND IMPORTANT VAN HOYTL

I think I must have read something about him somewhere, but I don't remember exactly what. Then, years ago, I stumbled across one of his books in a bookstore in Paris, and I read some pages. I loved his writing, right off the bat.

    Beware of Pity was the first one I read. At first I sort of thought maybe I might just adapt that book—just do a movie of it. But then I read more Zweig, and I started thinking, "I'm getting a sense of his whole body of work."

What impressions did you have of the quality of his prose, and the types of stories that he told?

My first reaction was that I liked the way you enter that book, *Beware of Pity*, because he does that thing: Somebody meets a mysterious stranger, who tells them their story. He does that in so many of the short stories. It's almost his default method.

I've been keeping a running list of Zweig stories that are told that way, where somebody is telling someone else's story verbally, or in the case of *Letter from an Unknown Woman*, via a mysterious letter that arrives at someone's home unsigned, with no return address. There are almost too many to count.
    This storytelling approach returns us to a subject we discussed in *The Wes Anderson Collection*, the idea of putting a frame around a story. You literally do this in *The Grand Budapest Hotel*, through the literary framing devices of having characters tell us stories, but also visually, by changing the shape of the frame.

That's something I think we should talk about: the aspect ratios. You've already got dates on-screen, and there's also visual production-design differentiations between periods, so, in theory, you didn't need to do that.

That's true. The characters tell you where you are in relation to the story, and when you change periods, there are different kinds of visual cues, and hopefully they're subtler: the colors and the treatment of it—not just the decay, but also the effects, and everything else. The change of aspect ratios, really, I just did it for fun. I did it because I thought it would be interesting. Also, I've always wanted to do a movie in 1.33, the Academy ratio, so here was the chance.

Why is the run-up to Gustave's death in black and white? I don't know if there are any other black-and-white scenes in the movie, are there?

I don't think so, apart from black-and-white photographs. That's the only scene. I don't know if I want to analyze that choice. I'd better just let it be.
    Have you ever read Roald Dahl's book *Henry Sugar*?

Absolutely! *The Wonderful Story of Henry Sugar and Six More.* That book haunted me as a child.

It's a strange book for children. I mention it because, like Zweig, it's a layered thing, where you've basically got a book within a book. It's one within another within another within another. It's got many layers of storytellers, that long short story.

That's the thing that immediately grabbed me with *Beware of Pity*. It's just a very strange, powerful story, *Beware of Pity*. And it's also a beautiful description not just of being in a cavalry regiment, but also of the whole Austro-Hungarian Empire experience. He's writing about a time and a place I don't think I'd read much about, and he puts you right there.

And he does a very concise, lyrical job of explaining that time and place.

Beware of Pity even begins with a note saying something like, "It's important to know the rules of a military officer, the rules of military life during that time."*** It actually has an introductory note that says something like that.

And then Zweig proceeds to unfurl an elaborate list on the reader, almost like an annotated narrative.

In his introduction?

No, just generally, as the whole story goes along.
    That's something that I've noticed, a characteristic of Zweig that stands out in pretty much everything he writes. He is an absolute master of the list.

Interesting. Give me an example.

Well, here's one from his memoir, *The World of Yesterday*. I marked this passage, where he's giving you sort of an anthropological tour of Vienna. He has this whole section about coffeehouses, and he talks about it being "an institution of a peculiar kind" and a "democratic club" where the price of admission is a cup of coffee. Then he goes on to list all the things you can do there: talking, writing, playing cards, getting mail, reading all the newspapers and other periodicals they have there. He says, "A Viennese coffeehouse of the better sort took all the Viennese newspapers available, and not only those, but the newspapers of the entire German Reich, as well as the French, British, Italian and American newspapers, and the literary and artistic magazines."
    And then, in the next section, he's cataloging the different kinds of intellectual competitions that go on in these Viennese coffeehouses, and describes how they're competing to see who can cite passages from the most underappreciated or obscure philosopher.

Right.

He seems very much a taxonomist, Zweig.

He's talking about a world that is so different from the one that he's writing from, in his present. He describes what these journals were like, the ones in Vienna, in particular. They're not like newspapers. They're more like daily literary magazines. These are publications that include philosophical texts, and they have stories and poems. That's what comes in the morning to your door. But the obsession isn't with something new. It's something in the past.

I love how he describes students in *The World of Yesterday*: the coffeehouse kids, all kind of one-upping each other. One of them talks about Nietzsche, and the other one all but declares Nietzsche to be yesterday's news and agitates for Kierkegaard. There are notes of triumph at having been able to read something that everyone else figured was unavailable. It's like those preening record store geeks in *High Fidelity*, but with philosophy.

That's right. And he says in the book at one point that very suddenly, the thing to do became sport.**** He feels like this thing he's describing, a sudden interest in physical culture, went hand-in-hand with nationalism—with this *rise* in nationalism. He says that at that point, the world split into teams, and that wasn't the way among artists—that even though there's *competition* among artists, he considers it completely alien to art for people to divide up that way, in teams, and what they'd originally wanted to be was international, cosmopolitan. For Zweig, that sudden interest in sports and nationalism was the beginning of what would become the end.

***The World of Yesterday* could be an alternate title for *The Grand Budapest Hotel*, it seems to me. It's so much concerned with looking backward, and explaining—well, not the world as it objectively *was*, but one person's selective impression of that world, and all the memories and sensations he carried with him from the past into the present, which are only a bunch of fragments, ultimately.**

Have you read Zweig's writing about his collecting? Have you come across that? I think he does get around to talking about it in *The World of Yesterday*, eventually, but you know, he collected manuscripts and musical scores. He was a big collector.

Yes—and in fact, you see Zweig throughout his various fictions projecting that part of himself onto his characters: the collector mentality. You sense that mentality in the way Zweig obsessively catalogs the belongings in someone's apartment, or the accoutrements in their wardrobe.

He felt a great sense of loss about having to abandon all his stuff when he fled, when he left Austria.

And it seems like his characters are always doing a lot of fleeing. They're fleeing history, war, and in a lot of cases, just personal disasters. They often have to leave under cover of darkness, with very little notice.

The Post-Office Girl has a very similar thing. The last section of that book takes that sort of form. *The Post-Office Girl* was a very late one.

Have you read *Confusion*?

That's the one with the student and the older professor and the professor's young wife.

Yeah, and the wife falls in love with the student, our narrator.

Confusion's a good one. The main character has gone to school in Berlin, which has turned into just debauchery, and his father comes to see him and kind of witnesses this, and so he decides to buckle down and pull himself together and heads for Heidelberg, which has a purity to it. A place to really study.

Yeah. I was really struck by how, in *Confusion*, Zweig's narrator describes being told a story by a learned, magnetic older man. I think this might have jumped out at me even if I hadn't seen *The Grand Budapest Hotel*, which of course is built around exactly those sorts of exchanges.

The older guy telling the younger guy stories.

OPPOSITE: **Still-frames from moments in the film in which newspaper headlines both convey important plot information and establish the film's fictional European world.**

OVERLEAF: **A gallery of covers from books published in English, French, and German—the novels, short stories, and essays of Stefan Zweig.**

***   "A large part of the mind automatically accepts impressions and influences made on us long before, and if a man has been brought up from childhood in the drill of military discipline, the psychological effect of an order from a superior officer is compelling and cannot be ignored. Every military command has a power over him that is logically inexplicable, but cancels out his own will. Even if he is well aware of the pointlessness of what he is told to do, in the straitjacket of his uniform he does what he is told to do like a sleepwalker, without resisting and almost unconsciously."

****   "People had discovered that up in the mountains winter, once a dismal season to be spent gloomily playing cards in taverns or feeling bored as you sat around in overheated rooms, was a source of filtered sunlight, nectar for the lungs that sent blood coursing deliciously just beneath the skin. . . . On Sundays thousands and tens of thousands, clad in brightly coloured sportswear, raced down the snowy slopes on skis and toboggans; sports centres and swimming baths were built everywhere. You could see the change clearly in those swimming baths—while in my own youth a really fine figure of a man stood out among all the bull-necked, paunchy or pigeon-chested specimens, nowadays athletically agile young men, tanned by the sun and fit from all their sporting activities, competed cheerfully with each other as they did in classical antiquity." Stefan Zweig, *The World of Yesterday* (Pushkin Press), 216–17.

Trans-Alpine Yodel

Monday, February 17th, 1936 — ALL THE NEWS FROM ACROSS THE NATION IN TWO DAILY EDITIONS — ½ kl-. Zubrowka nr. 546

IMMIGRANT CLAIMS FORTUNE

ZERO MOUSTAFA OF THE

FREE LUTZ UNDERGROUND

The war is over. Not merely on the battlefields from Lutz to Pfeiffelstaad, but also in the chambers of the high financial court where Mr. Zero Moustafa, hero of the Lutz Underground, won the decisive settlement that will now unquestionably lead to the transfer of the vast

into his two small hands. It was a fight from which he was absolutely determined and perhaps pre-destined to emerge victorious. "No, I can't say I deserve a penny or a square foot of any of it -- but it's mine, just the same." His comments, as always, were succinct. "My plans, at the moment,

Thank you for your time, gentlemen." When offered condolences for the recent deaths of his wife and child, his response was merely a sad smile, a nod, and a hasty exit out the back doors of the House of Justice. He sped away on a loud, black motorcycle. Sources within the in-

council revealed his intention to travel immediately to the Maltese Riviera where the most remote of his properties sits, mothballed, on a low peak at the end of the ancient promontory made familiar to all Zubrow-kans in the great poem of Mr. Darrellman: "Under

---

THE WEATHER—CLOUDY
unsettled, cooler tonight and
Thursday

THE CONTINENTAL DRIFT

PUBLICATION OFFICE
Lutz, Zubrowka
Telephone LZ 1234

VOICE OF FREE EUROPA

VOL 64. Nº 333 — COMPLETE EDITION — MONDAY 24TH MARCH 1940 — EIGHTEEN PAGES — PRICE In Alpine Sudetenwaltz ½ Kl. Elsewhere 1 Kl-

ZERO CORNERS MARKET

LUTZ — The acts and actions of Mr. Zero Moustafa are now known far and wide. Ten years ago, he was a mere page working on the fringes of the lobby of the Grand Budapest Hotel. Nine years ago, he inherited the entirety of the Desgoffe und Taxis fortune and became a millionaire in an afternoon. Eight years ago, he led a fringe division of the Lutz Underground to an historic victory

the Occupation. Last week, he cemented his monopoly in Eastern European Coal. Yesterday afternoon, during a quiet ceremony at an unknown and undisclosed location in the Zubrowkan-Alpine extremities, he politely accepted the current administration's highest honor: Medal of Valor, Republic of Zubrowka. Inspector A.J. Henckels, once of the Lutz Police Militia

of the Government-in-Exile, read a few brief words to the assembly. We reproduce them verbatim in his own words: "We were introduced on a train, a decade and a lifetime ago. In the interim we have all suffered losses which can never be regained -- but our dignity and our future will not be among them. I share the viewpoint of our friend the late Gustave H. in esteeming

of this singular young man. With respect: please, accept this symbol of our crippled nation's gratitude and respect. It is a mere trifle."

Moustafa's has been a discreet but resounding advance through the corridors of industry and commerce. Reared on the mean streets of Aq-Salim-al-Jabat, he survived the genocide of his people and the devastation of his country. He

his own two, shoeless feet. The story of his apprenticeship with the late Gustave H. has been described in these pages previously. M. H's death was a great blow to the young Lobby Boy, but it was the loss of his wife and infant child fourteen months later that, some say, permanently and irrevocably crushed his spirit. Perhaps this was, in its infinite sadness and mystery, to the benefit and

browka. He emerged from this tragedy fearless and bent on self-sacrifice, gave his life to the liberation of his adopted nation -- and lived.

On Tuesday morning Moustafa's chess game with Eastern European Coal came to a decisive conclusion. It is estimated that his personal wealth will increase by a quarter over the next fiscal term due to the radically favorable

---

TRUTH AND WISDOM ★ For the Workers of the World

DAILY ★LUTZ★ FACT

TRUTH AND WISDOM ★ For the Workers of the World

WEDNESDAY (SREDA), NOVEMBER 28, 1950 — ZUBROWKA — (NUMBER) 232

PACT WITH COMMISSAR

COMRADE ZERO M.

LUTZGRAD — In acknowledgement of his acts of bravery during the occupation and his eagerness to share his international assets and properties with his comrades in our new and ancient homeland, the Secretariat of Lands and Treasures has formally granted Mr. Zero

propriety and ownership to the Grand Budapest Hotel. It will be a place of refuge to all the People of Zubrowka.

Due to the abolition of private property within our commonwealth,

the administration and Moustafa's legal team have been exceedingly complex and peculiar. Records of the discussions between the parties are said to run to over eleven hundred

censored and sealed in the state vaults where they are expected to remain in deep storage indefinitely.

The Grand Budapest Hotel contains 228 rooms. Mr. Moustafa has agreed that the grand suites of the lower floors will be divided and partitioned in

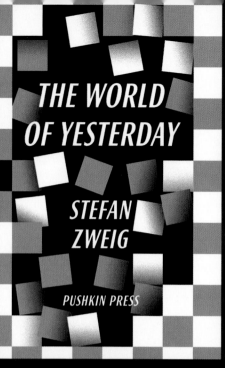

THE WORLD OF YESTERDAY

STEFAN ZWEIG

PUSHKIN PRESS

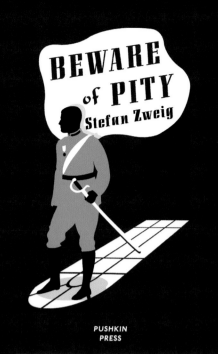

BEWARE of PITY
Stefan Zweig

PUSHKIN PRESS

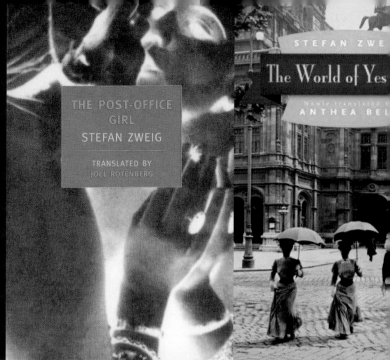

THE POST-OFFICE GIRL
STEFAN ZWEIG

TRANSLATED BY
JOEL ROTENBERG

STEFAN ZWEIG
The World of Yes
ANTHEA BELL

PUSHKIN PRESS

FEAR

STEFAN ZWEIG

STEFAN ZWEIG

DIE WELT VON GESTERN

ERINNERUNGEN
EINES EUROPÄERS

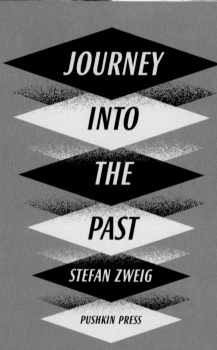

JOURNEY INTO THE PAST

STEFAN ZWEIG

PUSHKIN PRESS

Stefa
Zwei
Die V
von
Gest

G B. Fischer

LE JOUEUR D'ÉCHECS

NOUVELLE
DE
STEFAN ZWEIG

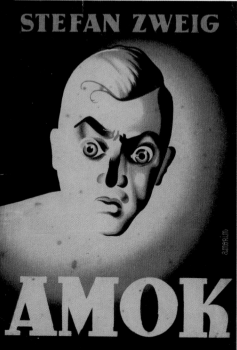

STEFAN ZWEIG

AMOK

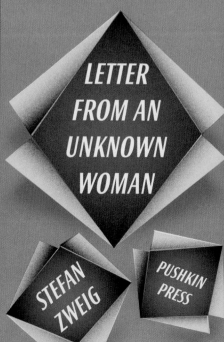

LETTER FROM AN UNKNOWN WOMAN

STEFAN ZWEIG

PUSHKIN PRESS

PUSHKIN

CONFU

STEFAN

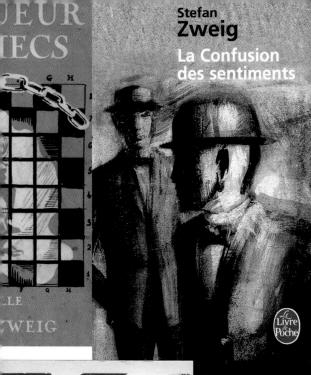

EUR
IECS

ZWEIG

Stefan
Zweig
La Confusion
des sentiments

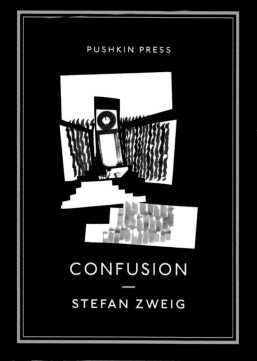

PUSHKIN PRESS

CONFUSION
—
STEFAN ZWEIG

STEFAN ZWEIG
SCHACHNOVELLE

STEFAN ZWEIG
UNGEDULD
DES HERZENS
ROMAN
FISCHER

Stefan
Zweig
Vingt-quatre
heures
de la vie
d'une femme

Le Livre de Poche

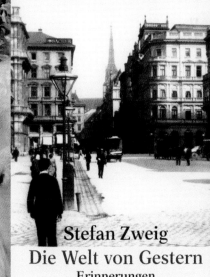

Stefan Zweig
Die Welt von Gestern
Erinnerungen
eines Europäers

Stefan
Zweig
Die Welt
von
Gestern

G B. Fischer

Stefan Zweig
Brennendes Geheimnis
Insel-Bücherei Nr. 122

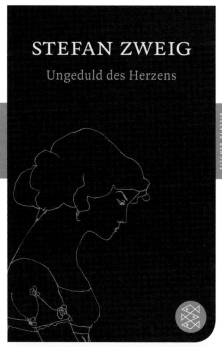

STEFAN ZWEIG
Ungeduld des Herzens

STEFAN ZWEIG
Angst
Novelle

RECLAM

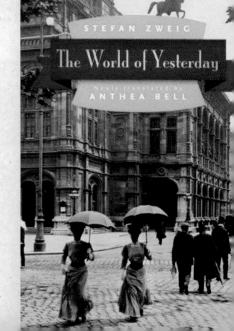

STEFAN ZWEIG
The World of Yesterday
Newly translated by
ANTHEA BELL

He writes, "How can I describe those hours? I waited for them all day long. By afternoon a heavy, unnerving restlessness was weighing electrically on my impatient mind; I could scarcely endure the hours until evening at last came. Once supper was over we would go straight to his study, I sat at the desk with my back turned to him while he paced restlessly up and down the room until he had got into his rhythm, so to speak, until he raised his voice and launched into the prelude. For this remarkable man constructed it all out of his musicality of feeling: he always needed some vibrant note to set his ideas flowing."

Zweig goes on: "He always needed some vibrant note to set his ideas flowing. Usually it was an image, a bold metaphor, a situation visualized in three dimensions which he extended into a dramatic scene, involuntarily working himself up as he went rapidly along. Something of all that is grandly natural in creativity would often flash from the swift radiance of these improvisations."

And in those scenes, what he's describing is the professor lecturing him. But what the professor is really doing is riffing on all his studies, and sort of just sharing his thoughts and ideas with our narrator, right?

Yes. Riffing. Privately—but in the classroom as well. If *Confusion* were a traditional love story, the story's "Eureka!" moment would be the moment where the guy realizes he's in love with the girl. Instead, the "Eureka!" moment—the moment that really draws the hero deeply into the story, and the reader as well—occurs in the classroom. Our hero is listening to the professor put Shakespeare within the context of Western literature.

Yes, that's right.

And he's treating that as the nexus point that everything else in the story flows in and out of.

I got on board the Stefan Zweig train during that passage. It captured what it feels like to become infatuated by somebody else's intellect. That's also what happens to the young Author in the 1968 sequences of *The Grand Budapest Hotel*. He falls in love with another person's intellect, with his power as a storyteller. And it moves him to the point where he feels he has to tell this man's story to the world.

At a certain point, the hero in *Confusion* starts helping the professor with his book, right? That's the scene you're talking about, right?

Yes.

That's when the two characters start to struggle a little more, because the professor has lost his confidence, and he hasn't been able to write for a long time. And then he gets it back, with the help of his protégé. But then the whole thing becomes a mess. *Confusion* is an interesting one, a strange one.

Related to what we've been talking about here is the idealization of youth, which is a factor in almost every piece of fiction I've read by Zweig. It's not an unreasonable idealization that he gives us, but it's very, very passionate.

There's a point in his short story "Forgotten Dreams" where he's describing this woman going into a reverie about her past, and he writes of how "a happy light plays over her whole face all of a sudden, her eyes sparkle with high spirits as she thinks of the long-ago days of her youth, almost forgotten now." Something like that happens when old Zero starts telling the Author his story. The light even changes on his face, the way it'd change on the face of an actor in a play. There are touches of that all through Zweig's writing, this romanticizing of youth. He's not just idealizing physical youth, as

in superficial beauty. He's idealizing the notion of a young society, too—a society that's just starting out, or maybe a society that's able to start over, in some way. Starting over and reinventing oneself—that's important to his writing, and it was important to Zweig.

Zweig wrote a book about Brazil that might have those kinds of ideas in it. I haven't read it. It's called *Country of the Future*. And I think that's sort of what it's about, a young society with enthusiasm and potential, and some purity.

The detail from Zweig that I always think of as one of the most telling ones is that, back then, in the 1920s, in Europe, they didn't have passports. They weren't issued. You didn't need them.

To Zweig, the passport represents the worst of everything. Suddenly, you're asked to prove your identity, justify your existence. Somebody has the power to say, "You can't cross that line; we control this." It just wasn't done.

I read an interview with you once where you were talking about traveling in Europe and how World War II is still very much a presence there. You said, "It's still right in the middle of our lives." What did you mean by that?

I wouldn't say it's just in Europe. I feel like it's that way in the United States, too. To me it is, anyway. I feel like some reference to the war and the Holocaust comes up most days, at some point during a day. I don't think the same can be said of Napoleon or George Washington. World War II is such a gigantic, horrific, insane episode that it's still kind of right there—or right *here*. It's an incalculably gigantic event.

It's certainly a presence when you travel in Europe. But in the states? Not so much. Except for Pearl Harbor in Hawaii, the United States was spared any direct physical impact by World War II. But there are still preserved ruins from that period in Europe. And people still stumble across bombs and mines.

That's true. In fact, in *Mr. Fox*, they blew one up in the canal next to the studio where we were. They found a doodlebug,***** I think it's called—that's the kind of bomb—that had not exploded, and they had to detonate it. And they had a humongous explosion. I mean, when they found it—I don't remember how it was discovered; I think it was because they were going to do some construction, and they drained a part of the canal, and it revealed this bomb.

We had to shut down the movie for X number of days, and it was a big thing. And then we recorded the explosion, and we used it in the movie twice. We have two bombs going off in the movie, and we used the doodlebug explosion both times.

I didn't know that.

They blow up the Fox family's tree; and then, later, Mrs. Fox does some detonating of her own. So we used the same bomb again. It was a local bomb.

But, you know, the war also lives on in another way, which is, the postwar borders. The First World War is when a lot of these countries were divided up.

And a lot of them were divided up again after World War II.

OPPOSITE: One of the most widely circulated portraits of Stefan Zweig.

***** The Vergeltungswaffe 1, or V-1 bomb, was a ballistics missile created by the Germans and lobbed across the English Channel; it was known colloquially as a "doodlebug" or "buzz bomb."

And now, they've split some of them back up to the borders before either one.

What happened in Germany was really amazing, the idea of a country that was, at the time, the most feared country on earth, defeated in the biggest war in human history, then divvied up, like a pie, and its most important city cut into quadrants.

This had a tremendous impact on the people of Germany. And it's hugely important for cinema. There's this entire tradition of East German art and West German art cinema that comes out of that period. Rainer Werner Fassbinder, Lina Wertmüller, Werner Herzog, Volker Schlöndorff, Margarethe von Trotta, Wim Wenders—it's just an incredible list of filmmakers. There is a substantial body of work dealing with the psychic impact of all that experience, the experience that shaped them all.

One of the most important European art films ever made is *Wings of Desire*, and it's all about that historical and personal experience. It's like a political poem. It's very much about that divided consciousness. And now the movie is nostalgia! When people look at it today, they're seeing a world that no longer exists. But at the time it came out, it was practically journalism. It was so raw. I saw it in high school. I was astounded that something so immediate could be up there on a movie screen.

And just five years after it came out . . .

. . . it was about something that was gone. A vanished way of life.

I'm trying to think of what the area is, I think it's Potsdamer Platz, that's just like a big empty ruin in the movie? And it's now the Sony Center—and that's where the Berlin film festival is currently held. That whole area is filled with new architecture. It's all right in the area where Peter Falk walked with Bruno Ganz in *Wings of Desire*, through the middle of nowhere.

"To smoke, and have coffee—and if you do it together, it's fantastic."

Is that what Peter Falk says in that scene?

Yes.
Here's another one of the ways in which your film demonstrates an allegiance to Zweig: It presents history as this enormous, very rude disruption in the private lives of your characters.

In our case, you could even say that the big movements of history are interfering with our little plot. I mean, even if it's just the littlest things of everyday life, even if it is about the time when this painting was stolen and an old woman died, what would be a big story in a person's life is, in the context of a war, just a tiny episode. It's of no significance compared to the big thing that's happening.

I'm reminded of my favorite moment in Terrence Malick's *Days of Heaven*: At the end, when Richard Gere gets shot, the film cuts to a wide shot of Gere's dead body floating downstream, and you see a bunch of people on a riverbank, watching the corpse float by.

That's a good bit.

You suddenly realize that, to the people on the riverbank, a character you've been invested in for ninety minutes is just a body. He means nothing to them. And the whole moment is infinitesimal in the context of World War I, which the United States is about to get into.

You've got two instances of that sort of thing in *The Grand Budapest Hotel*: the fate of both Gustave and Agatha. We care about

them very much. But they're just sort of cut down by the cosmos. Nobody has control over any of it. Their deaths happen offscreen.

The Life and Death of Colonel Blimp might be the movie that does the best job of conveying, in the context of this one person's story, these big historical forces that we're talking about here—just sort of taking us from war to war.

I feel like I might've stolen a whole bunch of stuff from that movie without quite meaning to, or without being very conscious of it.

On second viewing, I started to feel the loss of Gustave and Agatha *before* you'd killed them off. Along those lines, you do something with the narration that's interesting: That whole 1932 story is being told to us, by way of our surrogate, the young Author, and old Zero is very generous with the details of all that, but he doesn't tell us a lot about Agatha, or about the particulars of their relationship. He'll start to get into it, but then he'll say something like, "I never speak of Agatha." He talks *around* Agatha.

I guess the idea is that it's too painful for him to go into, but then finally he has no choice.

Would you say Zero is still nursing a broken heart at the end of the story he tells the young Author in the 1968 sequence?

I think so. I don't think he's really ever quite gotten over what happened to him, or the experience of losing all those people.

I wonder if that's why you put the run-up to Gustave's death in black-and-white? It seems like it's of a piece with old Zero talking his way around things that are too painful to dwell on at length.

I like that as an angle for it: That it's a little more austere.

[WES INSPECTS THE AUTHOR'S DRINK.]

What is that? Is that like a grappa or something?

It's sambuca.

That's a coffee bean floating in it, right?

Yeah. I'm into sambuca at the moment. I'm not sure why.

Do you know Dipak?

Dipak Pallana, Kumar's son? Of course.

Dipak used to drink sambuca. Or, actually, maybe that was the name of a nightclub where he used to go.******

Dipak and I hung out during the memorial service for his dad in Dallas last fall.

Was he overwhelmed, or was he kind of all right?

He seemed all right. I saw him on a book tour, when we went through Dallas. They showed *Bottle Rocket* on 35mm at the Texas Theatre that November. I went there, and afterward, I sat in on a panel. Kumar was going to be the guest of honor. But he died not too long before the event.
The panel turned into a tribute to Kumar. I was sitting there onstage with Dipak, and it became like *Dave Allen at Large* or

OPPOSITE: Three still-frames from the climax of Terrence Malick's second feature, 1978's *Days of Heaven*, in which Richard Gere's character is shot dead by police while indifferent citizens look on.

OVERLEAF: Still-frames: (TOP LEFT) M. Gustave, stopped by the police, seems to realize that this may be the moment of his death; (BOTTOM LEFT) M. Gustave posing for a group photo with his staff. Zero says, "He did not succeed, however, in growing old—nor did my darling Agatha. She and our infant son would be killed two years later by the Prussian *grippe*. (An absurd little disease. Today, we treat it in a single week; but, in those days, many millions died.)"; (TOP RIGHT) close-up of the Society of the Crossed Keys pendant given to Agatha by M. Gustave; (BOTTOM RIGHT) the marriage of Agatha and Zero, with M. Gustave officiating.

****** Sambuca is a jazz club on McKinney Avenue in Dallas, Texas, the city where Wes Anderson shot *Bottle Rocket*. Its regular acts include David Zoller, father of the author of this book.

something, a panel with me and Dipak and Robert Wilonsky, a guy who used to sit next to me at the *Dallas Observer* when you and I were coming up, and now he's an editor at the *Dallas Morning News*. So Robert and I were interviewing Dipak about his dad. And at one point I asked Dipak, "You know, your father was considerably older than I thought he was. I had no idea he was in his early nineties when he died, he seemed to be in such great shape, and when he appeared in his first film with Wes . . ."

When Kumar was in *Bottle Rocket* he was like, what, eighty?

Seventy-eight, actually. So I asked Dipak, "What was your father's secret? Is there anything you can share with us about Kumar Pallana's secret to his long and healthy life?" And he said something along the lines of, "To be honest with you, Matt, my father was a terrible yogi. He ate whatever he wanted. I don't even remember him really exercising all that much. I have no idea why he lived as long as he did! I wish I had a better answer for you, but I don't!"

I can see that. The yoga that you would do with Kumar was very gentle. It wasn't like a "jump to downward dog." It was not an athletic kind of experience. It was very gentle, reserved, and he used to make up different kinds of poses. It was really about meditation, breathing, and focusing.

And I don't know how focused Kumar was, but with him, it was all about being calm, And he was always upbeat, you know?*******

I mean, it wasn't like everything was easy for him. He had a divorce. He'd lived in this place and that place.

After his death, I learned that he'd fled from civil war in India as a young man, and that members of his family had been assassinated.

He wandered around India before he left. He set off on foot. He didn't used to talk—not about that part of his experience, anyway. Kumar used to talk about how he'd worked in Beirut and Las Vegas, and on *Ed Sullivan*, but I didn't often hear from him: "Here is my journey."

But then, over time, very slowly, you'd get the sense that there was this giant voyage he'd taken. An epic. You'd realize that when Kumar is sitting in a coffeeshop in Oak Lawn, here was a guy whose perspective was very different from all the other people sitting in that coffeeshop in Oak Lawn—

people who maybe had grown up in Oklahoma City and then made their way to Dallas, or something like that. Kumar had had a completely different experience.

Do you remember the first time that you met Kumar, or spoke to him?

I think it was the day after I had met Dipak. Owen brought Dipak into the mix. Dipak was friends with a guy who lived in the apartment above or across from us, back when we lived in that apartment on Throckmorton. I think his name is Darren? Owen played chess one afternoon with Darren, and then Darren introduced Owen to Dipak. Something like that. The next day, we went over to Cosmic Cup, and there was Kumar. Upstairs was yoga. The place was their house, *and* it was a yoga studio. Then, at some point, Dipak decided to open a coffeeshop inside it. But it wasn't *just* a coffeeshop. There were smoothies and samosas.

What was it about Kumar that made you think, "I've got to put this guy in a movie?" Did you already know he'd been an actor when he was younger, or did you discover that later?

I can't say I really remember when I learned he could act. I just remember that Owen and I had this conversation where we agreed that maybe Kumar could be a safecracker in *Bottle Rocket*. We thought it was funny, and suddenly we had a sense of the sort of movie we were going to try to do. It changed what we had in mind. That moment sort of located the tone of the movie.

What was Kumar's demeanor like when he was on a movie set?

Kumar was friends with everybody. By the time we were doing *Rushmore*, we were old friends. We'd known each other for some years by then, so Kumar was sort of like an insider on the set. But he still became friends, during *The Royal Tenenbaums*, with everybody. Gene Hackman liked him, and they had a nice rapport, even though it was definitely not that way from the start.

How so?

BELOW LEFT: Gene Hackman and Kumar Pallana shooting the prologue to *The Royal Tenenbaums*.

BELOW RIGHT: Still-frame from *Rushmore* of Kumar Pallana's son, Dipak, who, like his father, acts in the films of Wes Anderson.

OPPOSITE: Kumar Pallana's son, Dipak, provided these photos of his father and offered the following captions, which owing to the chaos of history, are somewhat incomplete.

(LEFT) "This was before he came to the United States, so this would have been in Puerto Rico, before 1947, when he was in his thirties."

(MIDDLE, TOP) "That was taken in Durbin, South Africa, just before he left for America. He took a German cargo ship from South Africa to Argentina."

(MIDDLE, CENTER) "I don't know where this was taken, but that's the one he used as his promotional shot. It could be in Vegas somewhere."

(MIDDLE, BOTTOM) "I'm pretty sure that one was in the US somewhere."

(RIGHT, TOP) "That was New York City in the late 1940s."

(RIGHT, BOTTOM) "That is where he was performing on *The Mickey Mouse Show*. He was on *The Mickey Mouse Show* twice. He also did an appearance in 1959 on *Captain Kangaroo*."

******* "My soul is my guru. My experience is my guru," says Kumar Pallana in the short film *The Rituals of Kumar Pallana*, which was produced by *Dark Rye* magazine, the online publication of Whole Foods Market. "Meditation is very important because without your concentration . . . you could not do nothing."

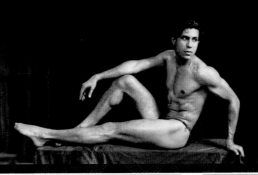

KUMAR

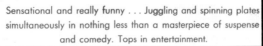

Sensational and really funny . . . Juggling and spinning plates simultaneously in nothing less than a masterpiece of suspense and comedy. Tops in entertainment.

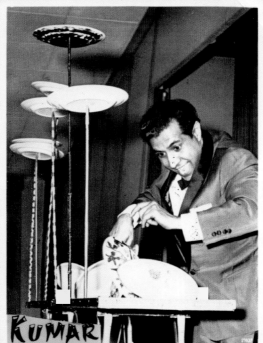

KUMAR

Gene and Kumar had this wonderful chemistry, and Gene was great with him on some level. But Gene also wanted to do his work and go home. He wanted to nail his stuff and be done. That's what made him feel good, I think. And working with somebody less experienced means we might have to do the scene a few more times, because we have to figure out how this other guy can do it. We have to figure out what *his* way is.

I would imagine that, given those proclivities, the scene where Gene Hackman has got to work with Kumar, and you're positioning Kumar so that he blocks the Statue of Liberty on purpose, must've been a strange day for Gene.

Well, it was the first day. I didn't direct Gene very well. I didn't present my thoughts well. But that scene was actually fine, because Kumar was in his own separate shot, which meant Gene didn't have to rely on him. I guess he was probably thinking, "This guy can't act!" or something like that. But I think Gene had a lot of personal affection for Kumar, and I think he even liked his performance when he finally saw the actual movie.

Did Kumar ever tell you any stories about his previous lives?

He talked about how he used to be on a full-fledged vaudeville-type circuit, doing the plate spinning and magic. He sort of went everywhere doing that stuff. I know he went all over Europe and the Middle East.

There was a clip reel that was shown right after they played your videotaped statement at the memorial, titled *The Rituals of Kumar Pallana*, narrated by Dipak, a thing that was actually produced by Whole Foods. It's on Vimeo, along with another nice short film called *The Secret of Life with Kumar Pallana*.

I did a little documentary thing about Kumar once, but it was not Kumar telling his life story. He just performed different things for me. I would be interested to see those other ones. I'm sure there's a lot about Kumar that I've never heard.

I want to try something different here. Over the past six months, readers have been sending me questions that they would like me to ask you, and I have a few of them here. Maybe I can just ask them, and you can answer them?

Sure.

Here's the first one: "Do you have particular writing rituals?"

I use little spiral notebooks of a particular kind. I have an odd sort of format. But I don't write out the entire script in a notebook and finish it that way and then start typing it. I write in the notebook, then I type some of it, then I go back to the notebook, and so on.

Although, on *Moonrise Kingdom*, I remember I had twelve or thirteen pages or something, the beginning of it, and I thought, "Now I should type this," but then I kept going, and I did it all in the notebook. And then suddenly I was faced with, "Now I have to type this whole movie."

THE MIDNIGHT COTERIE
OF
SINISTER INTRUDERS

IN THE FACE OF
UNSPEAKABLE EVIL

LITTLE FLAG

THE NEW YORK TIMES
"YOU HAD ME AT 'WES ANDERSON.'"

FANGORIA
"DA FUH?"

I'm fascinated by other writers' rituals. Writers all have their own rituals, and they're as charged with meaning as the rituals of an actor.

Another question: "This is the first script where you have a solo credit for the screenplay. Your others were collaborations. What is it like working with different writers versus writing by yourself?"

Well, you know, this movie wasn't actually that different of a process from other ones—different parts of different ones. Noah Baumbach and I, for *Life Aquatic*, really did sort of sit there together, all the way through the process. *Bottle Rocket*, certainly, and *Rushmore*: Owen and I were together while we were writing those.

But, on the other hand, at different phases of all of those scripts, there were times when I was working on my own a bit. So it's not like I felt, on this movie, "I'm on my own here." In fact, I had Hugo Guinness, who is a very old friend, hysterically funny and tremendously intelligent, working with me on the story from the very beginning.

"Will you ever write and direct a horror film?" And a related question: "Did you see *The Midnight Coterie of Sinister Intruders*, and, if so, what did you think of it?" Referring to the parody that *Saturday Night Live* did of your movies in fall 2013, starring Edward Norton as Owen Wilson.

Well, to answer that first question first, I would like to do a horror movie. And it would obviously not relate in any way whatsoever to what *Saturday Night Live* did.

Edward did ask me what title I might use for a horror movie, though.

Was he trying to get ideas for the *SNL* spoof?

Right. He didn't explain the context. I thought we were brainstorming together for a future project. But I was very happy to see the result. It looked like they spent some money on it.

Did they use the title that you suggested to Edward Norton?

No.

Do you remember what title you suggested?

Something like *The Whispen in the Stalking*. I think we sort of made up some words.

Have you given any thought to what a Wes Anderson horror film might look like, or what sort of general mood you'd go for?

I don't know. Maybe I might go for *Alien* or something.

OK, here's another one. "Why have you never made a musical?"

Because I never really loved musicals. I think I like them more now than I used to, but it was definitely not a genre that I was studying. I wouldn't mind doing a musical now, though, or, at least, throwing in a singing/dancing number here or there.

You could see there being musical interludes in your films, then, but you can't see yourself doing a start-to-finish musical?

I don't think so.

Do you believe in the idea of guilty pleasure films, and if so, what is one of *your* guilty pleasure films?

You know, the problem with my guilty pleasure films is that I don't feel guilty about them. I don't really experience that sensation. But, I guess, a movie like *Godzilla* might probably fit into that category. Any movie like *Deep Impact* or *I Am Legend* would fit into that category for me. Anything where the Earth is going to be obliterated or frozen or New York is going to be shaken to its foundation fits into that category. I'm drawn to that sort of stuff.

I feel guilty watching video of a tsunami flooding a city. Have you ever seen that kind of footage?

I have, and I can't tear myself away.

You're seeing reality turned completely upside down and inside out. The transformation is so total and so radical. Anyway, I guess that would be my guilty pleasure—so guilty that I'm extremely reluctant to use the word "pleasure."

I know what you mean.

OK, another one.

"How did your mother's job as an archaeologist influence you?"

Well, the mother is an archaeologist in *The Royal Tenenbaums*. Other than that, I don't know. I can't say I really ever knew that much about what she was doing, though I'm sure you can see some little influences here or there if you look.

"Why do animals have such a rough time of it in your movies?"

I don't think they necessarily do have a rough time of it. Compared to the humans, anyway. There's a cycle of life and death, and all aspects of existence might figure into it.

"Have you ever thought of starting your own fashion line?"

I prefer to work on costumes that go with a story.

"Would you ever direct a film based on somebody else's script?"

I would do that if I felt that I didn't have something to do on my own, or if I didn't have anything to adapt at that moment.

"How do you know if a gag is going to work in a movie?"

I don't know. There's a certain kind of joke where if the audience doesn't laugh, the movie's in trouble. And then there's another kind of joke where they might not laugh the first or second time, but eventually they'll say, "Oh, that's funny." And I guess there are also certain kinds of gags that are entertaining without having a punch line.

"You mentioned in an interview that you would like to make a science-fiction movie that is actually shot in outer space. Were you just messing with people?"

Well, I'm open to it.

OK, here's a big one: "In your filmic universe, is there a God, and if so, does God stand aloof or intervene?"

[LONG PAUSE.]

God intervenes.

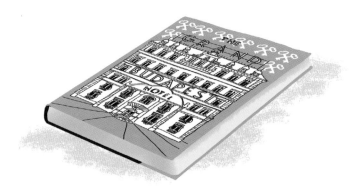

OPPOSITE: Wes Anderson going for a spin on Agatha's pink bicycle, freighted down with Mendl's boxes.

OVERLEAF: The hand-painted mural that hangs on the back wall of the Grand Budapest Hotel ballroom. Painter Michael Lenz modeled the image on *The Watzmann* by Caspar David Friedrich.

the grand
budapest
hotel

worlds
of
yesterday

ali
arikan

Worlds of Yesterday

"To be frank, I think *his* world had vanished long before he ever entered it—but I will say: He certainly sustained the illusion with a marvelous grace!" — ZERO MOUSTAFA

Worlds of Yesterday

by ALI ARIKAN

THE WORLD Stefan Zweig was born into and the world whose passing he lamented were two distinct entities. One might call the former "reality" and the latter "illusion," but we shouldn't. When the subject is storytelling, as it is here, the two tend to blur. To get a sense of how that happens, let us consider two images.

The first is Zweig's best-known headshot, featured on myriad editions of his books.* With his head turned forty-five degrees toward the camera, Zweig rests his index finger on his cheek and throws an enigmatic smile toward posterity. He seems both mischievous and melancholy. With his finely trimmed moustache, his starched collar and patterned tie affixed with a clip, and his hair brilliantined over his scalp, he also looks quite the dandy.

* See page 190.

The second image is one of the publicity stills released at the same time as *The Grand Budapest Hotel*'s theatrical trailer: a shot of Ralph Fiennes as M. Gustave, the concierge of the eponymous lodge. Fiennes's appearance is quite similar to Zweig's. I initially presumed this was a pleasant coincidence, but once I saw the film, I realized it wasn't. The film emanates a Zweig-esque aura in its mix of buoyant wit and melancholy longing, and in its preoccupation with loss. Wes Anderson admits as much (the neologism "Zweig-esque" is his, not mine) right at the top of *The Grand Budapest Hotel*. An unnamed bibliophile in the fictional Zubrowka visits the grave of the country's "national treasure," represented by a bust identifying him simply as "Author"; the sculpture resembles Stefan Zweig in his later years. Observed in the flesh in a 1985 framing scene, the Author faintly suggests photographs of Zweig, as do the young Author (identified in the credits as "young writer") and M. Gustave. "See the resemblance?" Gustave asks Zero, emulating *Boy with Apple*. And just in case the subsequent story doesn't affirm the Zweig allegiance beyond reasonable doubt, Anderson confirms it in a closing title card reading, "Inspired by the Writings of Stefan Zweig." Not content with that tribute alone, Anderson curated a collection of Zweig's writing for Pushkin Press, featuring prefaces by the writer-director and Hugo Guinness, who helped devise the film's story.

One wonders: What kinship did a filmmaker from Texas find with a foppish writer from fin-de-siècle Vienna who died seventy-two years before his new film came out, and whose prose, however adored, had yet to penetrate popular culture?

The answer to this question may be found by studying the twinned histories of Austria and Stefan Zweig.

VIENNA DEFENDED the European ideal against the East for centuries. Located at the easternmost extension of the Alps, the city was all that stood between the comparatively easily conquered European Plain and the oncoming Saracens. Vienna was the city the Romans fortified against Germanic tribes marching from the East, and the city that stopped the advances of the heathen Ottomans in 1529 and 1683.

By the time the Turkish threat subsided and the Age of Enlightenment started to take hold, Vienna finally had a chance to breathe and reflect. In 1804, during the Napoleonic Wars, Vienna became the capital of the Austrian Empire and, following the Compromise of 1867, the capital of the newly crowned Hapsburg Empire. Sixty-three years later, it became the capital of the Austro-Hungarian Empire, as well as a beacon for talent and genius.

With the arrival of new immigrants and the construction of the magnificent *Ringstrasse*, or Ring Boulevard, which incorporated former suburbs into the city, the city's population grew from 1870 through 1910 from nine-hundred thousand to more than two million. As its aura of possibility grew, subjects from the Austro-Hungarian Empire streamed into the capital. The empire consisted of fifteen nations, but only the Austrians and the Hungarians enjoyed a nation-state status, thus bringing rise to the term "Völkerkerker," or prison of nations.

That was not the case in Zweig's city. There was always conflict, but urban unrest was minimal. Vienna was peaceful, with an innate ability to create from supranational disorder a sense of cosmopolitan unity. In the last decades of the nineteenth century, liberalism, secularism, capitalism, urbanization, nationalism, and socialism were the predominant, somewhat conflicting developments, and they allowed members of previously stigmatized groups, Jews in particular, to succeed, despite centuries of exclusion.

One of the building blocks of Viennese culture was the coffeehouse. These were open to everyone. People would gather around the traditional marble tabletops, converse, play cards, read papers and books. Zweig attributed a good measure of Vienna's cosmopolitan air to the rich daily diet of international dispatches and cultural commentary offered in the coffeehouses. At one point, Hitler, Trotsky, Tito, Freud, and Stalin all hung around the same neighborhood, and probably drank at the same coffeehouses. Working in the city of dreams, Sigmund Freud turned interpretation of dreams into a science. The almost erotic contours of Jugendstil ("young style") snaked their way through the paintings of Gustav Klimt, the polyphonies of Gustav Mahler and Hugo Wolf, and the architecture of Otto Wagner. In literature, Arthur Schnitzler, Hermann Bahr, and Peter Altenberg produced innovative essays, novels, and monographs. This initial movement was challenged by an expressionist wave that cut through the old forms, as well as through the Jugendstil line. In music, Arnold Schoenberg and Alban Berg broke the tonal patterns of Western music. Painters Oskar Kokoschka and Egon Schiele did much the same for painting; Adolf Loos for architecture; polymath Karl Kraus for literature; and Ludwig Wittgenstein in philosophy.

It would be naive, however, to believe that fin-de-siècle Vienna was a city of triumphant upswing or unwavering faith in the future. Vienna's intellectuals were excited and happy, for the most part, but they also wondered how long this world could last, for the forces of irrationality and brute dominance were seething in the background, biding their time.

ZWEIG'S LIFE unfolded amidst Vienna's late-nineteenth-century transformation. He was born in the city in 1881. His father was a wealthy textile industrialist, his mother a scion of a Jewish-Italian banking dynasty. Their wealth granted them entry into Viennese society, but while they were happy to be spared some of the more blatant manifestations of anti-Semitism, they felt their tremors, anyway. The Zweigs knew they could never be part of the Austrian aristocracy or the gentry. They "knew their place," in the parlance of that time, which is why the gentile elite accepted them.

Other Jewish writers questioned the irony of this acceptance, but not Zweig. He was aware of it, of course, but not obsessed with it. "We were able to mould our private existence with more individual personality," he wrote. "We could live a more cosmopolitan life, and the whole world stood open to us." Zweig's youthful experience in late-nineteenth-century Vienna emboldened his pride all the more. "There is hardly a city in Europe where the drive towards cultural ideals was as passionate as it was in Vienna," he wrote. And by the turn of the century, a new understanding of the arts bloomed. "The truly great experience of our youthful years was the realisation that something new in art was on the way—something more impassioned, difficult and alluring than the art that had satisfied our parents and the world around us," Zweig wrote.

This state of affairs was so intoxicating to the young Viennese that they failed to notice that these "aesthetic changes were only the forerunners of the much more far-reaching changes that were to shake and finally destroy the world of our fathers, the world of security."

ALTHOUGH PATRIOTIC, Zweig refused to pick up a rifle at the spark of the First World War. He served in the archives of the Ministry of War and became a pacifist and an advocate for the unification of Europe. When his advocacy of nonviolence alarmed authorities, he moved, first to Zurich, and then, for a brief period after the war, to Berlin. He settled in a villa on the Kapuzinerberg mountain near Salzburg.

Zweig's mountainside villa became a cultural mecca for the European literati—the Playboy Mansion by way of the Algonquin Round Table, the place to be for stars and gadflies of European high culture. "Romain Rolland stayed with us," he wrote, "and Thomas Mann. Among the guests whom we welcomed to our house were H. G. Wells, Hofmannsthal, Jakob Wassermann, van Loon, James Joyce, Emil Ludwig, Franz Werfel, Georg Brandes, Paul Valéry, Jane Addams, Shalom Asch, and Arthur Schnitzler. Musicians included Ravel and Richard Strauss, Alban Berg, Bruno Walter, Bartók, and there were many other guests—painters, actors and scholars from all over the world."

When Zweig went out to his villa's terrace, he could see across the border into Southern Germany. "We spent so many happy hours with all our guests, sitting on the terrace and looking out at the beautiful and peaceful landscape, never guessing that directly opposite, on the mountain in Berchtesgaden, a man lived who would destroy it all," he wrote in *The World of Yesterday*. His alpine villa represented everything that Hitler was determined to annihilate, and not just because the landlord was Jewish: it was the cosmopolitan, egalitarian, socialist European ideal the Nazis wanted to stomp on.

The aftermath of the First World War had clarified national boundaries. Zweig detested this "modern trend." He saw the invention of the passport as the vector of this ailment. "Nothing more graphically illustrates the monstrous relapse the world suffered after the First World War than the restrictions on personal freedom of movement and civil rights," he wrote bitterly. "Before 1914 the earth

belonged to the entire human race. Everyone could go where he wanted and stay there as long as he liked. . . . No permits, no visas, nothing to give you trouble; the borders that today, thanks to the pathological distrust felt by everyone for everyone else, are a tangled fence of red tape were then nothing but symbolic lines on the map, and you crossed them as unthinkingly as you can cross the meridian in Greenwich." Nationalism, Zweig believed, emerged to agitate the world only after the so-called Great War. The first visible phenomenon spawned by this intellectual epidemic was xenophobia: morbid dislike of the foreigner. "All the humiliations previously devised solely for criminals were now inflicted on every traveller before and during a journey."

In 1934, following Hitler's rise to power in Germany, Zweig left Austria. He moved first to London and York, England, then to New York, and, eventually, to Petropolis in Brazil. He had always loved to travel, afflicted as he was by an ailment that can only be described in German: *fernweh* (literally "longing for a land unseen"). Both in England and in New York, he wrote that he hated "the wretched feeling of being a 'foreigner'." He posited that in a foreign land self-respect tended to diminish, "and I do not hesitate to confess that since the day when I first had to live with papers or passports essentially foreign to me, I have not felt that I entirely belong to myself any more. Something of my natural identity has been destroyed for ever with my original, real self."

History had made the younger Zweig prolific and confident, with faith in the future, and then it turned around and ran him over, robbing him of idealism and rosy thoughts, and leaving only the bittersweet consolation prizes of memories, which grew ever fonder in the retelling. Zweig penned many of his writings about the Vienna of his youth near the end of his life, in the late 1930s, as the specter of fascism loomed over Europe. He made his living fashioning vignettes and dioramas from the chaos of a remembered world, but he also remained aware of his own maudlin tendency to "conceive culture as a glass bead

game of the spirit."** His nostalgia for a bygone Vienna was dreamlike and unreliable, which he admitted in his autobiography, *The World of Yesterday*: "Now that a great storm has long since destroyed it, we know at last that our world of security was a castle in the air."

As admittedly subjective as Zweig's remembrances were, they were wound around a core of truth. Something glorious and good had indeed been toppled by the First World War, then ground into ashes by the second. In the aftermath of the Nazis' reign, much of the ornamental richness of the turn of the century had disappeared, along with the culture that birthed it. By the time Zweig killed himself, with his second wife beside him, in late 1942, he had spent many years despairing at the future of Europe and its culture. The past that Zweig eulogized was the moribund twilight of European high culture and human goodness. It was an innocence that was forever lost.

WELL, NOT FOREVER: The Vienna of Zweig's youth lives again in the *The World of Yesterday*. It lives, too, in sections of novels and short stories that recount the intellectual competitions and mutual exhortations of poets, philosophers, lovers of literacy, and literate lovers and that recount the splendors of a

place the narrator left long ago.

Are Zweig's storytellers trustworthy? They themselves wonder. His prose is filled with moments where characters struggle to remember things, or wonder if they're misremembering things, or take a while to dredge details from the unconscious. We are often aware that we are not seeing a representation of how things actually were, but a personal, lyrical evocation—a record in which feelings are equal to, in some ways more important than, facts. The telling matters more than the tale. The feelings experienced by the teller matter even more. The feelings that arise in the reader matter most of all.

The Grand Budapest Hotel understands this layering effect, embedding it in the plot. Layer one is the story of young Zero Moustafa learning from M. Gustave about life, love, and hotel management. The glory days of the Grand Budapest are the embodiment of high European culture—the film's transmogrified and compacted version of the Austria ecstatically recounted in *The World of Yesterday*. This is the bulk of the film. Our hero is M. Gustave, a charismatic fop who personifies everything Zweig thought stood for Old Europe: a sense of personal style; a knowing sense of humor; an infectious optimism tempered by wisdom; an appreciation of tradition fused with a refusal to let tradition constrain him; a resilience that lets him escape prison and scamper about the countryside, evading enemies to reclaim *Boy with Apple*.

Layer two is provided by the 1968 framing device of old Zero recounting his story to the young Author—a sentimental evocation of events that occurred more than three decades prior; or, to invoke the title of a Zweig story, a tale told in twilight.

Layer three belongs to the old Author, who in 1985 "presents" the other two layers; this positions Gustave and young Zero's adventures as an old

** Ritchie Robertson, *The 'Jewish Question' in German Literature, 1749–1939: Emancipation and its Discontents* (Oxford University Press), 127.

man's account of a story told to him decades earlier by a different old man.

The cemetery scenes constitute layer four: These frame the whole thing as a mind-film, imagined by a young woman who read the Author's book circa 2014 and was so moved that she visited his grave.

There is a fifth layer to the story, though. By identifying it, we can understand the mechanism through which a filmmaker transmutes his love for real art based on real life into a scripted film set in a Europe that never existed.

WHEREAS Zweig's biographies and monographs contain determined, straight narratives, his stories are like nesting dolls: tales within tales, told by diverse narrators, occurring in different times, in distant lands. *The Grand Budapest Hotel* utilizes this aspect by offering the aforementioned array of narrators, all of whom push the story along, in the process abstracting events into legend.

The Grand Budapest Hotel is not solely the vision of young Zero, old Zero, the young Author, the old Author, or that worshipful young woman in the cemetery, but an amalgamation of them all. It is also the vision of Wes Anderson. And its most salient virtue is its humility. It is a tribute to Zweig by an American filmmaker eight decades and an ocean removed from the events that shaped his fantasy. It is a fanciful feature-length motion picture by a writer of literate films who would not have made this one if he didn't adore Zweig, but who nonetheless seems conscious of himself as an image-maker—a storyteller for whom words are one part of the texture of movies whose stories unfold in realities adjacent to reality: One in which New York is not New York, the ocean is not entirely the ocean, and India is not exactly India. *The Grand Budapest Hotel* is correspondingly filled with allusions and homages to Zweig's work, but it is not a direct adaptation of any one of them.

And yet, in its calculated indirectness, *The Grand Budapest Hotel* captures a Zweig-like quality that seems, in retrospect, to originate in the feelings of loss that fueled so much of Zweig's writing. His fiction, and especially his memoirs, give the sense that what we are reading is an attempt to revive experiences that died the instant they happened, that only lived on in the storyteller's memory, and that the Author fears will disappear unless he fixes them to paper.

It is through the alchemy of the film's layering that Stefan Zweig's writing merges with Wes Anderson's filmmaking to become a story about the need for stories. In the 1985 "preface," as it were, the Author starts speaking into the camera, telling of the August he spent at the eponymous mountain lodge recuperating from "scribe's fever." A near-wreck close to demolition, the hotel plays host to a number of solitary guests. One evening, the young Author spots an old man with "an imperceptible air of sadness" sitting in the lobby. He is Zero Moustafa, the hotel's owner, who offers to tell the story of "this enchanting old ruin."

Throughout this initial interlude, Anderson plays with aspect ratios: 1.37:, 1.85:, and 2.35:1, one for each timeline, collapsing and expanding the space, cinematically expressing the nesting nature of this tale. The morphing rectangular borders of the screen literalize the phrase "framing device" and impart secondary significance to rectangles within the film's frames: the hotel rooms and elevators, the windows and doors, the paintings and boxes of confectionary. This is, of course, itself a sly allusion to Zweig's stories, which frequently contained tortured characters harboring secrets, and which were themselves often "framed" as memories recollected after the fact, or preserved in diaries or letters.

So we have layers upon layers, frames within frames, and stories within stories, yet the emotional core of the tale is never smothered. All the devices contribute to this story about stories. Zweig is the old Author is the young Author is old Zero is young Zero, and they are all the stylized essence of Europe fetishized by Ernst Lubitsch, Billy Wilder, Max Ophüls, and other directors to whom the filmmaker pays tribute alongside Zweig, his muse. Of course, just as the Grand Budapest's opulence will be ousted, in the wake of war, by regional brutalism, so M. Gustave's old-world charm will be replaced by an unhappy wage-slave, M. Jean, rushing around in a depopulated husk that once was a palace of hospitality.

There is a clear connection between Zweig's Alpine villa and the Grand Budapest. This connection manifests itself as a chain of associations: Zweig's mania was for exalting Europe's vanished past and commemorating his own; M. Gustave's is about forestalling the possibility that his beloved hotel will be overrun by "filthy, goddamn, pock-marked, fascist assholes" or incinerated by bombs; old Zero's is about carrying M. Gustave's story forward in time; the Author's is about performing the same service for future generations, represented by the grandson who disrupts his prologue and then stands by his side. All of these rescues are gathered in a pink Mendl's box and tied with a bow in the bracketing sequences at the cemetery. The film is the book, the book is Zero's story, Zero's story is Gustave's, Gustave's story is the Grand Budapest, the Grand Budapest is Zweig's Alpine villa is Austria is Europe is everything. And it's gone, gone, gone: all of it. Only the stories remain.

STEFAN ZWEIG
Excerpts

BEWARE OF PITY

"To him that hath, more shall be given." Every writer knows the truth of this biblical maxim, and can confirm the fact that "To him who hath told much, more shall be told." There is nothing more erroneous than the idea, which is only too common, that a writer's imagination is always at work, and he is constantly inventing an inexhaustible supply of incidents and stories. In reality he does not have to invent his stories; he need only let characters and events find their own way to him, and if he retains to a high degree the ability to look and listen, they will keep seeking him out as someone who will pass them on. To him who has often tried to interpret the tales of others, many will tell their tales.

The incidents that follow were told to me almost entirely as I record them here, and in a wholly unexpected way. Last time I was in Vienna I felt tired after dealing with a great deal of business, and I went one evening to a suburban restaurant that I suspected had fallen out of fashion long ago, and would not be very full. As soon as I had come in, however, I found to my annoyance that I was wrong. An acquaintance of mine rose from the very first table with every evidence of high delight, to which I am afraid I could not respond quite so warmly, and asked me to sit down with him. It would not be true to say that this excessively friendly gentleman was disagreeable company in himself; but he was one of those compulsively sociable people who collect acquaintances as enthusiastically as children collect stamps, and like to show off every item in their collection. For this well-meaning oddity—a knowledgeable and competent archivist by profession—the whole meaning of life was confined to the modest satisfaction of being able to boast, in an offhand manner, of anyone whose name appeared in the news-papers from time to time, "Ah, he's a good friend of mine," or, "Oh, I met him only yesterday," or, "My friend A told me, and then my friend B gave it as his opinion that . . ."and so on all through the alphabet. He was regularly in the audience to applaud the premieres of his friends' plays, and would telephone every leading actress next morning with his congratulations, he never forgot a birthday, he never referred to any poor reviews of your work in the papers, but sent you those that praised it to the skies. Not a disagree-able man, then—his warmth of feeling was genuine, and he was delighted if you ever did him a small favour, or even added a new item to his fine collection of acquaintances.

However, there is no need for me to say more about my friend the hanger-on—such was the usual name in Vienna for this particular kind of well-intentioned parasite among the motley group of social climbers—for we all know hangers-on, and we also know that there is no way of repelling their well-meant attentions without being rude. So I resigned myself to sitting down beside him, and half-an-hour had passed in idle chatter when a man came into the restaurant. He was tall, his fresh-complexioned, still youthful face and the interesting touch of grey at his temples made him a striking figure, and a certain way of holding himself very upright marked him out at once as a former military man. My table companion immediately leapt to his feet with a typically warm greeting, to which, however, the gentleman responded with more indifference than civility, and the newcomer had hardly ordered from the attentive waiter who came hurrying up before my friend the lion-hunter was leaning towards me and asking in a whisper, "Do you know who that is?" As I well knew his collector's pride in displaying his collection, and I feared a lengthy story, I said only a brief, "No," and went back to dissecting my Sachertorte. However, my lack of interest only aroused further enthusiasm in the collector of famous names, and he confidentially whispered, "Why, that's Hofmiller of the General Commissariat—you know, the man who won the Order of Maria Theresia in the war." And since even this did not seem to impress me as much as he had hoped, he launched with all the enthusiasm of a patriotic textbook into an account of the great achievements of this Captain Hofmiller, first in the cavalry, then on the famous reconnaissance flight over the river Piave when he shot down three enemy aircraft single-handed, and finally the time when he occupied and held a sector of the front for three days with his company of gunners—all with a wealth of detail that I omit here, and many expressions of astonishment at finding that I had never heard of this great man, decorated by Emperor Karl in person with the highest order in the Austrian Army.

Reluctantly, I let myself be persuaded to glance at the other table for a closer view of a historically authentic hero. But I met with a look of annoyance, as much as to say—has that fellow been talking about me?

There's no need to stare! At the same time the gentleman pushed his chair to one side with an air of distinct displeasure, ostentatiously turning his back to us. Feeling a little ashamed of myself, I looked away from him, and from then on I avoided looking curiously at anything, even the tablecloth. Soon after that I said goodbye to my talkative friend. I noticed as I left that he immediately moved to the table where his military hero was sitting, probably to give him an account of me as eagerly as he had talked to me about Hofmiller.

That was all. A mere couple of glances, and I would certainly have forgotten that brief meeting, but at a small party the very next day it so happened that I again found myself opposite the same unsociable gentleman, who incidentally looked even more striking and elegant in a dinner jacket than he had in his casual tweeds the day before. We both had some difficulty in suppressing a small smile, the kind exchanged in a company of any size by two people who share a well-kept secret. He recognised me as easily as I did him, and probably we felt the same amusement in thinking of the mutual acquaintance who had failed to throw us together yesterday. At first we avoided speaking to one another, and indeed there was not much chance to do so, because an animated discussion was going on around us.

I shall be giving away the subject of that discussion in advance if I mention that it took place in the year 1938. Later historians of our time will agree that in 1938 almost every conversation, in every country of our ruined continent of Europe, revolved around the probability or otherwise of a second world war. The theme inevitably fascinated every social gathering, and you sometimes felt that fears, suppositions and hopes were being expressed not so much by the speakers as by the atmosphere itself, the air of those times, highly charged with secret tensions and anxious to put them into words.

The subject had been broached by the master of the house, a lawyer and self-opinionated, as lawyers tend to be. He trotted out the usual arguments to prove the usual nonsense—the younger generation knew about war now, he said, and would not stumble blindly into another one. At the moment of mobilisation, guns would be turned on those who had given orders to fire them. Men like him in particular, said our host, men who had fought at the front in the last war, had not forgotten what it was like. At a time when explosives and poison gas were being manufactured in tens of thousands—no, hundreds of thousands—of armaments factories, he dismissed the possibility of war as easily as he flicked the ash off his cigarette, speaking in a confident tone that irritated me. We shouldn't always, I firmly retorted, believe in our own wishful thinking. The civil and military organisations directing the apparatus of war had not been asleep, and while our heads were spinning with utopian notions they had made the maximum use of peacetime to get control of the population at large. It had been organised in advance and was now, so to speak, primed ready to fire. Even now, thanks to our sophisticated propaganda machine, general subservience had grown to extraordinary proportions, and we had only to look facts in the face to see that when mobilisation was announced on the radio sets in our living rooms, no resistance could be expected. Men today were just motes of dust with no will of their own left.

Of course everyone else was against me. We all know from experience how the human tendency to self-delusion likes to declare dangers null and void even when we sense in our hearts that they are real. And such a warning against cheap optimism was certain to be unwelcome at the magnificently laid supper table in the next room.

Unexpectedly, although I had assumed that the hero who had won the Order of Maria Theresia would be an adversary, he now spoke up and took my side. It was sheer nonsense, he said firmly, to suppose that what ordinary people wanted or did not want counted for anything today. In the next war machinery would do the real work, and human beings would be downgraded to the status of machine parts. Even in the last war, he said, he had not met many men in the field who were clearly either for or against it. Most of them had been caught up in hostilities like a cloud of dust in the wind, and there they were, stuck in the whirl of events, shaken about and helpless like dried peas in a big bag. All things considered, he said, perhaps more men had fled into the war than away from it.

I listened in surprise, particularly interested by the vehemence with which he went on. "Let's not delude ourselves. If you were to try drumming up support in any country today for a war in a completely different part of the world, say Polynesia or some remote corner of Africa, thousands and tens of thousands would volunteer as recruits without really knowing why, perhaps just out of a desire to get away from themselves or their unsatisfactory lives. But I can't put the chances of any real opposition to the idea of war higher than zero. It takes far more courage for a man to oppose an organisation than to go along with the crowd. Standing up to it calls for individualism, and individualists are a dying species in these times of progressive organisation and mechanisation. In the war the instances of courage that I met could be called courage en masse, courage within the ranks, and if you look closely at that phenomenon you'll find some very strange elements in it—a good deal of vanity, thoughtlessness, even boredom, but mainly fear—fear of lagging behind, fear of mockery, fear of taking independent action, and most of all fear of opposing the united opinion of your companions. Most of those whom I knew on the field as the bravest of the brave seemed to me very dubious heroes when I returned to civil life. And please don't misunderstand me," he added, turning courteously to our host, who had a wry look on his face, "I make no exception at all for myself."

I liked the way he spoke, and would have gone over for a word with him, but just then the lady of the house summoned us to supper, and as we were seated some way apart we had no chance to talk. Only when everyone was leaving did we meet in the cloakroom.

"I think," he said to me, with a smile, "that we've already been introduced by our mutual friend."

I smiled back. "And at such length, too."

"I expect he laid it on thick, presenting me as an Achilles and carrying on about my order."

"Something like that."

"Yes, he's very proud of my order—and of your books as well."

"An oddity, isn't he? Still, there are worse. Shall we walk a little way together?"

As we were leaving, he suddenly turned to me. "Believe me, I mean it when I tell you that over the years the Order of Maria Theresia has been nothing but a nuisance to me. Too showy by half for my liking. Although to be honest, when it was handed out to me on the battlefield of course I was delighted at first. After all, when you've been trained as a soldier and from your days at military academy on you've heard about the legendary order—it's given to perhaps only a dozen men in any war—well, it's like a star falling from heaven into your lap. A thing like that means a lot to a young man of twenty-eight. All of a sudden there you are in front of everyone, they're all staring at something shining on your chest like a little sun, and the Emperor himself, His Unapproachable Majesty, is shaking your hand and congratulating you. But you see, it's a distinction that meant nothing outside the world of the army, and after the war it struck me as ridiculous to be going around as a certified hero for the rest of my life, just because I'd shown real courage for twenty minutes—probably no more courage, in fact, than ten thousand others. All that distinguished me from them was that I had attracted attention and, perhaps even more surprising, I'd come back alive. After a year when everyone stared at that little bit of metal, with their eyes wandering over me in awe, I felt sick and tired of going around like a monument on the move, and I hated all the fuss. That's one of the reasons why I switched to civilian life so soon after the end of the war."

He began walking a little faster.

"One of the reasons, I said, but the main reason was private, and you may find it easier to understand. The main reason was that I had grave doubts of my right to be decorated at all, or at least of my heroism. I knew better than any of the gaping strangers that behind that order was a man who was far from being a hero, was even decidedly a non-hero—one of those who ran full tilt into the war to save themselves from a desperate situation. Deserters from their own responsibilities, not heroes doing their duty. I don't know how it seems to you, but I for one see life lived in an aura of heroism as unnatural and unbearable, and I felt genuinely relieved when I could give up parading my heroic story on my uniform for all to see. It still irritates me to hear someone digging up the old days of my glory, and I might as well admit that yesterday I was on the point of going over to your table and telling our loquacious friend, in no uncertain terms, to boast of knowing someone else, not me. Your look of respect rankled, and I felt like showing how wrong our friend was by making you listen to the tale of the devious ways whereby I acquired my heroic reputation. It's a very strange story, and it certainly shows that courage is often only another aspect of weakness. Incidentally, I would still have no reservations about telling you that tale. What happened to a man a quarter-of-a-century ago no longer concerns him personally—it happened to someone different. Do you have the time and inclination to hear it?"

Of course I had time, and we walked up and down the now deserted streets for some while longer. In the following days, we also spent a great deal of time together. I have changed very little in Captain Hofmiller's account, at most making a regiment of hussars into a regiment of lancers, moving garrisons around the map a little to hide their identity, and carefully changing all the personal names. But I have not added anything of importance, and it is not I as the writer of this story but its real narrator who now begins to tell his tale.

THE WORLD OF YESTERDAY

The times provide the pictures, I merely speak the words to go with them, and it will not be so much my own story I tell as that of an entire generation—our

PREFACE

unique generation, carrying a heavier burden of fate than almost any other in the course of history. (p. 17)

For the very reason that for centuries Austria and its monarchy had been neither politically ambitious nor particularly successful in its military ventures,

CHAPTER ONE

native pride had focused most strongly on distinction in artistic achievement. Vienna, as everyone knew, was an epicurean city—however, what does culture

mean but taking the raw material of life and enticing from it its finest, most delicate and subtle aspects by means of art and love? The people of Vienna were gourmets who appreciated good food and good wine, fresh and astringent beer, lavish desserts and tortes, but they also demanded subtler pleasures. (pp. 35-6)

In fact we had a boundless capacity for enthusiasm. For years, we adolescents did nothing during our lessons, on the way to and from school, in the coffee

CHAPTER TWO

house, at the theatre and on walks but discuss books, pictures, music, philosophy. Anyone who performed in public as an actor or conductor, anyone who had published a book or wrote in a newspaper, was a star in our firmament. I was almost alarmed when, years later, I found in Balzac's account of his youth the sentence: "Les gens célèbres étaient pour moi comme des dieux qui ne parlaient pas, ne marchaient pas, ne mangeaient pas comme les autres hommes."* That was exactly what we used to feel—to have seen Gustav Mahler in the street was an event to be reported to your friends next morning like a personal triumph, and when once, as a boy, I was introduced to Johannes Brahms and he gave me a kindly pat on the shoulder, I was in a state of total confusion for days over this extraordinary event. (p. 63)

> * "Famous people were like gods to me who did not speak, did not eat like other men."

We young men, however, wholly absorbed in our literary ambitions, noticed little of these dangerous changes in our native land; our eyes were bent entirely on books and pictures. We took not the slightest interest in political and social problems; what did all this shrill squabbling mean in our lives? The city was in a state of agitation at election time; we went to the libraries. The masses rose up; we wrote and discussed poetry. We failed to see the writing on the wall in letters of fire. Like King Belshazzar before us, we dined on the delicious dishes of the arts and never looked apprehensively ahead. Only decades later, when the roof and walls of the building fell in on us, did we realise that the foundations had been undermined long before, and the downfall of individual freedom in Europe had begun with the new century. (p. 86)

What was suppressed found outlets everywhere, found ways around obstacles, ways out of difficulties. So ultimately the generation that was prudishly denied any sexual enlightenment, any form of easy social encounter with the opposite sex, was a thousand times more erotically obsessed than young people today, who have so much more freedom in love. Forbidden fruit excites a craving, only what is forbidden stimulates desire, and the less the eyes saw and the ears heard the more minds dreamt. The less air, light and sun was allowed to fall on the body, the more heated did the senses become. (p. 98)

CHAPTER THREE

I know, I know, Paris is not alone in its suffering today. It will be decades before that other Europe can return to what it was before the First World War. A certain gloom has never entirely lifted from the once-bright horizon of the continent since then, and from country to country, from one person to another, bitterness and distrust have lurked in the mutilated body of Europe corroding it like poison. However much progress in society and technology has been made during the quarter of a century between the two world wars, look closely and there is not a single nation in our small Western world that is not immeasurably worse off by comparison with its old natural joie de vivre. (p. 150)

CHAPTER FIVE

Then, on 28th June 1914, a shot was fired in Sarajevo, the shot that in a single second was to shatter the world of security and creative reason in which we had been reared, where we had grown up and were at home, as if it were a hollow clay pot breaking into a thousand pieces. (p. 235)

CHAPTER SEVEN

221

The war of 1939 had intellectual ideas behind it—it was about freedom and the preservation of moral values, and fighting for ideas makes men hard and determined. In contrast, the war of 1914 was ignorant of the realities; it was still serving a delusion, the dream of a better world, a world that would be just and peaceful. And only delusion, not knowledge, brings happiness. That was why the victims went to the slaughter drunk and rejoicing, crowned with flowers and wearing oak leaves on their helmets, while the streets echoed with cheering and blazed with light, as if it were a festival. (p. 250)

Was it not understandable for the new generation to feel no respect whatsoever for their elders? None of these young people believed their parents, the politicians or their teachers. Every state decree or proclamation was read with distrust. The post-war generation emancipated itself, with a sudden, violent reaction, from all that had previously been accepted. It turned its back on all tradition, determined to take its fate into its own hands, moving forcefully away from the old past and on into the future. An entirely new world, a different order, was to begin with these young people in every area of life, and of course it all started with wild exaggeration. Anyone or anything not their own age was finished, out-of-date, done for. (p. 322)

COLLECTED STORIES

During the increasingly agitated discussion the fugitive's timid gaze had gradually lifted, and his eyes were now fixed on the lips of the hotel manager, the only person in all this turmoil who, he knew, could tell him his fate in terms that he was able to understand. He seemed to be vaguely aware of the turmoil caused by his presence, and as the noisy argument died down he spontaneously raised both hands in the silence, and reached them out to the manager with the pleading look of women at prayer before a holy picture. This moving gesture had an irresistible effect on all present. The manager went up to the man and reassured him warmly, saying that he had nothing to fear, he could stay here and come to no harm, he would have accommodation for the immediate future. The Russian tried to kiss his hand, but the other man withdrew it and quickly stepped back. Then he pointed out the house next door, a small village inn where the Russian would have bed and board, said a few more words of reassurance to him, and then, with another friendly wave, went up the beach to his hotel. (pp. 584–96)

"INCIDENT ON LAKE GENEVA"

The story of how Leopold or Lämmel Kanitz became Herr von Kekesfalva and master of a landed estate begins in a passenger train from Budapest to Vienna. Although by now he was forty-two years old, and there were strands of grey in his hair, our friend still spent most of his nights travelling—the thrifty like to save time as well as money—and I don't suppose I have to point out that he always went third class. He was an old hand at travelling by night, and had long ago worked out a technique for it. First he would spread a Scottish tartan rug that he had once picked up cheap at an auction over the hard wooden seat, then he carefully hung up his inevitable black coat on the hook provided, to spare it wear and tear, put his gold-framed glasses away in their case, took a soft old dressing gown out of his canvas travelling bag—he never went to the expense of buying a leather suitcase—and finally crammed his cap well down over his forehead to keep the light out of his eyes. Then he would settle back into the corner of the compartment, used as he was to falling asleep where he sat, for little Leopold had learnt as a child that you can spend the night asleep without the comfort of a bed. (p. 149)

THE GOVERNESS AND OTHER STORIES

The old man, alone with himself, stared open-eyed at the endless void of the night. Beside him something lay in the dark, breathing deeply; he made an effort to remember that the body drawing in the same air in the same room was the woman whom he had known when she was young and ardent, who had borne him a child, a body bound to him through the deepest mystery of the blood; he kept forcing himself to think that the warm, soft body there—he had only to put out a hand to touch it—had once been a life that was part of his own. But strangely, the memory aroused no feelings in him any more. And he heard her regular breathing only like the murmuring of little waves coming through the open window as they broke softly on the pebbles near the shore. It was all far away and unreal, something strange was lying beside him only by chance—it was over, over for ever. (p. 570)

"DOWNFALL OF THE HEART"

But there it was—the sweet perfume that aroused a memory, or was it his half-numbed brain remembering forgotten moments?—and suddenly a terrible change came over the features that had looked happy only just now. (p. 576)

CONFUSION

And the formative word rang out, full-toned, as he launched himself with enthusiasm into the description of that barbarically primeval beginning. His voice, which at first raced along fast in a whisper, stretching muscles and ligaments of sound, became a metallically gleaming airborne craft pressing on ever more freely, ever further aloft—the room, the walls pressed close in answer, became too small for it, it needed so much space. I felt a storm surging over me, the breaking surf of the ocean's lip powerfully uttered its echoing word; bending over the desk, I felt as if I were standing among the dunes of my home again, with the great surge of a thousand waves coming up and sea spray flying in the wind. All the sense of awe that surrounds both the birth of a man and the birth of a work of literature broke for the first time over my amazed and delighted mind at this time.

If my teacher ended his dictation at the point where the strength of his inspiration tore the words magnificently away from their scholarly purpose, where thought became poetry, I was left reeling. A fiery weariness streamed through me, strong and heavy, not at all like his own weariness, which was a sense of exhaustion or relief, while I, over whom the storm had broken, was still trembling with all that had flowed into me

Both of us, however, always needed a little conversation afterwards to help us find sleep or rest. I would usually read over what I had taken down in shorthand, and curiously enough, no sooner did my writing become spoken words than another voice breathed through my own and rose from it, as if something had transformed the language in my mouth. And then I realized that, in repeating his own words, I was scanning and forming his intonations with such faithful devotion that he might have been speaking out of me, not I myself—so entirely had I come to echo his own nature. I was the resonance of his words. (pp. 78-79)

THE COLLECTED STORIES OF STEFAN ZWEIG

They went on talking. But there was already a warmth in their voices, an affectionate familiarity, that only a rosy if already half-faded secret like

"FORGOTTEN DREAMS"

theirs can allow. In quiet words, broken by a peal of happy laughter now and then, they talked about the past, or forgotten poems, faded flowers, lost ribbons— little love tokens that they had exchanged in the little town where they spent their youth. The old stories that, like half-remembered legends, rang bells in their hearts that had long ago fallen silent, stifled by dust, were slowly, very slowly invested with a melancholy solemnity; the final notes of their youthful love, now dead, brought profound and almost sad gravity to their conversation. (p. 11)

But how dark it is now in this room, and how far away you are from me in the deep twilight! I can see only a faint pale light where I think your face is,

"A STORY TOLD IN TWILIGHT"

and I do not know if you are smiling or sad. Are you smiling because I make up strange stories for people whom I knew fleetingly, dream of whole destinies for them, and then calmly let them slip back into their lives and their own world? Or are you sad for that boy who rejected love and found himself all at once cast out of the garden of his sweet dream forever? There, I didn't mean my story to be dark and melancholy—I only wanted to tell you about a boy suddenly surprised by love, his own and someone else's. But stories told in the evening all tread the gentle path of melancholy. Twilight falls with its veils, the sorrow that rests in the evening is a starless vault above them, darkness seeps into their blood, and all the bright, colourful words in them have as full and heavy a sound as if they came from our inmost hearts. (pp. 212-13)

Excerpts

But once more I feel I must pause, for yet again, and with some alarm, I become aware of the double-edged ambiguity of a single word. Only now that, for the first time, I am to tell a story in its full context do I understand the difficulty of expressing the ever-changing aspect of all that lives in concentrated form. I have just written "I", and said that I took a cab at noon on the 7th of June, 1913. But the word itself is not really straightforward, for I am by no means still the "I" of that time, that 7th of June, although only four months have passed since that day, although I live in the apartment of that former "I" and write at his desk, with his pen, and with his own hand. I am quite distinct from the man I was then, because of this experience of mine, I see him now from the outside, looking coolly at a stranger, and I can describe him like a playmate, a comrade, a friend whom I know well and whose essential nature I also know, but I am not that man any longer. I could speak of him, blame or condemn him, without any sense that he was once a part of me. (pp. 363–64)

"FANTASTIC NIGHT"

I will tell you the whole story of my life, and it is a life that truly began only on the day I met you. Before that, there was nothing but murky confusion into which my memory never dipped again, some kind of cellar full of dusty, cobwebbed, sombre objects and people. My heart knows nothing about them now. When you arrived I was thirteen years old, living in the apartment building where you live now, the same building in which you are holding my letter, my last living breath, in your hands. I lived in the same corridor, right opposite the door of your apartment. I am sure you will not remember us any more, an accountant's impoverished widow (my mother always wore mourning) and her thin teenage daughter; we had quietly become imbued, so to speak, with our life of needy respectability. Perhaps you never even heard our name, because we had no nameplate on the front door of our apartment, and no one came to visit us or asked after us. And it is all so long ago, fifteen or sixteen years; no, I am sure you don't remember anything about it, my beloved, but I—oh, I recollect every detail with passion. As if it were today, I remember the very day, no, the very hour when I first heard your voice and set eyes on you for the first time, and how could I not? It was only then that the world began for me. Allow me, beloved, to tell you the whole story from the beginning. I beg you, do not tire of listening to me for a quarter of an hour, when I have never tired of loving you all my life. (pp. 425–26)

"LETTER FROM AN UNKNOWN WOMAN"

But after all, time is strong, and age has the curious power of devaluing all our feelings. You feel death coming closer, its shadow falls black across your path, and things seem less brightly coloured, they do not go to the heart so much, they lose much of their dangerous violence.

"TWENTY-FOUR HOURS IN THE LIFE OF A WOMAN"

Growing old, after all, means that one no longer fears the past. (p. 441)

AN
INTERVIEW
WITH

TOP   Frequent Wes Anderson cast member Bill Murray on location with cinematographer Robert Yeoman at the Kunstmuseum in Dresden. This is where the lawyer Deputy Kovacs (Jeff Goldblum) is tailed by the assassin Jopling (Willem Dafoe).
BOTTOM   Edward Norton, with camera and monitor in the foreground.

A WHOLE DIFFERENT ELEMENT:

AN INTERVIEW WITH ROBERT YEOMAN

 Cinematographer **ROBERT YEOMAN** *started out in the early eighties working on low-budget exploitation pictures, then gradually moved up to independent films, such as William Friedkin's* Rampage *(1987) and Gus Van Sant's* Drugstore Cowboy *(1989), for which he won an Independent Spirit Award. His credits also include* The Substance of Fire *(1996),* White Lies *(1997), and* Dogma *(1999); two films directed by regular Wes Anderson collaborators, Roman Coppola's* CQ *(2001) and Noah Baumbach's* The Squid and the Whale *(2005); and several knockabout comedies, including* Get Him to the Greek *(2010),* Bridesmaids *(2011), and* The Heat *(2013). Yeoman has served as director of photography on every live-action Wes Anderson feature, starting with 1996's* Bottle Rocket. *His work on* Moonrise Kingdom *(2013) won him a citation from the British Society of Film Critics.*

MATT ZOLLER SEITZ: *Do you remember the first time you met Wes?*

ROBERT YEOMAN: I'm a little bit older than Wes—like, fifteen or sixteen years older. I'd been doing a series of low-budget movies that hadn't been that well received, and then he sent me the *Bottle Rocket* short and a script for the feature version. I read the feature script and thought it was great, and I liked the short, so I went to meet him. Wes was in an office at Sony Pictures, because James L. Brooks was producing the feature version, so I went over and met him there.

What was your impression of him?

When I first met Wes, he had these big glasses, and I was like, "Oh, man, another kid is going to make another movie that's not going to go anywhere." But I liked him, and the more we talked, the more I realized that this guy really had something going on. We found that we were drawn to the same things visually. We agreed on things we didn't like, as well as things we both liked. We just kind of hit it off, and I could see right away he had something special to offer—and good for me! I'm really happy I've been part of all his films. It's been one of the highlights of my career.

What is it like working with a guy who, in a sense, pre-edits the movie in his head? We've seen his storyboards. He's not a filmmaker who does a lot of "finding the movie in the editing room."

Yes—it's all very carefully planned out. On the past couple of movies, Wes has done these things called animatics, which are little hand-drawn cartoons that represent each shot and scene. He then adds all the voices of the characters himself, and that gives an "attitude" to the scene. He'd show the animatics to me and Adam and our first A.D. Josh, and sometimes even to the actors, and I think it gave everyone a sense of what we were going for. And it helped us in the shooting and during the prep.

Occasionally, as we worked on the film, we'd go out with just the assistant directors, the producers, and myself and Wes, and we'd shoot rough footage based on some of the animatics. It gave us a pretty good idea of how a scene was going to look when we

The Grand Budapest Hotel's cinematographer Robert Yeoman (right) lining up a shot of Agatha (Saoirse Ronan) opening up the hotel's vault.

photographed it with the actors. In the hotel shoot-out scene, for instance, we shot some of that with a camera without the actors, just to get a sense of how everything would come together.

Wes was pretty true to the animatics. Whenever we were shooting, if, for some reason, we had any doubt of what direction to go in, we'd get out the animatic for that scene and stay true to that. To work on a movie like that is refreshing, because most of the time, people don't really have an idea of what they want to shoot when they show up on the set. Wes has it all planned out so carefully in his head—and knows what shot to cut with what shot—so everyone knows exactly what we're going to be doing when we get there. He has a very strong vision of how the film is going to be, and we're all there to try to help him achieve that.

I'm sure you're aware that there's this stereotype of the cinematographer as the guy who's never happy with whatever the plan is and wants to do his own thing.

It depends on what movie you work on. I've worked on movies where the director is much more concerned with the actors and the writing, and so he more often leaves the visuals up to me and the production designer. That's not as satisfying.

I find the best movies come from people like Wes, who are directors with a very strong vision of the film. Certainly, I have more creative freedom on movies with other directors, but in the end, Wes pushes all of us—himself included—to do our best work, and so we're pushed into territories we wouldn't ordinarily think about, cinematically. I think the challenge and the excitement that comes from that adds a whole different element to the filmmaking experience for all of us.

Let's talk about the different aspect ratios in The Grand Budapest Hotel. *This is the sort of thing—the ratio of frame width to frame height—that a lot of viewers may not be aware of: that movies have different shapes depending on how they are shot or matted.*

A long time ago, I was really intrigued by the Academy ratio. In fact, on *The Royal Tenenbaums*, for the house, we talked about shooting that 1:37.

Which is more "square-ish" than people are used to seeing now. The "old-movie ratio," basically.

Right. We didn't do it on that movie, but it's something we'd talked about doing for a long time, When this movie came up, we first thought about the 1930s segment of it, and we decided to shoot 1:37 for those parts. Gradually, that idea kind of expanded to using 1:85 and 2:40 to represent the other time periods.

1:85, the ratio you use in the 1980s part of the movie with the older version of the Author, is slightly more rectangular—very close to 16:9, or the standard dimensions of contemporary televisions. 2:40 is Cinema-Scope, basically, the really wide format you and Wes used on his second, third, fourth, and fifth movies, and the ratio you use in the 1960s part of the movie with the younger version of the Author.

Right. The idea of changing aspect ratios from one time period to another was something Wes came up with. I was very excited about it, and I think it brought a lot to the film.

When we're looking at this movie, we're not actually looking at the Academy ratio, and 1:85 and 2:40, because all those different sizes of image have to fit within a 1:85 frame, right? So 1:85 is the basic frame for the film, and then the anamorphic and the old-movie, Academy ratio are sort of nestled within the 1:85 frame?

Yes. We nestled them all within the 1:85 frame, but the aspect ratios are still the same within the 1:85 frame. On the 1:37 footage, you get less on the side than you otherwise would, and on the 2:40 footage, you get more. But it all had to fit within the 1:85 frame.

How did that work, exactly?

Well, it's basically done in post-production. We shot three different formats, and in post, they just fit them all into 1:85. It was all done digitally. You can kind of combine all the formats into one format that way.

Was the entire movie shot on 35mm film?

Yes, with the exception of some of the miniatures. The film itself was shot on 35mm, but some elements of the miniatures—the skiing, the wide shots of the hotel exteriors—some of that was done digitally.

How was the skiing sequence done, exactly? Wes and I talked about the general outlines of that, but I thought maybe you could give us some more details.

The skiing sequence was a combination of a lot of different elements. We tried to shoot as much live, with the actors, as possible. We put them on a slant with the wind coming at them and the smoke coming at them, and with a white backdrop behind them. When you see the wide shots of them skiing, those are miniatures, done later. But as much as possible, when you see Ralph, when you see Tony, we wanted it to actually be Ralph and Tony. For example, we tried, first thing out of the shed, with the skies, to shoot that live. But then the wide shots and some of the more spectacular point-of-view shots were all done with miniatures later.

Can you talk about the use of paintings and films as reference points?

We looked at the Ernst Lubitsch films of the thirties. We looked at *Grand Hotel*, *To Be or Not to Be*, *The Shop Around the Corner* . . . those were our references. Wes got a lot of these photochrom pictures of old hotels from back in the thirties, and we used those as references, too.

In fact, at the beginning, we were toying with the idea of making the whole movie with a photochrom look. A lot of it would have been treated in post. We played around a little bit, but we never really came up with anything Wes was happy with, so we abandoned the idea. But it was certainly an inspiration to us, in the preparation of the film.

Cinematographer Robert Yeoman on location in Görlitz.

the grand
budapest
hotel

wes
anderson
takes
the 4:3
challenge

david
bordwell

Still-frames from *The Grand Budapest Hotel* demonstrating the film's various aspect ratios. From top to bottom: The present-day bracketing sequence, shot at 1.85:1; the 1985 sequence, also shot at 1.85:1; the 1968 sequences, shot at 2.40:1, and the 1932 section of the movie, shot at 1.37:1, sometimes referred to as the Academy ratio. Note that the 1985 sequence is slightly smaller than the "present day" sequence.

In the past, it would have been extremely challenging to show a film with changing aspect ratios. It would have required a well-rehearsed projectionist monitoring every second of the film as it went along, anticipating the moments before the story was about to change aspect ratios, and then switching the lens and gate on the projector to accommodate the different formats; and he would have needed to have reflexes faster than the Flash. It would have been a very bumpy ride at its best.

In the age of digital projection, however, *The Grand Budapest Hotel* is able to accommodate the 1.85, CinemaScope, and Academy ratio images simply by matting the images with vertical or horizontal black bars.

wes anderson takes the 4:3 challenge[1]

DAVID BORDWELL

As of this writing, *The Grand Budapest Hotel* is Wes Anderson's highest-grossing film. As such, it has introduced a broader audience to the director's idiosyncratic sensibility. Surprisingly, Anderson's biggest financial success has come without compromise. If anything, he's gotten bolder.

The audience-friendly *Fantastic Mr. Fox* and *Moonrise Kingdom* paved the way. Still, we should note how casually *Grand Budapest* flouts multiplex taste. It's not just a matter of featuring a protagonist who is apparently (and casually) bisexual. Or inventing an alternate version of the most harrowing period in recent European history. Or giving the bulk of the film's narration to a dark-skinned boy who falls in love with a European girl with a Mexico-shaped facial

birthmark and who ends the tale older, wiser, and sadder—having gained a hotel but lost his wife and best friend. In the spirit of Lewis Carroll's "The Walrus and the Carpenter," Anderson cuts his whimsy with grotesquerie. There are moments of offhand brutality and flashes of frank sexuality. And the film's retro leanings go beyond cozy citations. With its bustling ensemble cast, *Grand Budapest Hotel* suggests a postmodern remake of those sprawling, self-congratulatory spoofs of the 1960s: *The Great Race*; *Those Magnificent Men in Their Flying Machines*; *It's a Mad, Mad, Mad, Mad World*. (The film's title evokes another subgenre, the all-star movie set in a hotel, represented by *Grand Hotel* and *Hotel Berlin*.) In creating a comic-pathetic alternative account of Nazi imperialism, Anderson engages in a more serious, albeit roundabout, way with history than those inspirations do. He imagines the collapse of Europe as a sort of grave operetta, yet it manages to be ingratiating, even in its melancholy. Our most rigorous mainstream formalist shows just how much you can get away with and still leave an audience feeling affection for your people and their world.

fragile worlds

World building is at the center of much contemporary cinema. A studio can buy a world off the rack, as DC and Marvel franchises demonstrate. George Lucas—the creator of *Star Wars*, the dominant pop-culture influence during Anderson's 1970s childhood—taught us that you can create a world from scratch (or rather, from scraps of old cliffhangers and space operas. That approach forces an artist to be finicky. Inventing everything, from clothes and settings to machinery and tableware, demands a dedication to detail. Lucas remarked: "You can spend your entire life perfecting a new world when you create its every piece."[2] Anderson does that in every film he makes. The Tenenbaums live in a parallel-world New York, Steve Zissou sails to phantom islands, and *Moonrise* lovebirds Sam and Suzy find each other on the vaguely New England–ish island of New Penzance. Instead of being sleek, perfectly finished worlds, these realms seem handmade, fragile, in the manner of outsider art. Like illustrations in children's books, the rooms and landscapes evoke naive realism. The architectural spaces have a squat solidity, and they're stuffed with knickknacks, tchotchkes, and ephemera. The sense that each new release will transport us into a different topography is part of Anderson's appeal.

Having created a distinctive world in front of the camera, Anderson offers equally distinctive plots and visual techniques, drawing on old, even old-fashioned, storytelling strategies and film styles and sprucing them up.

Take his interest in what we might call "boxed-in" spaces. His story-world largely consists of squared-off, closed-in views, as if a buzz saw had sliced through chambers, tents, boats. The director's "dollhouse" shots yield cross sections of a family's home (the opening of *Moonrise Kingdom*), a submarine (*The Life Aquatic with Steve Zissou*), a passenger train (*The Darjeeling Limited*), and an underground community (*Fantastic Mr. Fox*). Thanks to right angles, central perspectives, and symmetrical layouts, his carpentered world gains a layer of formality, almost ceremony.

The plots are boxed, as well. Anderson uses flashbacks, voice-overs, and embedded stories to create partial or entire frames around each scene. This is not an innovation, but a continuation of a long tradition; since at least the 1940s, we've learned to follow stories within stories in movies, and Anderson's hearken back to the pre-TV way of doing things. He often uses one of the oldest conventions of Hollywood film, in which the story is visualized as a tale in a book, with the volume opening at the prologue and closing (perhaps uncertainly) at the end. He doubles the effect with *The Royal Tenenbaums*, presenting the entire movie as a book that's being read to us by Alec Baldwin's voice-over narrator. Sometimes, as in *Tenenbaums*, the narrative bracketing is consistent and orderly. Other times, the framing devices come and go. Bob Balaban's character in *Moonrise Kingdom* at first seems a detached narrator, delivering information as we need it, only to be revealed as a denizen of the island and a participant in the story he's been helping to tell.

Within each film, we may also find additional tales that enhance or reflect the main story. These stories-within-stories may be accompanied by spoken narration, on-screen titles, film or video footage, or excerpts from manuscripts and letters. This material can deliver exposition or embellish characters, especially when it's yoked to scenes that show other characters reacting to what they've seen or read. The festival screening of the unfinished documentary that opens *The Life Aquatic* sums up the loss that traumatized the hero; the reception afterward introduces us to nearly all the key players (including Zissou's maybe-son, Ned) in just a few minutes. In *Moonrise Kingdom* the Bishops' discovery of Sam and Suzy's correspondence leads to snatches of voice-over excerpts, which are in turn dramatized in crisp flashbacks that sketch the children's personalities and complicate the Bishops' reactions to their daughter's rebellious acts.

fixing the frame

Anderson has one of the most distinctive styles of any American filmmaker, partly because he always seems to have an answer to the central question of film direction: Where to put the camera? Anderson answers that question by committing himself to "planimetric staging" and shooting, matched by "compass-point" editing.

Most shots in most films present people in three-quarter

frontal views, in a dynamic, diagonal playing space. Here's a shot from John Huston's *In This Our Life* (1942) **[1]** that's as hyper-designed in its own way as Anderson's imagery.

1

As the eighteenth-century painter and social critic William Hogarth[3] pointed out, with a serpentine line in painting and drawing, such shots can lead our eye on "a wanton kind of chase." [4]

By contrast, "planimetric" shooting involves framing people against a perpendicular background, as if they were taking part in a police lineup. Usually they face the camera **[2]**, but you can rotate them ninety degrees to the left or right and show them to us in profile, or have them turn their backs to us.

When filming groups **[3]**, you can arrange the players in some depth, too, but again, they are stacked in perpendicular fashion, making each plane more or less parallel.

NEVILLE SMYTHE-DORLEAC

The decision to embrace "mug shot" staging limits a director's options. Characters stare directly at the camera, or seem to. Three-quarter views become rare, as their in-between-ness makes them feel like outliers. This visual style also sacrifices deep, sinuous compositions in favor of one-point perspective (or, alternatively, minimal depth). It's a surprisingly old strategy; Buster Keaton **[4]** used it occasionally, and Jean-Luc Godard **[5]** employed it in several films.[5]

4

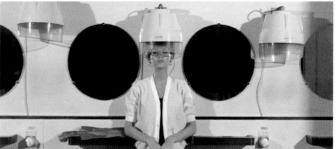

5

Planimetric shots became more common in European and Asian films from the 1970s onward. Today they show up as one-off effects in mainstream movies, too. A few filmmakers, however, make them the building blocks of whole films.[6]

In America, Anderson has become the most visible example of the style. While others use planimetric staging as visual punctuation, it is the basis of Anderson's vocabulary. This yields a formal and somewhat distanced quality—a sense that we are looking from a distance into an enclosed world that sometimes looks back at us.

This style also opens up comic possibilities that Keaton recognized in such films as *Neighbors* and *The General*. A rigid perpendicular angle can endow action with an absurd geometry and a deadpan humor, qualities that Anderson has exploited freely. **[6, 7]**

6

7

These apparently simple framings enhance the sense that we're looking at the world through a child's eyes, or the eyes of an adult with a childlike sense of innocence. Just as the Japanese thriller director Takeshi Kitano shows us gangsters behaving like little boys, Anderson's "dollhouse" frames combine with the planimetric look to turn adults into toy people, almost like items laid out in a Joseph Cornell box.[7] It's a style suitable for magical-realist environments like the world of Steve Zissou. In *Moonrise Kingdom*, it finds its echo in children's illustrated books.

But once you get beyond individual shots, how do you sustain the planimetric technique, through editing, within a scene?

One way is to make your cuts along the lens axis, straight in or straight back. Anderson sometimes does this. **[8, 9]**

8

9

You can also use what I call "compass-point" editing. This often involves cutting from a shot that's looking in a certain direction to another shot that's looking in the opposite direction, as if to reveal what was "behind" the camera in the first shot.

In effect, this option respects the implied "axis of action," an imagined 180-degree line that runs between the characters in classically staged cinema. But when a director is staging action planimetrically, as Anderson tends to do, the camera sits right on that line.

Parking the camera on the axis of action is a common tactic for subjective cutting, showing us first a person looking, more or less at the camera, then revealing what the character sees, from his or her vantage point. We see this technique used sporadically in many types of films. Often it's deployed to create momentary surprise, by showing us a character's reaction to a sight, then cutting to reveal what he or she is looking at.

If characters in such a scene are confronting each other, the camera is, in effect, sitting between them, so that each seems to be looking through the lens at the other.

This is a technique that Yasujirō Ozu favored in his late career. It was picked up by Kitano in *Sonatine* (1993) and other films. **[10]**

10

Filmmakers who work mainly in the planimetric tradition often use the approach for all types of scenes. When I asked Kitano why he used the technique, he explained that it was exactly the way people saw one another in ordinary life. He added that he was a novice director when he started, and this was the only way he knew to set up scenes. This tendency is one quality, perhaps the only quality, that Anderson and Kitano's films have in common. **[11]**

11

So you can preserve the planimetric layout shot-by-shot by cutting on the axis of a scene. But you can also do it by cutting at ninety-degree angles to the background plane or the figures' positions. Chantal Akerman does it throughout *Jeanne Dielman, 23 Quai du Commerce, 1080 Bruxelles* (1975). **[12, 13]**

12

13

Anderson exercises all these cutting options in *The Grand Budapest Hotel*.

Look at how this planimetric-profile two-shot **[14]** yields two frontal shots **[15, 16]**: we shift ninety degrees, then 180 degrees.

14

15

16

Now look at the images below **[17-19]**, from a scene at the front desk of the hotel. The first cut rotates ninety degrees. The second cuts in right on the lens axis. Cutting on the axis respects the lateral layout of the space.

In long shots, Anderson sometimes follows the classic Hollywood practice of allowing some decentering, as long as the cuts balance one off-center composition against another. Here, the changing angles obey the compass-point principle across three shots. **[20-22]** They shift the emphasis from the right side of the frame to the center, and then to the left.

17

20

18

21

19

22

Just as Anderson's occasional snap-zooms suggest the equivalent of axial cuts, ninety-degree shifts are sometimes enacted not through cuts but via hard, right-angled pans. In all, few directors have thought through the implications of the planimetric approach as thoroughly as Anderson has.

Does such an austere style risk monotony? Of course. Having imposed tight constraints on himself, Anderson is now obliged to show us, in scene after scene, that he can vary the approach, in obvious or subtle ways. The imaginative director can treat this as a challenge instead of a drag.

One source of variation is lens length. Most planimetric filmmakers use long lenses, which flatten the space severely. The figures can look like clothes hanging on a line. Anderson often counters this by shooting with wide-angle lenses. These exaggerate depth and make horizontal lines bulge, as in early CinemaScope films. **[23, 24]**

Another way Anderson varies his images is by departing from straight-on angles. As long as the framing maintains a planimetric geometry, we can look down or up at the action. **[25, 26]** That's what happens in this scene, which finds the camera making 180-degree reversals.

23

24

25

26

29

30

In this spirit, Anderson can give us bird's-eye views. Sometimes they do duty for long shots, as in Zero's brisk walk down the hotel carpet. **[27]**

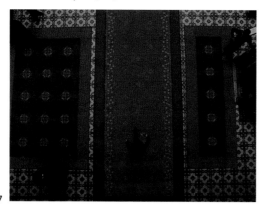

27

Though such shots aren't commonplace in modern cinema, there are precedents, as in the work of the Coen brothers. In this shot from *The Hudsucker Proxy*, the inflexible straight-down framing creates a joke. **[28]**

28

The Grand Budapest Hotel has room for some classically funny framings. Common practice says that you want somebody to look lonely, place the figure off center in a long shot. Here, Anderson seems to be playing a joke on the convention. **[29, 30]**

He presents it as a point-of-view shot, although presumably if the Author were looking at the mysterious man, he would center the object of attention in his field of vision.

Although three-quarter views in closeup are a common sight in Hollywood movies, they're rare in Anderson's. Yet he gives us a small, powerful dose at a key moment in *Moonrise Kingdom*: Sam and Suzy's declaration of love. **[31, 32]**

31

32

The same technique will reappear briefly for the young couple's dance and kiss on the shore of Mile 3.25 Tidal Inlet.

high or wide, and handsome

Something similar happens, without cutting, when M. Gustave interviews Zero. Zero's explanation of why he wants to keep the job as lobby boy warms the flinty concierge's heart. Then Anderson pans from a three-quarter close-up of Zero to M. Gustave's approving smile. **[33, 34]**

33

34

The turning point in their relationship is marked by a touch that would go unnoticed in a more conventional movie, but which stands out in *The Grand Budapest Hotel*. By using the device sparingly, Anderson restores its emotional power.

The Grand Budapest Hotel blends Anderson's distinctive visual style with his penchant for boxing up stories. For the first time, he builds a whole film out of embedded flashbacks, and uses them to guide us through several historical periods. We move from an older, now-famous Author giving an interview in 1985, then to the young Author's visit to the hotel in 1968, and eventually to the central tale, set in the 1930s and recounted by Zero Moustafa. Anderson has claimed his inspiration in Stefan Zweig's tales of interwar Europe, in which one character encounters another who tells of his past.

The eras are marked by Anderson's most complex narrational framing to date. The young woman paying tribute to the Author in the Lutz cemetery holds his book, *The Grand Budapest Hotel*. The Author's voice-over narration emerges to explain that writers often find people bringing them stories. But it's not clear that this narration is part of the book itself; the Author delivers it to us as if lecturing from his index cards, and a light is switched on as he starts, as if he were being filmed (shades of Bob Balaban's character in *Moonrise*). As the Author explains the bout of scribe's fever that led him to visit the Grand Budapest, his voice is replaced by that of his younger self. That narration, in turn, encloses the story told by the older version of Zero.

The film buckles shut as Mr. Moustafa ends his tale. Then the young Author concludes his story in his younger voice and then finishes it in the old Author's voice. ("But I never managed to see it again.") Then we return to the Lutz graveyard, where the young woman is reading the book that we have been hearing and seeing.[8] The sections neatly enclose one another, although the opening gives a glimpse of the hotel in its glory days, and the central 1930s story is occasionally interrupted by a return to Zero's 1968 conversation with the young Author.

Crucial to any frame-within-a-frame pattern is the point of attack. Whenever we get an embedded tale, we can always ask: Why start here? What motivates a character to recount the past at this point? The trigger might be a situation of crisis, a tranquil phase of life, or a moment when what happened can still arouse pain. Zweig and Anderson settle for the past recollected at a distance, a point at which everything is more or less settled. This way, we can see how the years take their toll. In 1968, the hotel is in terminal decline, so the young Author's faithful recounting of Mr. Moustafa's days as a lobby boy carries a pungent sense of loss. That is accentuated by our brief encounter with the Author several years later; now he's an old man, too, with his own uniformed companion. And in the film's ultimate present tense, the moment when the young woman pays homage to the Author, the past is irredeemably gone, recalled only in traces: the hotel keys festooning the monument, the book that is partly but imperfectly the story of the film we will see.

35

36

Boxes within boxes encase increasingly remote eras. As we'd expect, Anderson accentuates the different time periods through costuming and production design. He has also, more daringly, shot each era in a different aspect ratio. The ratio is about 1:1.85 for the present frame story and for the 1985 passage, when the Author begins to recount meeting Mr. Moustafa.[9] **[35, 36]** Their 1968 meeting is enacted in 1:2.40, the anamorphic widescreen aspect ratio. The central story, taking place in the 1930s, is presented in an approximation of classic 1:1.33, or 4:3, imagery.[10] **[37]**

With typical Anderson wit, each period gets a ratio that could have been used in a movie at that time. He subtly distinguishes the 1985 layer from the ultimate frame, that of the prologue showing the young woman adding a hotel key to the many others at the monument. The Author's 1985 interview sequence has about the same proportions as the statue scene, but it's a slightly smaller image. Thus Anderson's boxes-within-boxes screenwriting technique finds its visual equivalent.

37

Mixing ratios offers both problems and opportunities for composing the images. Most commercially released films from the 1950s onward were filmed in some widescreen ratio. In the early days, a popular pictorial option was a sort of clothesline staging, centering a single character or balancing others around the central axis: two side by side, three across, four as a pair of pairs, and so on, as in this still-frame from *How to Marry a Millionaire* (1953).[11] **[38]**

38

Thanks to the widening of the frame, there's less air above the characters and less ground below them. Any empty spaces are typically on the sides. Eventually, some directors solved this problem of filling the frame by moving the camera very close to the actors. Steven Spielberg remarked that he began shooting more close-ups when he began filming in anamorphic.[12]

The planimetric approach, which favors symmetry, suits the wider formats of 1.85 and 2.40 nicely, as Anderson found in previous films. He wasn't worried by the extra acreage; he just used items in the set or empty areas to balance one side against the other. Shots of only one character could be more or less centered, as if posed, and shots of groups could be arranged somewhat symmetrically. [39, 40] Central perspective also helps drive your eye to the main items, as several of the images here indicate.

39

40

As we'd expect, in *Grand Budapest*, Anderson's signature framings click into place in the 1.85 and 2.40 sections. But what about the 1.37 scenes?

In *The Wes Anderson Collection*, Anderson expresses an interest in making a film in the classic 4:3 aspect ratio. Seitz points out that, after decades of the wider rectangles of post-television cinema, older films shot in the boxier "Academy" ratio can look surprisingly tall. Anderson agrees, saying that he had wanted to shoot *The Royal Tenenbaums* in 4:3 to emphasize the verticality of the house.[13] Echoing this, cinematographer Robert Yeoman said he and Anderson prepared for *The Grand Budapest Hotel* by watching a lot of films from the 1930s, especially those directed by Ernst Lubitsch.

> *We looked at those more to familiarize ourselves with the 1.37:1 aspect ratio, which Wes wanted to use for the 1930s sequences. This aspect ratio opens up some interesting compositional possibilities; we often gave people a lot more headroom than is customary. A two-shot tends to be a little wider than the same shot in anamorphic. It was a format I'd never used before on a movie, and it was a fun departure. You can get accustomed to 1.85 or 2.40 to the point that the shots become more predictable.*[14]

You might think that Anderson's penchant for centering and symmetry in the widescreen formats could be adapted to fit the 1.37 ratio simply by cropping on the left and right. His single characters and huddled groups would remain, much as before. But in more distant framings, the filmmaker might get a lot of extra space at top and bottom—areas that simply aren't there in the wide ratios. And close views would look odd if the heads weren't somehow fitted into the top half of the picture. Pouring the central 1930s tale into the 1.37 box gave him a new problem in maintaining his signature style.

How did he solve it? Many *Grand Budapest* shots leave considerable headroom, as you see in some of the 1.37 examples throughout this book. But other shots show Anderson composing his 4:3 frame in varied and engaging ways.

For instance, a planimetric filmmaker can fill the frame's upper area by setting camera height below eye level. During the conversation in the limousine, Anderson puts the head of M. Ivan (Bill Murray) in the top of the frame, thanks to a low angle. In other scenes, a low camera position helps fill the upper reaches. [41]

41

Alternatively, headroom can become comic. In this elevator shot below [42], we get M. Gustave and Madame D. seated on the right, the morose bellboy filling the vertical area on the left, and Zero in the middle. The empty space above Gustave and Madame D. creates a lively imbalance with the other two characters in the elevator, and emphasizes them in a different way from the very balanced framing that centers Inspector Henckels among his men.

42

The sets can cooperate with the shots. During the climax of *The Grand Budapest Hotel*, Zero and Agatha's centered embrace leaves lots of headroom [43], but the slightly disheveled stack of pastry boxes in the upper background contributes to the sense that they're engulfed.

43

In this shot from the prison-break sequence, part of the humor comes from the rigid geometry of the grid and the way M. Gustave and his colleagues fill in the matrix with their intent faces and busy hands. [44]

44

In all, Anderson gets elaborate, even virtuoso results from rudimentary cinematic choices. Centered symmetry, coupled with compass-point editing, may seem a fairly easy strategy—the answer to the question "What is our shot?" is always, "Some variation of what we usually do"—but there's a stubborn artistry at work here. The very perpendicular framings and cutting patterns seen in Anderson's features weren't used much in the mainstream tradition because many filmmakers, and some viewers, fear that they're too artificial and confining; perhaps only with the rise of art cinema and widescreen formats was this sort of look welcomed. It remains for the ambitious filmmaker to show us what can be done with this "simple" cascade of forced choices. Do many modern day filmmakers think much about frontality, spacing, symmetry, headroom, and the like? I suspect not. Fewer still are willing to create problems for themselves by adopting a limited visual toolkit and accept the creative challenges that invariably accompany such a choice. Most filmmakers today are eclectic maximalists, not stringent minimalists. They want to do more with more, not more with less.

We should, then, welcome a director who narrows his range of creative choices, to the point of seeming to make trouble for himself. Call it the Ozu strategy: By refining your means, you discover nuances that less constrained directors might never see. This is what happened during the creation of *The Grand Budapest Hotel*. By sticking to his signature look, but reimagining it in the rarely-used 4:3 ratio, Anderson assigned himself a problem that didn't exist for his contemporaries, and solved it adroitly. By pursuing the multiformat strategy in *The Grand Budapest Hotel*, he gave new resonance to narratives that come to us boxed and bookended—tidy display cases preserving wildly untidy lives.

1　　　"The 4:3 Challenge" is a play on the "Pepsi Challenge," a recurring bit in ads for Pepsi-Cola wherein random people were asked to compare it to Coca-Cola and discovered, to their surprise, that they liked it just as much or better.

2　　　Quoted in David Bordwell, *The Way Hollywood Tells It: Story and Style in Modern Movies* (Berkeley: University of California Press, 2006), 58.

3　　　William Hogarth (1697–1764) was a painter, cartoonist, and social critic, and a pioneer in what is now called "sequential art." His best known works are *A Harlot's Progress* and *A Rake's Progress*. In his 1753 book *The Analysis of Beauty*, Hogarth originated the idea of "The Line of Beauty," a term describing an S-shaped, curved line appearing within an object, as the boundary line demarcating an object, or as a virtual boundary line formed by the composition of several objects. Horgarth inveighed against symmetry and regularity in visual art, writing, "It is a constant rule in composition in painting to avoid regularity," adding, "regularity, uniformity, or symmetry, please only as they serve to give the idea of fitness."

4　　　William Hogarth, *The Analysis of Beauty*, ed. Charles Davis (Heidelberg: Artdok, 2010; orig. 1753), 45.

5　　　I discuss the history of planimetric framing in *On the History of Film Style* (Berkeley: University of California Press, 1998), chapter 5. See also the blog entry http://www.davidbordwell.net/blog/2007/01/16/shot-consciousness/.

6　　　One film using planimetric techniques throughout is *Napoleon Dynamite* (2004). Another example is Manoel de Oliveira's *Gebo and the Shadow* (2012), discussed in "VIFF 2013 finale: The Bold and the Beautiful, sometimes both together," at http://www.davidbordwell.net/blog/2013/10/21/viff-2013-finale-the-bold-and-the-beautiful-sometimes-together/.

7　　　The Surrealist-influenced artist and filmmaker Joseph Cornell (1903–1972) was a pioneer in the field of "assemblage," creating two- or three-dimensional art out of found objects. Cornell's work in this field was often bordered by or enclosed within boxes. His signature works include the *Pink Palace* series, the *Hotel* series, the *Observatory* series, the *Medici Slot Machine* series, *Soap Bubble Sets,* and the *Space Object Boxes.*

8　　　She sits, intriguingly enough, on a bench that wasn't there in initial shots of the Author's monument.

9　　　The mix of aspect ratios is idiosyncratic. The Fox Searchlight logo, at 1.85:1, was the reference point for the maximal image to be projected. Deluxe Digital Laboratories sent to theaters showing *Grand Budapest* a briefing sheet explaining that all the ratios in the film lie within the 1.85 (1998 x 1080) surround. The letter warned against reframing the picture, top or sides, to fit any of the scenes after the studio logo.

The prologue and epilogue in the cemetery are formatted at 1.80, leaving a bit at the sides as well as the top and bottom. Many directors would have kept this framing situation at the full 1.85, but it's typical of Anderson, with his interest in Russian-nesting-doll structure, that he makes the prologue and epilogue themselves a slight "embed" within the overall picture format.

Within the 1.80 picture is the 1985 Author interview, which also comes in at about 1.80, but it, too, is embedded: it's smaller in dimensions than the prologue. The 2.40 scenes are the only ones in the film that fill the horizontal extent of the master 1.85 frame. (But of course those scenes leave the top and bottom areas of the full frame blank and aren't as tall as scenes in other ratios.)

Interestingly, release copies came with a customized framing chart that has its mate at the start of the DVD and Blu-ray disc release. The DVD release, framed at 16 x 9 (that is, closer to 1.75:1) has reduced the black areas around the embedded frames a little.

10　　　The 1932 events in the central story are presented at a little more than 1.30:1. Interestingly, Anderson has tweaked orthodox ratios before. *The Life Aquatic with Steve Zissou* presents portions of the jaguar-shark installment in 1.5:1, neither 1.33 nor the nearest standard alternative, 1.66.

11　　　For more on CinemaScope staging options, see my "CinemaScope: The Modern Miracle You See Without Glasses," at http://www.davidbordwell.net/books/poetics_10cinemascope.pdf and the web lecture of the same title at http://vimeo.com/64644113.

12　　　See David Bordwell, *Figures Traced in Light: On Cinematic Staging* (Berkeley: University of California Press, 2005), 27. I discuss the modern history of planimetric framing in chapter 4.

13　　　Matt Zoller Seitz, *The Wes Anderson Collection* (New York: Abrams, 2013), 324.

14　　　Iain Stasukevich, "5-Star Service," *American Cinematographer* (March 2014) at http://www.theasc.com/ac_magazine/March2014/TheGrandBudapestHotel/page1.php.

The
SOCIETY OF THE
CROSSED PENS

1

2

3

4

5

6

[1] ALI ARIKAN is the chief film critic of *Dipnot TV*, a Turkish news portal and iPad magazine, and one of Roger Ebert's Far-Flung Correspondents. Ali's work has appeared in *IndieWire*, *Slant* magazine, *The House Next Door*, *Fandor*, the *Chicago Sun-Times*, *Vogue*, and the *Times* (UK). Ali currently resides in Istanbul, Turkey.

[2] ANNE WASHBURN's plays include *Mr. Burns*, *The Internationalist*, *A Devil at Noon*, *Apparition*, *The Communist Dracula Pageant*, *I Have Loved Strangers*, *The Ladies*, *The Small*, and a transadaptation of Euripides' *Orestes*. She lives in New York City and, occasionally, Buenos Aires.

[3] STEVEN BOONE, currently of Los Angeles, is a critic and filmmaker. He has written for RogerEbert. com, the *Village Voice*, the *Star-Ledger*, *Time Out New York*, *The House Next Door*, Fandor's *Keyframe* blog, and *Salon.com*.

[4] OLIVIA COLLETTE is a Montreal-based journalist and a classically trained pianist. Her writing on film and other subjects has appeared in *Montreal Gazette*, *Sparksheet*, *The Scrawn*, *Press Play*, the *Spectator Arts Blog*, and in the book *World Film Locations: San Francisco*. Although she already owns six musical instruments, she'd very much like to add a cimbalom to her collection.

[5] DAVID BORDWELL is a Madison, Wisconsin-based film theorist and scholar. His books include *Narration in the Fiction Film*, *Ozu and the Poetics of Cinema*, *Making Meaning*, and *On the History of Film Style*. He and his creative partner and spouse, Kristin Thompson, wrote the textbooks *Film Art* and *Film History*.

[6] CHRISTOPHER LAVERTY is a style and costume consultant, and the creator of the blog *Clothes on Film*. He is currently writing a book about designer fashion in cinema, to be published in 2016. He lives in Dundrum, Down, United Kingdom.

The
INDEX

About the
AUTHOR

A Brooklyn-based writer and filmmaker, **MATT ZOLLER SEITZ** is the editor-in-chief of RogerEbert. com, the TV critic for *New York Magazine*, and the author of *The Wes Anderson Collection*, a *New York Times* bestseller. He is the founder and original editor of *The House Next Door*, the cofounder of *Press Play*, and the author of the forthcoming *The Oliver Stone Experience* (Abrams, Fall 2015).

About the
ILLUSTRATOR

MAX DALTON is a graphic artist living in Buenos Aires, Argentina, by way of Barcelona, New York, and Paris. He has published a few books and illustrated some others, including *The Wes Anderson Collection* (Abrams, 2013). Max started painting in 1977, and since 2008, he has been creating posters about music, movies, and pop culture, quickly becoming one of the top names in the industry.

The
IMAGE CREDITS

Max Dalton: Front and back cover illustrations, endpaper illustrations; illustrations: pp. 4, 6, 8, 12, 14–15, 24–25, 94–95, 168–169, 208, 209, 210, 211, 212, 213, 251, 254; spot illustrations: pp. 32, 34, 46, 48, 51, 61, 102, 105, 117, 175, 186, 191, 192, 202. • Still photographer: Martin Scali: pp. 2–3, 18, 28–29, 30, 35, 46 (top left), 47, 48, 51 (top), 51 (bottom), 52, 55, 58–59, 62, 63, 66, 75, 80 (center), 81 (top left), 81 (top right), 81 (bottom), 82, 83 (top left), 83 (bottom left), 91 (top right), 101, 104 (top), 104 (bottom), 105, 106, 107 (bottom), 114, 116, 142, 144, 146–147, 150 (top), 150 (bottom), 153, 170, 171, 172–173, 174, 177, 182 (top), 201, 203, 228 (bottom), 230, 233, 237, 256. • pp. 16–17, 80 (bottom), 108 (bottom left), 145: Photographs by Francesco Zippel. • p. 26: Production art by Michael Taylor. • pp. 27, 98–99, 100, 102 (bottom left): Courtesy of the Library of Congress Photochrom Print Collection. • p. 31 (bottom left): Courtesy of the Stefan Zweig Centre Salzburg. • pp. 38–39, 184 (center bottom): Production art by Wes Anderson. • pp. 40–41: Storyboards by Christian De Vita. • pp. 46 (bottom right): Courtesy of Graphic House, New York. • pp. 80, 81, 83: Production sketches by Juman Malouf. • pp. 86, 88 (top left), 88 (top right), 88 (bottom left), 88 (bottom right), 91 (top left), 91 (bottom left), 91 (bottom right): Production sketches by *The Grand Budapest Hotel* costume department. • pp. 90 (top), 90 (bottom), 159 (bottom right): Photographs by Ben Adler. • pp. 96, 228 (top): Photographs courtesy of Robert Yeoman. • p. 97: Photograph by Jeremy Dawson. • p. 102 (bottom right): *Morgen im Riesengebirge* by Caspar David Friedrich. Courtesy of the Nationalgalerie, Berlin, Germany. • pp. 108 (top), 111 (top): Production sketches by Carl Sprague. • pp. 107 (top), 115 (top left), 115 (center left), 115 (bottom left): Storyboards by Jay Clarke. • pp. 108 (bottom right): Photograph by Alex Friedrich. • pp. 109 (top left), 109 (top right), 110 (bottom left), 110 (bottom right), 111 (center left), 111 (bottom left), 112 (top left), 112 (top right): Photographs by Simon Weisse. • pp. 132, 139: Photographs courtesy of Alexandre Desplat. • p. 154 (top): Jacket design by Annie Atkins. • p. 159 (bottom left): Mendl's box design by Annie Atkins and Robin Miller. • p. 182 (bottom left): Illustration by Hugo Guinness. • p. 182 (bottom right) Photograph courtesy of *The National Interest*. • pp. 184–185: Stamp, flag, ZigZag banner, and passport designs by Annie Atkins. Zero's migratory visa made by Liliana Lambriev. • p. 190: © Hulton Archive/Stringer/Getty Images. • p. 196 (bottom left): Photograph by James Hamilton. • p. 198 (top): Photograph by Merrick Morton. • p. 197: Photographs courtesy of Dipak Pallana. • pp. 204–205: Production art by Michael Lenz.

The
COPYRIGHT

The Editor: ERIC KLOPFER
The Designer: MARTIN VENEZKY'S APPETITE ENGINEERS
The Production Manager: DENISE LACONGO

Library of Congress Control Number: 2014948522
ISBN: 978-1-4197-1571-6

Printed and bound in the United States
10 9 8 7 6 5 4 3 2 1

ABRAMS
THE ART OF BOOKS SINCE 1949
115 West 18th Street — New York, NY 10011
www.abramsbooks.com

The
ACKNOWLEDGMENTS

The author wishes to thank the following people and institutions that helped bring this book to life:

Thanks to Josh Izzo, Melissa Quinn, Amanda Silver, and Ruth Busenkell at Fox.

Thanks to the many kind and attentive people in Wes Anderson's corner, including Kimberly Jaime, Jim Berkus, Rich Klubeck, Jacob Epstein, and Cait Ringness.

Thanks to all the folks in my corner, especially my agent Amy Williams of McCormick-Williams; Tony Zhou and Tony Dayoub, who helped source high-quality images on short notice; Max Winter and Rebecca Carroll, for their editorial advice; and David Schwartz, Dennis Lim, Jason Eppink, and Livia Bloom, for their tireless support of my work at the Museum of the Moving Image, which helped make this book and *The Wes Anderson Collection* possible. Thanks to my assistant, Lily Puckett, for helping make the trains run on time, and my former assistant and still-transcriber, Jeremy Fassler, a wizard who might type faster than Clark Kent.

Thanks to *New York* and *Vulture* publisher Adam Moss and editors Gilbert Cruz, Lane Brown, and John Sellers, as well as to RogerEbert.com publisher Chaz Ebert and content editor Brian Tallerico, all of whom allowed me the latitude necessary to produce this book while keeping my day jobs. Thanks are also due Ali Arikan, Steven Boone, Olivia Collette, Christopher Laverty, and Anne Washburn for their exemplary contributions to the Society of the Crossed Pens, and to the most exalted member of that group, David Bordwell, for his scholarship and keen insight on all matters film-related.

Thank you, Wes, for having another go at this, and for your time and guidance. To the inimitable Molly Cooper, ditto.

Thanks to this book's designer, Martin Venezky, for taking your already extraordinary work to the next level, sometimes under impossible circumstances, and to Max Dalton, whose illustrations brighten my days as well as the pages of this book. Thanks to The Outsider Agency, Paul Colarusso, and Marisa Dobson, for their brilliant promotion of *The Wes Anderson Collection*. Thanks also to Michael Clark, Denise LaCongo, and Zach Greenwald at ABRAMS, for helping to pull this all together.

Thanks to my dear friend and editor, Eric Klopfer: Murtaugh to my Riggs, or Riggs to my Murtaugh, depending on the day.

Finally, thank you to my family, in particular my father, Dave Zoller, and his special lady Elizabeth Sutherland; to my children, Hannah and James, for their devotion and patience; and Amy Cook, whose love and wisdom have made my life make sense again.